Another Liberalism

Another Liberalism

*Romanticism and the Reconstruction
of Liberal Thought*

Nancy L. Rosenblum

Harvard University Press

*Cambridge, Massachusetts
and London, England*
1987

This book is printed on acid-free paper, and its binding materials
have been chosen for strength and durability.

Library of Congress Cataloging-in-Publication Data

Rosenblum, Nancy L., 1947–
    Another liberalism.

    Includes index.
    1. Liberalism.   2. Romanticism.   I. Title.
JC571.R755   1987   320.5'1   87-365
ISBN 0-674-03765-0 (alk. paper)

For Richard and Anna

Acknowledgments

As befits a work on romanticism, this book was a labor of love, and I am especially happy to thank my friends for their help. Sherry Turkle lent her intelligence and sympathy to the project and was my model of discipline for the absorbing business of writing and rewriting. Michael Stein offered useful advice on the manuscript at different stages; his enthusiasm for it brightened my task always. Some friends read parts of the manuscript and offered specific suggestions, while others in conversation after conversation shared their ideas about liberalism with me. I am grateful to Samuel Beer, Mary Gluck, Harry Hirsch, Stephen Holmes, Bradley Honoroff, Susan Okin, and Judith Shklar. My talks with them helped to shape this work; they were also a very great pleasure.

I am indebted to the National Endowment for the Humanities for a summer grant in 1980. An early version of Chapter 2 appeared in the April 1982 *Journal of the History of Ideas,* and portions of Chapter 6 appeared as "Thoreau's Militant Conscience" in *Political Theory,* February 1981. I presented a paper covering many of the ideas in Chapter 4 to the New York area Conference for the Study of Political Thought in 1983, and I am indebted to the members for their helpful comments. I have also benefited from comments on another version of that paper by my colleagues in a faculty study group on social and political thought at Brown University.

Finally, I want to thank Aida Donald of Harvard University Press for her support, Elizabeth Suttell for her editorial suggestions, and Suzannah Ringel and Anna Rosenblum for their help with the notes.

Contents

Another Liberalism

INTRODUCTION

Making Peace with Liberalism

This book describes the romantic response to liberalism. It is a distinctive response, expressive and intuitive. It has more to do with personal than political expectations, with taste and sensibility than with independent political values. Romantic attractions, and more particularly romantic aversions, to liberalism are immediate, affective, and sometimes aesthetic. Political theorists seldom capture spontaneous responses to the experience of political life. Most often they subject the conceptual apparatus of political thought to formal argument, or defend or attack institutions and principles, or study the traditions of thought that provide their rationales. These approaches to political theory may betray pride or disappointment; they are not always coolly analytic in tone or purpose. But, refracted through systematic ethical and political categories, they are not purely personal, intimate responses of individual sensibilities. Romantic responses are. The picture of liberalism that can be distilled from them is unlike any other. This picture is the focus of this book.

Many readers will find familiar the romantic experience of liberalism I describe. In fact it may be easier to recognize some of its elements in ourselves than to identify political thinkers who fully embody them. In this work, I want to capture an array of feelings I believe are common, even everyday, although often diffuse and elusive. My interest is thus descriptive, but prescriptive as well; romantic responses to liberalism offer powerful resources for the reconstruction of liberal thought.

From the perspective I call romantic, certain qualities of liberalism stand out. They are recognizable from any view, but from the romantic perspective they appear so vivid and compelling and dominate responses so thoroughly that the liberalism that emerges amounts to "another liberalism." How does liberalism appear to romantic sensibilities? The initial romantic picture is negative. Liberalism is legalistic. It values regularity, impersonality, and impartiality; preoccupied with securing expectations, it inhibits spontaneity and self-expression. Liberal theory gives a fearful, self-protective rationale for limited government. It gives an instrumental rationale for a sphere of personal liberty, which does not prize privacy and detachment as goods in themselves, elements of the sort of fulfillment that comes from inwardness and self-cultivation. Liberalism portrays men and women as legal persons bearing rights or as moral agents capable of rational choice, as consumers or as possessive individualists, but these representations acknowledge only what is general among people, not what makes them unique, various, and original. In short, liberalism does not take individuality, spontaneity, and expressivity into account. Its political society is cold, contractual, and unlovely—without emotional or aesthetic appeal.

I call this perspective romantic, understanding that "romanticism" is a notoriously elusive term. I do not identify romanticism with a particular artistic period or movement. For purposes of literary criticism, the designation "romantic" is too broad. Perhaps its connotations are so varied that it cannot serve in writing intellectual history, either. For my purposes, though, its resonance is important. I give romanticism central place precisely because it is luxuriously evocative. It brings to mind the emotional, aesthetic, and personal. I call "romantic" attitudes and feelings that combine to make liberalism appear unbearably arid and cold, impersonal and unexpressive. I call a "romantic sensibility" the person who is disposed to suffer and confess these aversions. Typically expressions of discontent take the form of personal history or *Bildungsroman*. Here I describe romantic responses in a more systematic fashion and I present them as a prism through which liberalism is refracted. Most important, I present them as a resource for recasting liberal thought.

For some romantic sensibilities, the disaffected experience of liberalism is constant; for others, it is only episodic. It is possible not to be consumed by romantic preoccupations and to see liberalism through romantic eyes without losing sight of its historical political advantages—constitutionalism and civil liberties, religious toleration and representative government. Still, individuals may be unwilling to repress other romantic reactions that are distressing and recurrent.

They may be unwilling to set aside the perfectly reasonable expectation that political theory should mirror their experiences of political life, including affective ones. The problem with orthodox liberal thought is that some men and women cannot recognize themselves in it.

Thus, I take up one of the neglected tasks of political theory—capturing our intuitive reactions to political life. And I show that under the impetus of romanticism, conventional liberalism can be recast. Liberal thought has always invited political agreement and the independent assent of reason. Reconstructed, it can also evoke genuine personal affinity.

Liberalism has many faces, and corrective portraits appear regularly in political thought. Ordinarily this reform is self-reform. In defense against political challenges, theorists borrow and incorporate ideas from their critics—socialists and egalitarians, mainstream participatory democrats and those nostalgic for civic virtue. Along with others of my generation whose formative political experiences occurred in the 1960s and 1970s, I have witnessed a succession of attacks on conventional liberalism—radical, neoconservative, republican, and libertarian. During the same period, political theorists have produced dramatic evidence of liberalism's resilience, accommodating democratic claims and demands for distributive justice and researching and reclaiming the foundations of liberalism's moral norms.

The relation between liberalism and romanticism too is one of mutual tension, reconciliation, and reconstruction. But its story can only be told by identifying a particular experience of liberalism that is not immediately discernible from within conventional political thought. So the story I tell falls outside the usual frame. Even theorists interested in reforming liberalism are liable to overlook very common romantic responses to political experience and to discount their potential as constructive forces for theoretical change.

I have distilled a vision of liberalism as an evolving theory. It is only one vision among others, which is why I call this book *Another Liberalism*. It does not refer to a formal tradition of thought; its coherence is psychological, and not a matter of intellectual history. Yet "another liberalism" is built on the sensibilities of historical individuals; I could not have captured this vision of liberalism without recourse to their experience. And it answers compelling contemporary needs that political theory has the capacity to address if only it would attend to them.

In capturing this vision of another liberalism, two themes converge: first, how open liberal political thought is to the claims of romantic sensibilities and how permeable to romantic ideas; second, the distinctive personal and political motives for making peace that arise within romanticism.

Traditionally liberalism has vigorously warded off everything affective, personal, and expressive. That is the promise of impersonal government, and that is what the discipline of tolerance and impartiality requires. Liberalism erases individuality and extinguishes spontaneity from its legalistic, utilitarian conception of politics. The vehemence with which this is done suggests that romantic responses may have a special, intimate connection with liberalism. Perhaps liberalism spawns its counterpart; perhaps romanticism is the return of the repressed.

What is certain is that at the heart of liberal thought lie concepts that can speak directly to romantic sensibilities, even if they do not always do so. Liberalism can appropriate what its first impulse was to expel: romantic connotations of individualism, for example. It can recast the public sphere as an arena for heroic self-display and the private domain as a scene for cultivating "beautiful individuality." It can reclaim romantic rationales for institutions traditionally justified in other ways—rationales for pluralism, freedom of association, and separate public and private spheres. Liberalism makes it possible for romantics to make their peace.

Romanticism's motivation for coming home to liberalism grows out of the painful failure of pure opposition. In reaction against the prosaic character of liberal society, romanticism invents stances of aesthetic detachment, militancy, and arrant emotionalism. But instead of satisfying longings for free expressivity, these poses often bring personal frustration and threats to liberty. Militarist stances reflect the feeling that a tame bourgeois existence is unbearable; but when heroic self-assertion fails, the result is melancholy and real self-loathing. The law of the heart as an alternative to legalistic rules and rights is warm and spontaneous; but it can be isolating and paralyzing when emotional imperatives are exhausted. Romantic discontents arise not only in response to liberalism, then, but also in response to romantics' own compensatory visions. Recognizing that longings to escape the discipline of liberalism can be self-defeating is crucial—only chastened romanticism can be brought home.

Throughout this book I assume familiarity with conventional liberal thought, both classical liberalism and contemporary reworkings. I focus on the border areas where liberalism and romanticism meet and where both prove to be more nuanced and many-sided than standard accounts suggest. Romanticism provides a unique stand-point, close to but outside liberalism, from which its ideas appear in a fresh light; and the reverse is also true. Juxtaposing ideas brings out aspects imperceptible from within—aspects of individualism revealed by romantic preoccupation with individuality and self-expression, for example, or aspects of private life illuminated by romantic tendencies to detachment, or aspects of pluralism brought out by romantic dread of definition and longing for infinite possibility. By juxtaposing ideas, affinities emerge and possibilities for reconciliation become clear. My strategy is to move from one standpoint to another, identifying the outer limits of liberalism and romanticism and exploring the way each can be used provocatively to define the other.

This strategy informs my choice of references, and I have selected works because they contain ideas that are in some way "at the margin" or because they can help to fix some of the important points along a boundary that is permeable and shifting. Thus, among romantics, I appeal to those who describe the motivations to escape romantic extremism. This, after all, is what makes a return to liberalism conceivable. The most fruitful romantic challenges to liberalism do not conform to familiar images of escape into pastoralism or medievalism, or to images of insular nationalism or totalitarianism. Instead, the romantic sensibilities that interest me seize on elements of liberal thought and exploit them in the revolt against conventional liberalism, at the same time suggesting that these ideas, suitably transformed, could enable them to make a new peace. In the same way, for me the most interesting liberal theorists exhibit some degree of sympathy with romantic longings or awareness of the incompleteness of liberalism's traditional agenda and appeal. I refer to particular thinkers to show that the impulses to recast liberalism or to abandon the pose of pure romanticism are not disembodied. I refer to them illustratively, without intending to label them revisionists, much less pretending to offer a complete exposition of their intentions and ideas.

My aim is not to identify a fully realized intellectual tradition, define doctrines, or classify political theorists, but to capture a certain kind of experience and its implications for political thought. I use literature as well as political philosophy, historical works as well as contemporary ones. I appeal to unconventional sources, such as aesthetic and psychological theory, for the ways in which romanticism can be brought home are not always found ready-made in political theory proper. To have done anything else—to have simplified types and periods of literature—would have given a false impression of the dimension of romantic claims. It would have suggested, falsely, that liberal responses to romanticism are neatly contained within the political philosophy of a particular period.

Studying romanticism and liberalism at the margins is problematic. It demands alertness to ambiguity and complication rather than to essences. Appreciation of this complexity led me to the conclusion that there are several divergent paths for bringing romanticism home to liberalism.

The existence of more than one path should not be surprising. Access to liberal political thought has always been pluralistic. Theorists have approached it through Kantian moral theory, through utilitarianism, through contract theory, and through natural rights. Outside philosophy they have found their way to liberalism by means of arguments for limited government and civil liberties inspired by current political events, by the experience of oppression and fear. Allegiance to practical institutional arrangements has also been a force. History as well as contemporary debates in philosophy teach that there is nothing unusual about liberalism's springing from more than one source or resting on more than one kind of justification.

With this in mind, and inspired by variations among romantic responses to the experience of liberalism, I propose a typology for reconciling liberalism and romanticism. Heroic individualism, shifting involvements, and communitarianism are all aspects of "another liberalism." Before engaging in the business of reconstruction, however, it is necessary to describe the dynamic of liberalism and romanticism: the conflict, self-doubt, and internal movement on both sides that make reconciliation possible. I begin with the romantic sensibility confronting conventional liberalism—with militarist opposition to prosaic peace and the law of the heart's opposition to legalism—suggesting both the limits of romantic revolt and liberalism's openness to romantic claims. I go on to survey the marginal area where both tensions and affinities between romanticism and liberalism show up most sharply. This is the area having to do with the separation of public and private spheres. I explore romantic longings for privatism and detachment, the elements of private life that have a privileged place in conventional liberal theory and how this category has expanded, and romantic disenchantment with its own pose of inwardness and retreat. Against this background romanticism appears as a powerful impetus for recasting liberal thought. And heroic individualism, shifting involvements, and communitarianism emerge as imaginative ways of making peace.

PART I

The Romantic Sensibility
Confronts Conventional
Liberalism

CHAPTER 1

Romantic Militarism
versus Civil Society

Glorification of militarism strikes directly at certain liberal values. Liberalism stands for, among other things, security of expectations, civilianism, and peace. In contrast to these prosaic promises, romantic militarism holds out heroic dreams. It substitutes extravagant self-assertion and self-display for more benign forms of the pursuit of happiness. It is an imaginative response to the dull routines of a utilitarian existence. Romantic militarism is the invention of sensibilities who usually were not inclined to real aggression, but who imagined war as the prime occasion for perfect freedom and self-expression. "The true sorrow of humanity consists in this;—not that the mind of man fails; but that the course and demands of action and of life so rarely correspond with the dignity and intensity of human desires," Wordsworth wrote in "The Convention of Cintra."[1] For some, war answers these longings.

Militarism is not an obvious response to romantic longings. After all, the military is hierarchical and severely disciplined. Historically, it was the first state bureaucracy, and it became synonymous with organization and service. The military is traditionally a profession—indeed a whole way of life—marked by coercion, obedience, and routine. Romantic sensibilities disregard all this, just as they disregard the political ideology of militarism and the actual uses of organized violence.[2]

There are as many idealizations of soldiering and war as there are frustrations with ordinary civilian life. Some stress the exhilaration of combat, the intimacy of esprit de corps, and homoeroticism. Romantics focus instead on war as the experience of freedom from inhibitions and conventional constraints. They look upon warfare as liberation, and on militancy as spontaneous self-display. This preoccupation with personal liberty suggests why romantic militarism poses a provocative challenge to liberalism. In liberal thought liberty is inseparable from legal security and peace. Romantics reject this pairing.

It is easy to see that romantic militarism is opposed to the prosaic promises of civil society. But opposition is only part of the story. Romantic militarism can also appear as a series of exuberant variations on liberal themes. For example, for the generation of romantics whose formative experience was the French Revolution, liberalism was a revolutionary doctrine. They fixed tenaciously on resistance to government as the supreme experience, however, and were unwilling to give up the excitement of liberation for the mundane business of instituting and constituting. For these romantics militarism meant perpetual insurrection, wars of independence that do not end in establishments. Romantic militarism is an exaggerated echo of a fundamental liberal dilemma—that the ideal of personal freedom can never be fully encompassed by any catalogue of rights and benefits, and will always be frustrated by the actualities of even limited government.

Another type of romantic militarism also relates to liberalism in a complex fashion. It opposes civil society even more emphatically, this time in the name of heroic individualism. The generation that came of age with the French Restoration replaced the revolutionary vision of militarism as popular liberation with militancy, the permanently defiant stance of extraordinary souls who cannot abide the ordinary experiences of conventional society. This militancy also exploits liberal ideas. Romantic militants start from the assumption of individualism, but purge it of its moderating elements. From the familiar idea of the pursuit of happiness they isolate the ethos of endless, insatiable striving. They blur the divide between unrestrained self-assertion and the politically recognizable claims to liberty embodied in rights. They replace moral autonomy with amoral expressivism. Romantic militancy is such a lavish departure from sober individualism that it amounts to an exploitation of liberal ideas. Still, it offers a perspective on the limits of liberalism that is impossible from within.

In this chapter I discuss several types of romantic militarism, focusing on their excesses. When romantic militarism is thoroughly antipacifist and antibourgeois, its extravagances become clear even to romantics themselves. Militancy generates its own motives for ap-

preciating civil society and the experience of limited government. From
its failings emerge some of the reasons for making peace. Like other
romantic inventions—such as pastoralism and the myth of Hellas—
romantic militarism is at once an ideal of perfect freedom and an
expression of despair.

Wordsworth and Inspired Revolution

Wordsworth's "Convention of Cintra" is the exemplary account of
militarism as liberation, in which revolution is less a struggle against
authorities than an expressive act. "The Convention of Cintra" takes
its title from the armistice signed by Britain and France to put an end
to their hostilities in Iberia. The Spanish were fighting the Napoleonic
invasion, and the British were allied with the Spanish efforts. For
Wordsworth the war had everything to satisfy longings for action
commensurate with the "dignity and intensity of human desires," and
he writes about it in language associated with romantic descriptions
of artistic creation. The Peninsula War was proof to Wordsworth that
"there are golden opportunities when . . . the beauty of the inner mind
is substantiated in an outward act" (p. 167). It was inspired. In his
vision an expedient act of state is transformed into an expression of
genius.

In order to ascribe genius to whole peoples, Wordsworth first had
to detach them from every civil and military authority and institution.
Just as the artist must be isolated from philistine society in order to
be creative, an inspired people can have nothing to do with officialdom
or ordinary political intentions. The significance of the Convention
of Cintra for Wordsworth was that it was a ministerial act, the work
of generals and officials who "stepped in with their forms, their im-
pediments, their rotten customs and precedents, their narrow desires,
their busy and purblind fears" (p. 168). What gripped Wordsworth
about the Peninsula War was that after the convention was signed
the British, acting as men and not as soldiers, refused to abandon
their fight.[3] The Spanish army fought on, too; it was a people "gath-
ered under the authority not of generals but of their country and
human nature" (p. 133). And a people cannot be crushed or dispersed
when it is moved by the force of inspiration.

"Inspiration" means here just what it does in the context of literary
romanticism—a spontaneous, intangible, uncontrollable force.
Wordsworth transfers romantic imagery wholesale from poets to people at war: they are moved by a "correspondent breeze"; they are "a

mass fluctuating with one motion under the breath of a mightier wind"; they have "a genius for spontaneous resistance" (p. 164).⁴ Inventing the simile J. S. Mill would later use to describe genius in *On Liberty*, Wordsworth describes the Spanish forces as "not confined like an ordinary river in a channel, but spreading like the Nile over the whole face of the land" (p. 133).

Wordsworth's militarism has its source in the experience of resistance to mundane constraints. It is about exalted states, not actual political outcomes. Nothing could separate romantic militarism more clearly from ordinary views of military action than his rejection of instrumentalism and his separation of war from calculated political purposes, even historically momentous ones. The battle against France was not fought to secure Spain's political independence: "Riddance, mere riddance, safety, mere safety are objects far too defined, too inert and passive in their own nature, to have ability either to rouse or to sustain" (p. 62). Instead, the Spanish were "roused more instantaneously from a deadly sleep to a more hopeful wakefulness"; they were enlightened from old superstitions and released from old loyalties (p. 164). Spain arose not only to be free of the French armies "but, in the act and process of acquiring freedom, to recompense herself, as it were in a moment, for all she had suffered through the ages" (pp. 161–162). Romantic poets often represent violence in nature—earthquakes and volcanos, pestilence and fire—as creative forces, and Wordsworth brings this dramatic imagery to war. It is transforming, redemptive. In war the British experienced a "conversion of love" and "perfect brotherhood" with the Spanish, solemnized by combat side by side (p. 129).

Any revolutionary movement can be idealized, of course. But what stands out in Wordsworth's romantic account is its complex relation to liberalism. One possible reading of "The Convention of Cintra" is as a classic republican warning: if a people has nothing to fear from without, it risks enervation within. But it would be a mistake to think that Wordsworth intended to draw the moral lessons of republicanism. His model of a people is not the Romans, as it was for the civic humanist tradition that saw militarism as a way to resist corruption. For Wordsworth, inspiration, "intensity of desire," and not virtue, is at stake. Other passages of "Cintra" evoke conservative nationalism, in which genius attaches to the historic spirit of a homogeneous people. But even when inspired, Wordsworth's people preserve the ethos of liberalism. They are private individuals united in their enthusiasm for liberty. What makes them a people is combination in resistance and love of freedom. His idealized people are suspicious of government and opposed to tyranny, a nation of men and not citizens, and certainly not anticivilian. "National Happiness [is] the end, the conspicuous crown, the ornament of the whole" (p. 193).

Still, this is not liberalism as usual. It is revolutionary liberalism taken to heart. For liberation takes priority over the peaceful enjoyment of liberty. Wordsworth dismisses concerns for security and prosperity: "It is not with security that Genius most loves to hold intercourse" (p. 180). He denounces those who "hoard up life for its own sake" (p. 146). Romantic militarism is a standing criticism of utilitarian calculation. Paradoxically, Wordsworth echoes the liberal tradition of popular resistance that has precisely the pursuit of security and happiness as its justification and end. But for Wordsworth, the pursuit itself is important. Being inspired is what matters. The point is to love independence, not to use it. In this way Wordsworth makes liberation rather than distinct liberties the ever-expanding, always-receding goal. Liberation—passionate intensity, striving, and resisting constraint—becomes the ideal.

Contemporary social science can sometimes illuminate romantic responses to liberalism. Samuel Huntington has analyzed how liberalism actually creates the conditions for revolutionary passion because it contains an inherent tension between expectations of freedom and any constituted political authority. Liberal, democratic, and egalitarian values conflict with the practical requirements of government. "No government can exist without some measure of hierarchy, inequality, arbitrary power, secrecy, deception, and established patterns of superordination and subordination," Huntington insists. In liberal society there is a permanent gap between institutions and ideals, and the setting exists for a particular view of politics where "what is important . . . is not that the dream is realized but that it is not and never can be realized completely."[5] Huntington's thesis helps us to see the resonance of Wordsworth's romantic militarism with this liberal dream. For Wordsworth too, a people's genius, its identity as an inspired nation, is expressed in pursuit of this elusive sense of liberty.

Wordsworth's is one of several versions of romantic militarism that oppose brilliant expressionism to business as usual. However, romantics cannot always convince themselves that inspired action is possible; sometimes militarist longings end in privatism and retreat.

Humboldt: Enervation and Self-Cultivation

Wordsworth's militarism would have been impossible without the patterns of popular resistance associated with the French Revolution and the nationalist wars of independence that followed. It is also indebted to British political history, with its tradition of limited government and civilian control. Neither strong centralized government, with its administrative zeal, nor the professional aristocratic army that formed a separate caste in continental Europe figured prominently in England, which helps to explain why Wordsworth's vision of militarism as spontaneous popular action differs from those of other romantic sensibilities. Political experiences such as German statism and princely absolutism generated the militarist vision of Wordsworth's contemporary Wilhelm von Humboldt. In "Cintra" Wordsworth distinguishes people from governments, inspired action from official purpose, and asserts the possibility of spontaneous revolution. Humboldt is more scrupulous about insulating individuals from government and less sanguine about their capacity for genius. The result is a kind of romantic militarism that is almost the reverse of Wordsworth's, though it has its source in the same longing for action corresponding to "the dignity and intensity of human desire."

For Humboldt, modern states regardless of their constitutional form are enlightened despotisms obsessed with what Mirabeau called "fureur de gouverner." Princely despotism and, even more, administrative efficiency are the enemies of independence. Governments fetter the free play of personal energies and homogenize individual differences. The results for individuals are crippling: "uniformity aggravated by the evil of diminished energy."[6] Because even the most benevolent state action results in enervation and passivity, Humboldt depreciates the goods governments promise—comfort and ease, tranquility and security, property and repose. For him, even more than for Wordsworth, the true nature of happiness has nothing to do with these but lies in striving and continual exertion. It must be thrilling: "the essence of man's value is that he can risk himself, and, when necessary, play freely with his own life."[7] Humboldt regrets that war is disappearing as society becomes increasingly legalistic, because with it passes the opportunity for the moments of greatest danger that are also the moments of highest ecstasy.

In the face of German efficiency, order, and uniformity, he composed a compensatory picture of soldiers cultivating individuality through war. In war, they throw off passive attitudes, disdain common pleasures, initiate actions, and experience personal freedom. Humboldt knows that this vision of liberated action is imaginary. Ecstasy, risk, and playing freely with one's own life are impossible in the wars of modern states, and conformity is nowhere more apparent than among soldiers. Antiquity knew warriors, but modern soldiers are machines who know only the abject submission of slavery.

If soldiering in the modern state is just another form of homogenization, where does Humboldt get his image of war as a brilliant occasion for self-cultivation? Why does he propose that in war personality expands, energy revives, and "beautiful individuality" is recovered? Unlike Wordsworth, he had no fond example of an inspired people close at hand. Instead, like many romantic sensibilities, he looked to the ancient Greeks for his standard. His image of self-cultivation through war has its source in the myth of Hellas. The Greeks combined bloom of fancy, depth of thought, and strength of will. They attained "perfect oneness of the entire being." For them, war was both an expression of the common life of the city and the premier opportunity for exhibiting personal perfection and attaining immortality.

Humboldt contrasts the Greeks with modern men, who are weak and fragmented, fallen off from "beautiful individuality." He reasserts wholeness as an ideal in the famous proposition that "the true end of man . . . is the highest and most harmonious development of his powers to a complete and consistent whole." At the same time he departs dramatically from the classical notion of character. There is nothing Greek about Humboldt's longing for the "greatest ecstasy" that comes with moments of greatest danger. Ecstasy, after all, is not courage. There is nothing classical about the claim that "energy is the chief virtue."[8] Despite his preoccupation with *Bildung*, Humboldt's notion of self-cultivation does not imitate the Greek ideal. For the ancients, self-development followed a fixed cultural pattern. Personal excellence meant participation in a definite catalogue of virtues, and virtue meant civic virtue. It was inseparable from the ethical life of the city. The Aristotelian catalogue of virtues and the classical ideal of one right and harmonious character made sense only in the context of a public culture. Moreover, good character was a duty, and it was the result of pedagogy, of authority.

For Humboldt, however, character is no longer exemplary; the end of self-cultivation is uniqueness, manifold diversity. Emphasis is on spontaneity and individuality, not training. Humboldt wants nothing so much as variety, and this idea is built into his definition of character as "all those peculiarities and individual traits which distinguish one man . . . absolutely from all other men."[9] This could hardly be farther from Hegel's defense of *Bildung* as the development of a man "who without the obtrusion of personal idiosyncrasy can do what others do."[10] For Humboldt, originality is "that towards which every human being must ceaselessly direct his efforts."[11]

Throughout these imaginings Humboldt continues to describe himself as free of illusion. His image of Hellas is delightful and personally satisfying; immersion in Greek literature "stills the heart's longings." He adores the ancients and prescribes classical education. But he knows that Hellas was a myth that cannot be brought back. The failed republican ambitions of the French Revolution reinforced the lesson that energetic militarism is inconceivable because modern men are unfit to be ardent citizen-soldiers. They are weak and fragmented. They need to recover energy, not tax it. Fallen off from Greek wholeness, they cannot be both men and citizens. They must make themselves into men first. They must detach themselves from political direction and demands, not submerge themselves in consuming public tasks like war.[12]

Finally Humboldt resigns himself to the view that individuality and spontaneity must be cultivated privately, apart from war. With this he charts a course back to liberalism that will be taken by other romantic sensibilities, moving from the exuberant dream of heroism to a stern recommendation of private life under limited government. He reconciles himself to legalism and to the pacific private sphere liberalism provides.

The Sphere and Duties of Government is the result of this odyssey. It presents Humboldt's theory of the liberal "nightwatchman state," in which a minimal government provides security against external enemies and a framework of laws to regulate conflict. It does not attempt to form character, but leaves the inner person alone. This picture of liberalism is traditional enough, but the motive and justification for limited government and personal liberty that lie behind it are not. They have little to do with protecting individuals from political tyranny. Happiness is not the justification for liberalism here; neither is minimizing political cruelty and fear. Instead, the rationale for limited government is the possibility of retreat to private life in order to cultivate depth of feeling and originality. Humboldt wants to restrict government because both its demands and its benefits are enervating, because it is an obstacle to uniqueness and spontaneity. No action is beneficial, he warns, unless it is "essentially individual." The libertarian nightwatchman state provides the necessary minimum of order and social welfare, leaving a free private sphere of action. More important, where the spheres and duties of government are contained and social control is exercised through the impersonal rule of law, individuals have the best chance of being left in peace. Limited government allows a free private sphere of inaction, detachment, and self-cultivation.

The essential characteristics of liberalism are evident in Humboldt's political thought: absence of positive duties, freedom from the demands of civic virtue and the inspections of close community, a protected sphere of private life. But the benefits of his private liberty are unconventional. Humboldt insists that men should not concern themselves about comfort and security; he calls possessions and repose unworthy objects of desire. Limited government and private liberty are transformed into conditions for the development of beautiful individuality. In this reconstruction, the *Rechtsstaat* no longer appears unbearably cold and unlovely. It provides a place to nurture variety, which is the greatest good social life can offer. Humboldt gives traditional liberal theory nothing less than a fresh rationale.

Wordsworth and Humboldt represent the two faces of romantic militarism of the revolutionary generation: revolutionism and privatization. Both seize on elements of liberal thought; Wordsworth exaggerates the promise of liberation, Humboldt exaggerates the promise of private liberty. They transform liberalism, but not in a spirit of unrelieved antagonism. The next romantic generation was more defiant; its aversion to liberalism ran deeper. For its members the experience of civil society was loathsome, and they actively longed for war as relief from routine civilian existence. Neither Wordsworth's liberation nor Humboldt's libertarianism could satisfy them. Their opposition was ferocious.

Heroism and Ennui

For the romantic generation that came of age after the Napoleonic wars and the Restoration, peace was an intolerable commercial necessity that brought no hard tasks, only ennui. While others described the century of relative peace following Napoleon's defeat as golden, these romantic sensibilities felt they had been born for extraordinary things and now were doomed to watch "the foaming billows which they had been prepared to meet subside." They "felt in the bottom of their souls an insupportable wretchedness."[13] Benjamin Constant judged war an anachronism: "the special goal of modern nations is tranquility, with tranquility affluence, with industry as its source. From day to day war becomes a less efficient means of attaining this goal."[14] Others could not resign themselves to such a view. They could not abide a society dedicated to the regular and ordinary pursuit of happiness. With this generation romantic militarism becomes uncompromisingly anticivilian and antibourgeois. Its ethos becomes heroic.

Historically, civilianism had evolved as an antiheroic set of values. The transition from a militaristic to a commercial society has a long history, and readers of Albert O. Hirschman's *The Passions and the Interests* will recognize the story in its main outlines. The medieval chivalric tradition and the aristocratic ideal of military service both looked upon the pursuit of glory as the most laudable passion—the one that, unlike lust or greed, had "redeeming social value." In the seventeenth and eighteenth centuries concern grew over the virtually permanent state of war, and to combat its attractions cupidity was rehabilitated. From a vice it became a virtue. The pursuit of wealth came to take the place of glory as the least malignant passion, the one that could tame the others "by imposing restraints on princely caprice, arbitrary government, and adventurous foreign policies." The "douceur" of commerce could replace violence. Finally, the desire for wealth—the regular desire, the one that requires reflection and calculation, constancy and predictability for its satisfaction—engulfed all the others, and the term "interest" replaced "passion" as a way of talking about human nature.[15]

As this narrative suggests, commercial economies were justified by their social effects: money-making activities were rational and benign compared with disruptive military enterprises. The connection to liberal political thought is not hard to discern, and the beneficiary of this shift from passions to interests is less liberalism narrowly conceived as a bourgeois ideology than liberalism broadly conceived as a political theory of legalism and limited government. For the unhindered pursuit of self-interest requires order, which requires good government, meaning government that guarantees the security and the liberty of individuals.[16]

Heroism was resurrected as a challenge to economic man. From one political quarter came attacks on civil society by republican advocates of civic virtue, for whom a military ethos and personal courage are the disciplines that best resist corruption.[17] From another quarter came the ancien régime's challenge. It identified heroic virtue with aristocratic honor and argued that since the nobility is by definition the only group that participates in honor and is prepared for self-sacrifice, its restoration to power is the only way to recover national glory. And from a third direction came the romantic attack on commercial peace, armed with yet another heroic ideal.

Romantic heroism is distinguished by the fact that it has no concrete historical and social content; it is distinct from civic virtue and aristocratic honor and has nothing to do with effecting common purposes or embodying common values. In fact, its appeal for romantics is precisely that it is remote not only from productive activity but from collective action and goals altogether. Heroism means just one thing: unconstrained self-assertion. Unlike republican courage and aristocratic service, romantic heroism is opposed not to egoism, but to the narrow selfishness of commercial types.

Heroic self-assertion reflects romantic longings because it offers external proof of the romantic's inner sense of limitless power, possibility, and independence. Every other sort of action in the world is constraining, sadly incommensurate with this grandiose sense of self. Apart from its anti-instrumentalism and its opposition to the regular advance of interests, self-assertion is an amorphous idea. The true Homeric hero had a destiny, but the romantic hero imagines a protean self and infinite possibilities for expressing it. Where utilitarian man pursues discrete interests, the romantic seeks self-expression. For romantic sensibilities, the alternative to the passions, especially glorious self-display, is not "interests" at all. Nor is it the spiritual alternative to interests—beatitude and repose. It is frustration and ennui.

Alfred de Musset's description of war as a glorious opportunity missed tells the whole story. His "ardent, pale, and neurotic generation" was "condemned to inaction . . . delivered to vulgar pedants of every kind, to idleness and to *ennui*." All that was left was contempt for the signs of civilian life: "that vestment of black which the men of our time wear is a terrible symbol; before coming to this, the armour must have fallen piece by piece and the embroidery flower by flower."[18] This is not historical memory, or even true nostalgia; it is mythmaking. Alfred de Vigny was one romantic poet who knew that military life bore little resemblance to his contemporaries' sweet dreams: "the gigantic conception of war . . . was actually Homeric and fit to take in schoolboys with its dazzle of multiple activities." It provides a myth of "magnificent uneasiness" that delivers the beautiful soul from boredom.[19]

At the heart of this myth was Napoleon. He was the model of what French romantics especially imagined they might have been in an age of war, and the measure of their misery. "His fatal memory will keep us from ever being happy," Julien Sorel says in *The Red and the Black*, where Stendhal dissects the social conditions of romantic militancy. Whether or not individual romantics actually subscribed to the cult of Bonaparte, their recollections of Napoleon are of a piece. His achievements as a strategist and his imperial ambitions are ignored; romantics draw their inspiration instead from Napoleon as an exemplary personality. He stood for free self-expression. He was, Chateaubriand wrote, "a poet in action."[20] To Chateaubriand, the royalist statesman and "moralist of the heart," Napoleon had been a political scourge. Even so, Chateaubriand was disenchanted with the Restoration and peace: "the palace of the Tuileries, so clean and soldierly under Napoleon, began to reek, instead of the smell of powder, with breakfast odours which rose on every side . . . everything resumed an air of domesticity."[21]

Nothing could express loathing for domestic peace better than militarism, or loathing for common productive activity better than uncommon heroism. War is not work. Heroism is not business as usual. However, there is another even starker way militarism reflects romantic disaffection: through its association with death.

Since Hobbes, fear of death had been represented in liberal thought as a constructive political force. It provided the origin and justification for modern political society, for liberal society in particular, as it is often said by liberalism's critics that only the desire for security could justify living in common without genuine common life.[22] Romantic flirtation with death shatters assumptions about the universal desire for security. The sensitive soul "half in love with easeful death" is a familiar theme in romantic literature. For the philosophical idealists among them, death means becoming one with the universe, as in Shelley's "Adonais." For others it is an escape from ennui; Werther's suicide in Goethe's early novel was the first of many such final retreats.[23] Death has a somewhat different significance for romantic militarists. The dream of heroism is a dream of self-assertion, not self-transcendence or self-annihilation. Unlike suicide, which is retirement from the world, death in battle is manifestly in the world. It is exhibitionist. It opposes banality. Where suicide suggests that the romantic is unfit for life, heroism pronounces his efficacy.[24] Romantic heroism is unrestrained self-affirmation, in which the exquisite inner self is forcibly felt and displayed.[25]

With this, another relation between romantic heroism and liberalism emerges—their connection through individualism. Heroism is not suggestive of every sort of individualism, of course. It rejects acquisitiveness, the core of personality in possessive individualism. It has little in common with individualism understood as legal personhood or moral autonomy, and nothing at all to do with individualism as a political ideology opposed to collectivism. But a romantic heroism that identifies personal dignity with independence, and independence with extraordinary action, is not as remote from liberal individualism as might seem. After all, classical liberal thought describes an individualism for the strong. This is especially true of Locke and Kant, for whom enlightenment requires "heroic" action, the throwing off of priestly and political authorities and striving for personal independence. Autonomy demands struggle against tyrannies on every front and against ingrained habits and prejudices. Enlightenment is something that can only be done by oneself, not by or for others. Individuals are not simple beneficiaries of liberty, then, but aggressive personalities who need to assert themselves to win it in the first place. And when they do, they are thrown back on themselves.

This is not to underestimate the differences between romantic heroism and liberal individualism. Liberal individualism does not always have this ethos of being for the strong, nor does it always have quite the same masculine aura. Although liberal individualism historically attributes rights and liberty to men, there is no conceptual barrier to extending them to women. At least the obstacles to considering women as persons are more likely to break down when independence means pursuit of happiness and not militarism. Plainly, part of the attraction of romantic militarism is its elitism, at whose heart is exclusion of women. Women embody the mundane. They are responsible for the breakfast odors and air of domesticity Chateaubriand despised.

Moreover, no matter how much liberal thought may identify individualism with the strong, with self-won independence and the emancipation of desires, it entails respect for others. It entails a minimum of utilitarian attention to the general happiness. Liberal individualism is inseparable from calculation and self-control. These are missing from romantic heroism. Missing too is the recognition that every action comes up against the actions of others. In liberal thought, neither civil society nor war could ever be a scene of pure self-assertion, because wherever there is more than one person, there is external resistance and constraint. Action in the world means acknowledging the limits of one's powers and the impossibility of self-sufficiency. Recognition of these limits impels men and women to give up natural freedom in the first place; it is what makes consent to government possible.

By contrast, the romantic hero is an anticivic, antisocial consciousness. Heroism is not burdened by any of the necessities of actual warfare. Self-assertion is unsullied by calculation of consequences. It is expressive, not purposive. In romantic dreams the soldier is perfectly self-sufficient and acts alone; he makes his own opportunity, and victory depends on his own initiative. Musset describes his generation as potential gladiators, and Stendhal's Julien Sorel imagines Napoleon as a hawk circling alone in the sky.

Honor and Resignation

Romantic sensibilities may feel aversion to prosaic civil society without accepting heroic self-assertion as a satisfying compensatory vision. The poet Alfred de Vigny warns against it: he knew that romantic heroism is a sad self-delusion. Vigny had experienced the frustrated longing for glory that fed romantic discontents: "I belong to that generation born with the century, which, fed upon the Emperor's bulletins, always had a drawn sword before its eyes, and which came to take it up at the very moment when France resheathed it in the Bourbon scabbard."[26] Fourteen "lost" years in the army cured him of his yearnings; although Vigny was not active in battle during his service in the royal guard, he did witness the routine degradation of the ordinary soldier. In *Military Servitude and Grandeur* he determines to dispel the myth that militarism is an invitation to heroic self-assertion.

Military life means monotony and idleness and everything cold, uniform, and adverse to intelligence. In modern commercial society, diplomacy and compromise replace combat. The army is reduced to inglorious police and parade functions. Soldiers are despised as idle and useless by the public. And when the army does act, it is on the orders of some political authority embroiling it in domestic disputes; in Vigny's tales the king, the emperor, and the directory deploy the military against their internal political enemies to serve their own ambitions. Musset imagined heroic action, but Vigny portrays the soldier reluctantly engaged in civil action, "employed to maltreat his mother" (p. 313). In place of self-assertion, Vigny describes self-abnegation. The man is effaced beneath the soldier, who acts never willfully or expressively but strictly in accord with duty. The soldier must resist the promptings of his heart and conscience. He is a martyr to discipline. "The Army is blind and dumb. It strikes where it is put ... It is a big thing that others control and that kills" (p. 31). Self-effacement has a rich spiritual history, but the soldier's renunciation is degrading.

Disillusioned with heroic dreams, Vigny is still enough of a romantic to invent a vehicle to express his own loathing of prosaic civil society. If one face of the military is servitude, the other is grandeur, and Vigny creates his own romanticized account of honor and esprit de corps. Military esprit is his answer to bourgeois society. A hierarchy of officers and men is structurally without a middle class. Military discipline is a standing criticism of egotism and materialism. The army is a "sacrificial family" where soldiers deny themselves daily comforts and luxuries, the pleasures of nature and of family life. No ethos is more antibourgeois than the one created by "vows of poverty and obedience," or more opposed to the social styles of both court and bourgeois than officers constrained to perpetual gravity, permitting themselves no familiarity or "friendly grace and gossip" (pp. 107, 34). Vigny calls the army a convent; once again, exclusion of women, even if unspoken, is central to the rejection of civil society.

Vigny's officer recalls older premodern characters—stoics or monks. But he is a genuine romantic type, a beautiful soul whose only peer is the artist. Vigny draws an explicit parallel between soldiers and poets. Like the outcast *poète maudit* who figures in Vigny's other works, the soldier is a pariah in civil society. Esprit de corps cannot protect them from the hatred or the hatefulness of the surrounding utilitarian universe, which makes the soldier an unhappy soul, aware of his "abnormal and absurd" situation set apart from the rest of the nation (p. 25).[27] Soldiers and poets suffer most acutely from the disenchantment of modern life. They are its real victims because they are deprived of opportunities for self-expression. Soldiers are forced to endure idleness or to perpetrate political crimes, and poets are condemned to soliloquy. Vigny's recommendation to both is stoic resignation.

We know from John Stuart Mill's essays that liberals perceived a deep conflict of values between militarism and commercial society. Mill is typically averse to the republican ideal because he associates the ethos of democratic republics with militarism and war. Whatever its limitations, he prefers commercial society, with its ideology of comfort, security, and personal liberty. And Mill insists that civic republicanism never enjoyed a strong hold on the English political imagination; the common response to the English Republic, he observes, was the desire for repose.[28] We also know from his essay "Civilization" that Mill saw romantic militarism as hopelessly anachronistic. In modern warfare "results are decided by the movement of masses," and individuals "sink into insignificance."[29] Both heroic self-assertion and esprit de corps are obsolete. Mill has no regrets; the practical advantages of modern military organization compensate for the demise of glory and devotion. Whereas Wordsworth described the irregular actions of the Spanish partisans as "a mighty engine of Nature" and thought them inspired, Mill calls the Spanish inept. They were incapable of acting together and of executing even the simplest rules of the military art. He dismisses romantic militarism from the standpoint of social progress: by definition civilization excludes romantic ideas of heroic self-sufficiency and inspired action. Civilization means differentiation and large-scale combination, and with these the inestimable benefits of order, prosperity, gentleness, and comfort.[30]

Even more striking than Mill's practical argument against militarism is his devastating response to the romantic sensibility itself and to its longings for heroism and honor. Mill reviewed Vigny's work for the *Edinburgh Review* and judged his picture of military grandeur and esprit de corps harshly. What Vigny portrays as noble self-effacement is really unmitigated self-absorption. The devoted soldier is focused entirely within. What he defends, after all, is his own honor. For Mill, Vigny describes antisocial detachment, not service—escape from the material and moral connectedness of life in civil society. Mill wants to point up the distance between ordinary self-interest and romantic self-concern: as a general state of mind, romanticism seemed to him "morbid and overcharged."

Things are complicated, however, because Mill was not always intolerant of romantic detachment. Vigny identified soldiers with poets, and Mill assents readily to half of this description. He is in perfect sympathy with Vigny's characterization of artists as inward, sensitive souls averse to society. He accepts without question the claim that detachment is the necessary condition for inspiration and creativity. Poetry, he writes, is "the natural fruit of solitude and meditation."[31] Mill applies this reasoning in his analysis of Vigny, remarking that when the Revolution of 1830 destroyed the elements of the past— royalist and Catholic—that Vigny loved, he became a sort of exile. This was for the best, Mill judges, because an unhappy state of mind is not an unfavorable one to poetry.[32] In adopting this connection between artistic creation and privatization, Mill suggests that liberalism might be open to a romantic justification of private liberty as the condition for imaginative expression. He suggests the possibility of an even more generous openness to romanticism if the benefits of detachment can be enjoyed by everyone, not just artists. But Mill has no patience with romantic sensibilities turning their desire for self-expression into wholesale opposition to commercial society or looking for opportunities for self-assertion in war. Between heroic longings and liberal promises of peace, there is no peace to be made.

There is, however, a position that shows sympathy for romantic longings yet is more conciliatory than Vigny's stern recommendation of silence and retreat. After all, stoic resignation to marginality holds out little satisfaction to either romantics or conventional liberals. The liberal politician and author Benjamin Constant offers something to both. He is able to chart a course from militarism home to liberalism while remaining faithful to romantic needs.

The Spirit of Conquest and the Spirit of Liberalism

Constant had many of the inclinations and antipathies of a true romantic soul. He agreed with the most ethereal German romantics that religious sentiment was nobler than calculating self-interest and that the rule of law was incommensurate with longings for self-expression. Like Humboldt he lamented the loss of the public life of the Greek polis and the falling off from "beautiful individuality." Before Musset's generation confessed its unhappiness, he had experienced for himself the terrible paralysis and ennui that would make progressive individualism such as Mill's alien to many romantics. Constant, however, was alert to the real political consequences of this disposition. He rejected heroic dreams on two grounds: that they were illusions, and that they were politically dangerous. He shared the sentimental life of romantic sensibilities, their psychology of longing, but not their excited political conclusions.

In *L'Esprit de Conquête* Constant argues that heroism is anachronistic because war can no longer provide occasions for exhilaration and self-display. Esprit de corps is also obsolete; where Vigny saw nobility in the military's separation from civil society and called the army a convent, Constant sees a hostile state within a state. Soldiers think of civilians as vulgar, laws as useless subtleties, and civil forms as insupportable burdens. These attitudes are dangerous. They subvert "regular and pacific liberty," which is in part what liberalism is about.[33] Constant also explains why romantics should care for regularity and peace, and why liberalism should be protected. He is insistent: because the romantic sensibility is safe under no other system.

For Constant, romantic illusions are not innocent. The world *is* disenchanted. There is nothing but the pursuit of self-interest. Under these conditions romantic dreams of popular wars of liberation, heroism, or esprit de corps will be manipulated by political men, resulting in awful invasions of personal liberty, not free expressiveness. Demagogues will talk about the genius of the people and promise fresh opportunities for glorious self-assertion. They will cloak their ambitions in the rhetoric of republicanism, exciting hopes for a joyous citizens' community. These are only pretexts for tyranny, to which romantics are peculiarly vulnerable. In the face of intense politicization under Robespierre and the calculating ambitiousness of Napoleon, militarist myths must be seen as politically treacherous and personally destructive.[34] For passionate politics does not leave men and women alone. Modern despotism "pursues the vanquished into the interior of their existence, it maims them spiritually in order to force them to conform."[35] The only hope for romantic souls is the peace and privacy of liberal society. That is what Constant thought liberalism can mean for romantics—protection from having their passions exploited and their grandiose sense of self seduced.

Out of this combination of romanticism and political scepticism, Constant organizes a defense of the entire framework of liberalism— of commercial society and constitutional government, representative institutions and the rule of law. Constant is too wary of rulers to want privatism exclusively. Self-government is necessary, but ideally its motivation is fear. Constant travels much the same course Humboldt did when he abandoned the cult of antiquity and argued for the nightwatchman state. Both justify liberalism negatively. It has no grandiose purposes and does not excite popular enthusiasm. It does not multiply duties or call up civic loyalties. It does not enervate, inspire, or give men and women "second natures." Its aim is to create the preconditions for commercial freedom, and in doing so it tends to leave people alone. The value of liberalism is its promise of personal liberty—not for the sake of legal persons or possessive individualists, though—for romantics.

Humboldt was optimistic that, left alone under the benign protection of the nightwatchman state, men would develop themselves into beautiful individualities—various, unique, and harmonious wholes. Constant is less sanguine about self-cultivation. His goal is modest. He limits the claims of politics in order to protect what there is of genuine personal feelings and imagination by providing time and space to explore one's inner self. Expressive political action, intense popular exaltation, and heroic display can produce only tyranny and deceit. Romantic longing is safe when there is a safe separation between public and private spheres. Constant adds a purely personal rationale for private life to the standard political ones.

From Militarism to Militancy

What if romantic sensibilities give up militarism but continue to resist dull routines and indulge heroic longings? What if they accept that life in civil society is the only possibility, but are not resigned to quietly tending their own gardens? Then militarism is transformed into militancy, and romantics escape ennui by investing ordinary existence with defiant energy. Then romanticism and liberalism clash directly.

Militancy can take several forms. The aesthetic form of defiance known as "épater la bourgeoisie" has antipathy to civil society built into its name. Exotic personal style is turned into a provocative assault on the philistines who constitute society. "Épater la bourgeoisie" means glorifying the obscure and nocturnal, the eccentric, demonic, bizarre, or pathological.[36] The bohemian modeled after the proletariat or outlaw, or the leisurely dandy modeled after the nobility, uses aloofness and stylistic nonconformity to shock and to draw attention to the uniqueness and the frustrations of the sensitive soul. "Épater la bourgeoisie" expresses both injury and pride.

Aesthetic defiance is essentially apolitical, gesture rather than action. It does not propose social reform, not even alternative social orders like Vigny's brotherhood of soldiers. However, there is a path from aesthetic provocation to the organized politics of resistance. In a pluralistic society, reactions of shock may be difficult to produce and still more difficult to sustain. Because defiance is unsatisfying unless it meets resistance, romantics may engage in action that is more than metaphorically violent, pushing liberalism beyond the limits of tolerance. Heroic defiance can also be lonely, leading romantics to invent affinities between their impulses and revolutionary socialism or anarchism. The sensitive soul may identify with others who are despised, and some suffering group becomes the recipient of the romantic's own anger and starved passions: "I was poor and desperate, life had no pleasures, the future seemed hopeless, yet I was overflowing with vehement desires, every nerve in me was a hunger which cried to be appeased . . . I identified myself with the poor and ignorant; I did not make their cause my own, but my cause theirs."[37] Finally, the practical limitations of aesthetic revolt are plain. If society appears as a philistine mass, a powerful social force must be amassed to oppose it—armed with an alternative social ideal as well.[38] But romantic sensibilities give up their identity as romantics when they subscribe wholly to the doctrines of a party, or when they adopt a style for its power to illustrate ideology, or when they look to political results rather than to self-expression.[39]

More common and more interesting than the aesthetic form of militancy is an aggressive, overcharged individualism. This militant individualism is very clearly a romantic exploitation of liberal ideas. Individualism is expressed, as it often is in liberal political thought, as the pursuit of private happiness. But romantics undertake the pursuit ferociously, seizing on pursuit of money and career, social advancement, and even love as opportunities for heroic self-assertion. Julien Sorel, the hero of Stendhal's *The Red and the Black,* is the militant individualist incarnate, and in Stendhal's story the romantic militant's strange affinity with liberal individualism emerges. Stendhal does for militancy what Vigny and Constant did for militarism proper— points to its internal failings and thus to the romantic sensibility's motivations for reconciliation.

Julien Sorel belongs to the generation that looks back on the Napoleonic wars as an opportunity lost: "I, condemned to wear this dreary black outfit forever . . . Alas! Twenty years sooner and I would have worn a uniform like them! In those days, a man like me was either killed in battle, or a general at thirty-six." Now the only struggles are narrowly political. Hypocrisy and talk are the weapons for victory in society. Eloquence replaces "the swiftness of action found at the time of the Empire," and Julien is so skilled in this peacetime form of aggression that he is "bored with the sound of his own voice." He cannot hide from himself his own disgust: "in another age, I would have earned my bread in the face of the enemy, by actions that speak for themselves." Although fellow romantics succumb to ennui, Julien Sorel remains faithful to his sense of personal power and infinite possibility, and asserts himself in the world. For Sorel life is a battle— even love—and Stendhal describes him seducing Madame de Rênal with "gaze atrocious, face hideous, instinct with unalloyed crime."[40] Sorel is at war with all of society.

Sorel does not employ the standard romantic weapons in his personal war from within: he does not produce subversive art like the *poète maudit,* or flout conventions like the dandy; he does not dream of the exaltation of popular wars of liberation, or immerse himself nostalgically in visions of military heroism and honor. Instead, he determines to exploit the social promise of liberal society—advancement by merit—to stake his immense, immodest claims. Society promises careers open to those with talent; Sorel will force society to recognize his genius and thus the inadequacy of its own measures, because genius cannot be encompassed in any single career. He will conquer every available social milieu and institutional domain, winning by the sheer force of his incomparable personality all the substitutes for glory that civil society offers. Rules and respectable forms have no meaning to him; they are things to be manipulated to suit his will. That is his revenge for having been born into a utilitarian universe. In Stendhal's character we see liberalism "elevated from a politics into a personal strategy, a way of outwitting the dullards who control things."[41]

Sorel's self-assertion bears an obvious resemblance to individualism, from which it springs, but to what kind of individualism, specifically, and exactly how does heroic self-assertion diverge from it? In the context of traditional liberal thought, individualism refers to moral autonomy and the capacity for rational consent, to possessive individualism and the claims of conscience. In every case individualism signifies a masterless person, free of deference and ascriptive attachments and privileges, though not without norms and attachments altogether. Atomistic individualism is a darker version. Antiliberals often attribute abstract, atomistic individualism to liberalism wholesale, as if liberal thought prescribed anomie as a norm, or as if the condition followed necessarily from some liberal theory of human nature, according to which all preferences and attachments are arbitrary, contingent, and insubstantial. To these critics atomistic individualism seems to speak for itself of liberalism's failings. It is this classless, placeless individualism without moral content that Stendhal portrays in Julien Sorel. He is an atom, a man without associations or property, interest-group loyalties or profession—without all those connections that bind individuals to others and to a social order.

Sorel's militant self-assertion bears an even more complicated relationship to liberal individualism. In its endless, insatiable striving it evokes the pursuit of happiness at the heart of liberal thought. Activism without a definite end is part of the notion of liberation and inherent in the idea of progress. Personal liberty is inseparable from the assumption that there is no fixed or natural limit to desires or to the advance of interests. Incessant willing is strongest in utilitarianism, which unleashes desires, proclaims the sovereignty of pleasure and pain, and proposes maximizing satisfaction as the sole imperative.

The romantic image of an unrestrained self—militant, sentimental,

or creative—would have been unimaginable without Jeremy Bentham's devastating attack on asceticism and his emancipation of desires. Utilitarianism assumes variety. It seems to admit a fantastic
array of pleasures, values, and ends. And it seems to require the outside
world to yield to internal imperatives, opening up possibilities for a
fantastic company of relations and schemes to maximize happiness.
Once again, the antagonism between romantic and liberal ideas con-
ceals a deep affinity. Julien Sorel would have been simply inconceivable if utilitarianism had not conquered asceticism and liberated
desires—if individualism had not been tied so securely to the pursuit
of happiness.

Yet the utilitarian portrait of men and women in society is nothing
like Stendhal's. In Bentham's arid fantasy of reason, calculation secures common expectations, and rules reign. What began with the
sovereign individual, and with justice tied to respect for variations
among individuals, ends by making the aggregate supreme. Moral
philosophers have argued against the principle of utility in terms of
the right to equal liberty, pointing out that a logical consequence of
the doctrine is the sacrifice of some individuals to the greatest happiness. But for romantics, failure to secure equal liberty for everyone
is not what matters most. The trouble rests with the whole idea of
maximizing happiness.[42] Both elements of the idea are abhorrent: the
calculation itself, and the elements of happiness that ordinarily enter
into it. If militant individualism can be traced to the notion of pursuit
of happiness, its excesses stem from antiutilitarianism.

Romantics insist that the scales of utilitarianism cannot weigh inestimable pleasures like beauty, and that calculations of the greatest
happiness—in which each person counts for one—do not take genius
into account.[43] All the "little employments" to accumulate pleasures
have the character of endless dreary misery: "The twelve labors of
Hercules were trifling in comparison with those my neighbors have
undertaken; . . . but I could never see that these men slew or captured
any monster or finished any labor," Thoreau wrote.[44] His revulsion
at his Concord neighbors suggests that liberalism can seem a dreary,
unheroic philosophy of anxiety: "It was anxiety which drove liberal
man to unrelenting activity—anxiety from struggling to eke out existence in the face of a hostile nature, anxiety from the precarious
state of possessions in a society where the masses were often desper-
ately hungry, and, equally strong, anxiety stemming from the appetites
instilled by society."[45]

Altogether, utilitarianism seems to romantics to describe a person who is wholly reactive, who acts only in response to sensations. Attention is turned perpetually outward to the mundane sources of pleasure and pain, rather than inward. This individualism is mechanistic and ignoble. The "tyranny" of pleasure and pain and the "subjection" of men and women to their imperatives—Bentham's extended metaphor for mental operations—can seem to romantics a perfectly accurate description of the condition of their contemporaries. Against this they propose alternative notions (really, alternative metaphors) of mental activity in which imagination or another inner resource—energy, emotion, or some unnamed power—informs the world.[46] Where utilitarians diminish the self to empirical pleasures and pains, romantics give the self a deep generative center. One notion of self is inert and reactive, the other expressive.

Utility, summed up as instrumentalism, is as old as human action. As part of the systematic conceptual apparatus of modern thought, however, it is self-conscious, formalized, and the source of norms. Bentham did more than pronounce the sovereignty of pleasure and pain; he also assigned reason the role of obeying their imperatives and made it a principle of morals and legislation to advance the greatest happiness of the greatest number. In liberal thought the pursuit of happiness may be endless, but as a mode of conduct in the world it is the essence of rationality. It means self-interested action, and the very term "interest" points to something definite and limited; it was invented to distinguish regular ends from inordinate ones like glory or religious zealotry. Julien Sorel lives out a romantic version of the pursuit of happiness extravagant to the point of violation. He asserts his claims to willfulness and gratification but is averse to calculation and self-control. For Julien Sorel pursuit is expressive, not instrumental, and distinct from utilitarianism.

Julien Sorel abandons the inherent restraints of instrumentalism. He gives little thought to particular interests he wants to promote. His striving is unrelated to making a living or acquiring possessions or maximizing general happiness. The injustice he rages against is not that society has failed to make him secure or to reward some particular labor or service, but that society has failed to recognize his extraordinary self. And as he imagines it, his self is not benignly desirous but satanic. He is charged with a passion for something the conventional pursuit of happiness simply does not take into account: distinction and self-display. He embodies a certain kind of structural impediment to calculation and satisfaction, which makes incessant pursuit inevitable. He is manic. For him "life is a fever."

Militancy means self-assertion and the willful exploitation of liberty; but conflict is its essence and, finally, the truest measure of its distance from a liberal politics designed to maximize happiness by adjusting and reconciling interests. Julien Sorel must come into conflict with society. He has a sense of himself only when he feels resistance; his individuality depends on it. Hence the contradiction that always threatens to undermine militant individualism: social success and recognition cut the ground from under the militant's stance. If liberal society is sufficiently tolerant or admiring, frustration is guaranteed. In Julien Sorel, Stendhal demonstrates how the romantic militant needs the constraints of conventional liberalism, how militancy cannot exist without the liberal ethos of calculation and self-control. Legalism and utilitarianism provide the necessary resistant context within which romantic sensibilities can work out their own immoderation.

The militant is stranded between pure romantic expressivism and liberal individualism. And because he is self-divided in this way, he is thwarted. Sorel is a model of failed defiance; his character helps to explain why some romantics become chastened and susceptible to the appeals of liberalism. For Stendhal tells a story of bruising self-defeat. Julien Sorel fails to find enduring love, to amass wealth, or to ascend in society for two opposite reasons, each associated with one part of his character as a militant individualist. He fails first because in trying to exploit the promises of a utilitarian universe he does not calculate well—because he is not sufficiently reasonable and self-interested. He also fails because he is unfaithful to his imagination and passionate sensibility by calculating at all. He is both too little and too much a strategist; too little and too much a romantic soul.

One way to uncover this devastating self-division in Sorel is through the female characters in *The Red and the Black,* who are corrective portraits: Madame de Rênal is the genuine romantic and Mathilde de la Mole the successful opportunist.[47] Like Julien, Mathilde is all energy and indomitable will, a solitary figure bent on distinguishing herself. She too is moved by imagination, by her identification with a sixteenth-century ancestor; acutely aware of the ridiculousness of the aristocracy in bourgeois society, she revolts against it, but she puts her intelligence and social acumen to work. Compared to her calculated self-serving, Sorel's conduct is wild, compulsive self-assertion.

The portrait of genuine emotion and spontaneity is Madame de Rênal, the conventional provincial wife. Until she falls in love with Julien Sorel, she submits to the stupid opinion of small-town France.

Then she follows the dictates of her heart unselfconsciously, setting aside the claims of reason, custom, and law. For Stendhal, Madame de Rênal's passion is more subversive than Sorel's heroic self-assertion. Pure feeling makes her the true independent spirit and the real social threat. She embodies the romantic "law of the heart," which Stendhal rightly depicts as an even more powerful attack on civil society than romantic militarism. It challenges liberalism at its legalistic core. Of romantic attacks on liberalism, none is more devastating.

CHAPTER 2

The Law of the Heart versus Liberal Legalism

The same longings for perfect freedom and unconstrained self-expression that inspire romantic militarism are at work in what I call "romantic anarchy," only here opposition is less to peace and the prosaic routines of civil society than to their underpinnings in legalistic culture. Romantic anarchy opposes law, its attendant ethos of fairness and impartiality, and the disposition to make and obey rules.[1] It rejects legalism for its own characteristic reasons: rules are insufferably dry and impersonal, and rule-following stifles individuality. In place of general, impersonal laws romantic anarchists want to obey the commands of feeling. In place of predictability they want spontaneity. Here the response to liberalism is not militant self-assertion but the gentler, anarchic "law of the heart."

For these romantic sensibilities, legalism is anathema in any department of life, not just the juridical state. Romantics would purify religion of ritual and doctrine, separating spirituality from form. They are repulsed by bureaucratization. They cannot abide social artifices and conventions. In art, they flee official academies and defy rules of style. They attack the propensity to look for universal laws of human nature or of morals. They find intolerable a political society that gives central place to lawyers and courts, claims and counterclaims. Romanticism addresses its challenges to legalistic culture generally and to liberalism in particular, since liberalism is the political philosophy par excellence of constitutionalism and rights, due process and the rule of law.

For its part, liberalism distrusts the law of the heart. Whereas romantics resist legalism, liberals promote it. In fact, the whole tendency of liberalism is antiromantic. It is designed to suppress the affective and personal from social life. Circumscribed political authority and settled standing rules eliminate the personal from the use of power. Legal formalism insures that relations among men and women are impartial and indirect. Rules value the general, and they speak impersonally to men and women in general. In the last chapter I showed that one justification for possessive individualism was that it protects against heroic virtues. In the same way, one justification for legalism is that it protects political society from the intrusion of emotional inclinations. Liberalism is not ignorant of the power and appeal of individuality and spontaneity; on the contrary, it is intent on containing them. Consider Jeremy Bentham, who writes about the sovereignty desires but whose real business is translating subjectivity into objectivity. Bentham's fervor is for legal formalism, and his work demonstrates that legislation, classification, and codification add up to a strategy for suppressing every trace of the personal and spontaneous from political life.

Romantic objections to law and legal processes differ from those that usually occupy political theorists. Adherents of radical and conservative political ideologies dispute the substantive content of legislation. Their concern is the injustice of liberal society, and they call for systematic changes in the institutions or social classes that make and enforce laws. Philosophers critical of certain liberal theories of justice argue that where "the right" has priority over "the good," where fairness has greater weight than agreement about the collective ends of a community, justice is barren. And from within liberal jurisprudence, legal theorists object to formalism when it eclipses informal ways of reaching decisions and resolving disputes. Unlike these critics, romantic anarchists do not challenge particular laws, or even particular systems of law. Their complaint is not injustice, but the personal inhibitions created by the social ethos of rules.

The romantic fear that legalism affects men and women personally is not groundless. Liberalism imposes the discipline of legalism. It expects more of its citizens than just the law-abiding behavior that any regime, including the most authoritarian, wants and enforces. Liberalism expects in addition an active disposition to respect rules and rights. It assumes personalities for whom making and following laws feels comfortable, as well as practical and just.

Antilegalism provides another window onto the complex, reciprocal way romanticism and liberalism work on each other. Neither their opposition nor their reconciliation is one-sided. Like romantic militarists, romantic anarchists can be chastened and brought home to liberalism. The painful failures of the law of the heart become apparent to even its most sympathetic followers. And liberalism has self-doubts too. Legal formalism protects against some tyrannies, guarantees certain forms of liberty, and supports a sophisticated commercial economy, but even correct procedures can be oppressive. Legalism has excesses and unintended consequences of its own.

The Impersonal Ethos of Liberal Government

Historically, liberal commitment to legalism comes from experience with political tyrannies that have one thing in common—arbitrariness. Legal formalism is one way to prevent governors from acting on their personal inclinations.[2] Constitutional divisions of power, systematic checks and balances, impersonal offices, rights upheld by independent courts of law, periodic elections, and ministerial responsibility are all techniques for containing arbitrariness and dissociating power from persons. That is one of the promises of limited government. Alongside the balancing of ambitions and interests is the institutionalization of impersonality, and with it impartiality and predictability. "Government of laws not men" rests less on distrust of power than on distrust of personality.

Liberal theorists often have a mistrustful, even misanthropic view of human nature, which is why suppression of the personal and expressive is so urgent. Montesquieu, Madison, and Kant were all concerned that government be organized so that even intelligent devils could manage it. The most intractable source of arbitrariness is not simple egotism, still less moral corruption or the absence of civic virtue, but the inescapability of intense personal emotions and attachments. Everything personal is irrational and dangerous, a potential source of unsafety, cruelty, and repression. Experience with both monarchic and revolutionary politics taught liberals that kinship and friendship, love and abomination give rise to partiality. They are fervent and unpredictable. Threats to impartiality and rights arise not only from private interests, but also from private passions. Liberalism's task is to protect against personal politics and the chaos of unconstrained self-expression. That is why "everyman" should be able to govern a well-organized liberal state, and why no one should be personally evident in the process of government.

It seems strange to speak of zeal for impersonality, but that is what inspires liberal theorists to insist that rules prevail even in areas beyond the laws of the state. When Locke advocated the separation of public and private spheres by separating civil from ecclesiastical power, he conceived of church and state as distinct societies, each making its own laws though they enforce them by different means. Civil society comprises the activities of men and women who respect rules and expect fairness, who plan, predict, and build institutions to ensure regularity. Private life is legalistic too, and if not all "private governments" are democratic or even liberal, they should be formally organized and operated in accordance with rules. Clearly, sophisticated economic pursuits depend on a complicated web of calculations, contracts, and forms. Legalism makes good faith and trust rational. It also imposes on men and women the discipline of thinking and acting *as if* they were abstract individuals, requiring them to disregard character and beliefs, loyalties, loves, tastes, and aversions. Looking on one another as legal persons for purposes of law and exchange requires self-control; that is why legalism is the "discipline" of liberalism. The social ethos of rules is pervasive.

When everything personal and affective is perceived as disturbing and potentially despotic and cast outside the bounds of political thought, certain experiences are left out of the official subject matter of political theory though they continue to have a bearing on political life. Liberalism has difficulty assigning a place to the family, for example, or patriotism, or the politics of personal leadership—except to warn against it. There is no intellectual justification for ignoring these elements of experience. But there are good reasons for valuing legal formalism and for thinking that everyone benefits when government must act according to rules and in conformity with rights rather than with the inclinations of rulers. The trouble is that these traditional reasons may not always be strong enough to convince romantic sensibilities that for many purposes individuality is safely ignored. Romantics are disinclined to agree that the constraints of impersonality are wholly beneficial, that "as citizens there is no one who feels this deprivation as a loss to himself."[3] For Schiller, the sense of deprivation was real: "Compelled to disburden itself of the diversity of its citizens by means of classification, and to receive humanity only at second hand, by representation, the governing section finally loses sight of it completely . . . and the governed cannot help receiving coldly the laws which are addressed so little to themselves." The state, he insists, should respect "not merely the objective and generic, but also the subjective and specific character" of individuals.[4]

From the point of view of conventional liberalism there are also good reasons to value the spread of legalism throughout the secondary associations of society. Formally organized groups provide sources of power outside of government to limit it. They provide supportive contexts for developing habits of making and following rules for individuals who would otherwise be strangers to one another, unable to form expectations and unable to engage in regular, productive relations at all. But from the point of view of romantics for whom the constraint of rules is an intolerable inhibition, it means that pluralism is experienced as uniformity—as the social ethos of rules taking over the whole fabric of private as well as public life. They are repulsed by Weber's observation that in a legalistic culture we need to retain "a legal father confessor" for all the contingencies of life.[5] Legalism can seem imperialistic; its discipline intrudes everywhere.

Some of the excesses of legal formalism are felt most acutely by romantic sensibilities who insist, with Schiller, that "the law of uniformity extinguishes in men . . . the last glimmering sparks of spontaneity and individuality."[6] Other kinds of excess emerge from and are acknowledged by liberalism itself. The problem is to sort out these distinct reactions.

The Limits of Legal Formalism

Legalism is central to liberalism, but even traditional liberals harbor misgivings about law and see laws as (necessary) evils. Bentham reminds us that since every law is an infraction of liberty, every law causes some people to suffer. Conventional liberal theory also recognizes the need for exceptions to law and for discretion in practice. Liberalism's first objective may be impartial laws enforced without discretion, but no rule of law can prescribe for every potential set of circumstances. That is why trust is an important part of Lockeian liberalism.[7] Locke makes the standard argument for executive prerogative: some actions necessary for public order simply cannot conform to rules. Liberals point out further that not all social disputes can be resolved through litigation. Miscarriage of justice, the pain of punishment, and the rigor of *fiat justitia* also inspire criticisms of legal formalism.

So, from within liberal political theory and jurisprudence come justifications for legal departures from rules by both officials and citizens.[8] Perhaps the oldest arguments for modifying legal formalism recommend discretion in the administration of justice. The broad discretion enjoyed by juries is one example.[9] Another is the periodic attempt by judges to make every individual a separate case and to adapt punishment to the individual offender. Legalism confronts its own limitations most dramatically with the power of pardon, which allows officials to exempt individuals from punishment. Pardon originated as the most personal exercise of power by the king, the one most entirely his own, and most often referred to when kings laid claim to the personal loyalty and affection of the people.[10] But as it has evolved, the pardon is neither a personal exercise of executive power nor intended to be in the personal interest of the pardoned, which is why it is enacted without regard to the criminal's own desires.[11] The executive must refrain from bringing to bear reasons or feelings extraneous to his or her official role, under penalty of impeachment. The pardon is to be used only to avoid mistake, undue prejudice, or needless severity.[12] The justification for discretion is that the public good is better served by inflicting lesser punishment than by carrying out the judgment formally fixed. The pardon power is also justified politically, as a way to facilitate a return from civil conflict to order so that the regular rule of law can be restored. This was Hamilton's reasoning in *The Federalist* 74: it is "a timely amnesty" to insurgents to restore public tranquillity. These deviations from legal formalism are employed to strengthen legal obligations by reducing tension between the law's formal demands and its agreed-on ends.[13] This antiformalism is still legalistic.

Proposed alternatives to litigation are usually legalistic as well. The title of Jerold Auerbach's recent work on the subject, *Justice Without Law*, is misleading.[14] "Alternative dispute resolution" does not reverse the history of legalism at all.[15] Even in arbitration, justice involves discovering a norm according to which each party gets its due, a norm that could be applied again in similar instances. Mediation too deals in claims and counterclaims. Courts have never been the sole institution upholding justice and law, only the most formal, and both arbitration and mediation have a secure place on the continuum of legalistic institutions.

Recent interest in informal justice reflects a curious mix of pragmatic and romantic concerns. One practical intention is to put some parties (chiefly low-income minority groups) in an allegedly better position to press their claims than they would have in a court of law. Another is to provide quicker and less costly justice in the face of overloaded court dockets. Clearly, these are attempts to improve due process, not transcend it. Perhaps the most common motive for advocating informal justice is animus against legalism seen as the self-serving ideology of lawyers; the subtitle of *Justice Without Law* is "Resolving Disputes Without Lawyers."

Alongside these practical arguments against legal formalism is one that echoes Schiller's romantic lament that law is as "cold and dry as a shackle." According to this thinking, litigation expresses "a chilling, Hobbesian vision of human nature." Laws exist only at the margins of community, where "solitary individuals feel the need to protect themselves against one another."[16] The unmistakable hope is that social relations will lose their adversarial character if formal legal processes are replaced. Impersonal respect and formal equality will give way to mutual empathy and trust. What is wanted is warm, affective community. The whole argument evokes romantic claims that law inhibits feeling.

From the point of view of genuine romantic anarchy, however, the difference between courts and arbitration or mediation is trivial, because these informal processes do not begin to address the longing for affect and spontaneity. Vigny's compensatory image of justice is a much more dramatic departure from legalism: "the simple and serious opinion handed down to his family by a desert Fellah, giving the judgment of his heart." In sharp contrast to this vision is legislation, "the flabby sinews of the Assemblies, whose limp, vacillating, ambiguous, misguided, corrupt, bewildered, limping, choleric, sluggish, vapid, cheerful, but always and eternally common and vulgar ideas" regulate conduct in modern society.[17] Vigny's dream of personal "Kadi-justice" may not appeal to all romantics, either, since the law of the heart rejects any external judgment. Romantic anarchy is typically unconcerned with justice. The law of the heart is expressive, not an alternative source of social norms.

This concern with individuality and spontaneity rather than social order is clearer still in contrast to conservative arguments against legal formalism. Edmund Burke advised that the laws of the French National Assembly were frail because they were supported only by punishment and "by the concern which each individual may find in them for his own private speculations or can spare to them from his own private interest."[18] The conservative view of legal positivism is that it is strictly utilitarian, and as such brittle. Law, it is argued, cannot compel obedience unless it is loved. In this spirit, customary law became the mark of what was called the romantic theory of jurisprudence in Germany, which subordinated positive law to organic laws that were the outgrowth of *Volksgeist*.

Plainly, the conservative quarrel is not with legalism, but with the liberal view of law's origin and force. What conservatives want is more hierarchy, not less; concrete duties, not freedom from formal obligations. Conservatism opposes sentiment to formal rights and abstract equality, but the point is for sentiments and obligations to coincide, not for raw sentiments to reign. In conservative thought, sentiments are a source of cohesion, not personal self-expression; they attach to a definite social order of rules. Spontaneity means organic growth rather than willfulness, inspiration, or irrepressible passion, and it is a quality of historical communities, not individuals. Romantic anarchy shares only conservatism's disdain for ordinary self-interest. The source of romantic anarchy is its striving for boundlessness, not order.

Unconcern for social order also separates romantic antilegalism from most forms of anarchist political thought. Traditional anarchist theorists such as Proudhon or Kropotkin want what the state provides—security and social order—only without government. In contemporary anarchist theory the two alternatives to the state are libertarian and anarcho-capitalist models, in which private firms compete in the market to provide social services, and community models in which members share beliefs and practice reciprocity. Both types of anarchism eliminate the state, but neither eliminates legalism. There are laws of the marketplace predicated on rational and efficient behavior; more important, expectations and voluntary contractual arrangements to meet them require forms and rules. Reciprocity and mutual aid, the most common anarchist alternatives to formal rules, are not spontaneous either. They entail counting on others to conform to a code of action against which claims and counterclaims can be made. Anarchism illustrates Weber's description of legalism as a continuum of law, convention, and usage.[19]

It should not be surprising that most anarchist thought remains legalistic. Anarchists oppose the state, but they have a definite vision of social order. Maximizing personal liberty may be one aim among others, but not always; in any case coordination takes priority. That is why anarchism does not ordinarily do without coercion any more than it does without rules. Socialization is rarely considered an adequate substitute for the official use of force by the state, and in anarchist communities it is supplemented by severe measures such as retaliation, withdrawal of reciprocity, and sanctions of approval and disapproval.[20] By contrast, romantic anarchy has nothing to do with social order and control. It is concerned with individuality and self-expression, with perfect freedom.

I use the term anarchy to describe this aspect of romanticism because for liberalism especially the term evokes lawlessness and chaos. In fact, chaotic emotionalism accompanies the law of the heart. But liberalism, despite its concern for security and regularity, is able to tolerate individuals' exempting themselves from the obligation to follow rules. Recognizing the limitations of legalism, it legitimates disobedience. Not every sort of extralegal conduct is antilegal, as romantic anarchy is. The question then becomes how romantic anarchy relates to the types of disobedience that have a firm place in traditional liberal thought.

Individualism and Disobedience

Liberal self-reflection recognizes not only some of the limitations of legal formalism and the need for exceptions in practice but also grounds for certain illegal departures from rules. The rationales for civil disobedience in liberal thought include appeals to higher law and appeals from actual political practices to some original political standard or ideal.[21] Legislation in liberal societies is not always faithful to the promise of generality, and legally designated classes are not always fair ones. The question of substantive equality—of the social conditions necessary for enjoying theoretically universal rights—is pressing too. Civil disobedience is also justified in terms of individualism. The formulation of the individual's right to personally consent to the rules he or she must obey invites comparison with romantic antilegalism, with its focus on one person's disposition to throw off the shackles of law.

According to consent or social contract theory civil disobedience arises in objection to specific laws, either because the dissenter feels that no one should consent to them or because of the absence of institutions by which individuals could consent to them if they would.[22] Civil disobedience is selective. It does not object to consenting to laws altogether, as romantic anarchy does, nor does it proceed from revulsion at rule-following. In fact, in moral and political theory consent is the condition for taking on legally defined duties. Autonomy is typically demonstrated by agreeing to be bound by selective obligations, not by refusing to be bound altogether.[23]

On this view, obligations are experienced as alien and coercive when individuals do not agree to accept them. The absence of personal consent justifies civil disobedience, but the right to disobey does not usually imply the right to legislate for oneself. Civil disobedients refuse to recognize the absolute supremacy of legal obligations which they have not agreed to assume—without claiming that they, personally or individually, are the source of authoritative norms or enjoy the right to perfect arbitrariness. Romantic anarchy takes the metaphor of the sovereign self more seriously. Where the law of the heart is the only law, personal feelings reign. The romantic self is the sole source of imperatives.

An early literary model of romantic anarchy is Robber Moor, the hero of Schiller's drama *The Robbers*. In response to betrayal by his tyrannical brother the prince, the Moor escalates his defiance from libertinism to crime. He is inspired less by injustice, however, than by his sense that prosaic laws are impossible constraints: "Am I to squeeze my body into stays and straitlace my will in the trammels of law? What might have risen to an eagle's flight has been reduced to a snail's pace by law. Never yet has law formed a great man; 'tis liberty that breeds giants and heroes."[24] Romantic anarchy does not usually take the form of such heated defiance. Nor is it always grandiose; more often it is sentimental. Robber Moor's band, for example, follows him out of loyalty and love, not egotism; still, for them, too, arrant emotionalism and lawlessness are allied. The Moor is an exemplary romantic anarchist because he is beyond the reach of rules, a literal outlaw. The histrionic Moor also embodies romantic anarchy's preoccupation with self-display. In political thought, civil disobedience is always socially conscious—to borrow terms from Albert Hirschman, it is a matter of voice, not of exit or escape.[25] Romantic anarchy disregards public purposes and political reform; like Schiller's Robber Moor, it is self-absorbed.

Conscientious objection is the form of civil disobedience recognized by liberal theorists that most resembles romantic anarchy, for one thing because it is self-centered. It is often described as an obligation to oneself, in which the chief concern is less political change than personal purity. The conscientious objector opposes obligations imposed by law in order to avoid complicity in evil. Conscience may be personal and exclusive; conscientious objection does not necessarily imply that the same inner voice speaks to everyone, or that others should object to the law if they are not impelled by some inner voice of their own. Conscientious objection demands personal exemption, not reform.

Of course, conscientious objection is often a collective affair. It can be based on "common Christian conscience" or the shared moral outlook of members of a community rather than on private judgment, and the resulting exemptions often have political purposes and effects indistinguishable from those of civil disobedience. Dissenting sects in England exemplify the stand of a religious group dissociated from the dominant religious culture. In *Obligations* Michael Walzer interprets the history of liberalism in these terms, as a process of gradual toleration by the state of claims for exception by marginal groups. He also argues that liberal society provides particularly fertile ground for civil disobedience based on conscience. Pluralism and freedom of association encourage the claims of divergent groups. Membership in these secondary associations is often dependent on consent to definite obligations, while citizenship in a liberal state is ordinarily a matter of birth and imposes only minimal duties. As a result citizenship is a weak and partial sort of membership compared to membership in these other, stronger groups, which Walzer calls "internal emigration." This produces the hard politics of pluralist societies—political conflict and civil disobedience.

Walzer proposes that liberal society could safely allow conscientious objection to every law and obligation, not just extraordinary ones like military service. However, not all who abandon a legal duty in order to be true to themselves merit the title "conscientious." Walzer is consistently communitarian; for him, civil disobedience is always a collective act and is justifiable only in terms of an overriding obligation to a group other than the state.[26] Hannah Arendt argued in the same vein: the civil disobedient "never exists as a single individual; he can function and survive only as a member of a group."[27] More than just a strategic argument about the necessity for group support in effecting reform, this assertion reflects assumptions about the origin and nature of conscience itself. It links obligation to legalism by assuming that conscience must be distinguishable from unique and spontaneous personal impulses to count as a justification of disobedience. Walzer discounts heroic encounters between the sovereign personality and the law. His conscientious objector, who is affiliated with an organized group, represents himself as someone who typically acts according to rules. He articulates strong reasons why an exception to the law should be made in his case, and shows that these reasons constitute a clear standard he can regularly adhere to. Here legitimate disobedience is manifestly legalistic, like the conscience that inspires it.

Of course individual conscience and individual disobedience have a respectable place in liberal thought, but the legalistic individual conscience resembles Walzer's notion of group values more than it does romantic anarchy and the law of the heart. The Kantian notion of conscience is at least as formal as the collective conscience of a religious community. Even at its most individual, conscience is a form of rectitude with imperatives that are often universal. It can be as impersonal as Kant's legislating will, whereas the point of the romantic law of the heart is its personal imperatives. The romantic anarchist is undermined rather than strengthened by agreement, by the fact that his or her feelings are shared by others. The law of the heart is an exclusive personal guide to what is right; if its sentiment turns out to be a common moral imperative, it loses its force and appeal. If it corresponds to a conventional principle of action or produces co-operation and general assent, then it is no longer a spontaneous personal directive, but an external law like any other.

Conscientious objectors ask for exemption from a particular law, not from being law-abiding. They want toleration, not perfect liberty. Conscience is not supposed to be an alternative to law, after all. It is not a positive guide to conduct: "conscience speaks only to forbid." A tender and self-absorbed romantic sensibility who wants to substitute spontaneous feelings for following rules will not be content with exemption or toleration. Every law and convention will be experienced as an unbearable constraint. The only imperative is the law of the heart.

The Law of the Heart

The romantic law of the heart makes faithfulness to feelings the measure of all things. Under its reign, actions spring from impulses, not purposes. They are lovely and sincere, not dutiful or instrumental. Spontaneity is crucial because the immediacy of feelings is proof that they are authentic and uncontaminated by law, convention, or calculation. Sincerity is opposed to artifice and, more important, connected with genuine self-expression. The point is not that sentiments be natural, in Rousseau's sense, but that they be personal. The law of the heart is opposed not to vice but to hypocrisy. And every action conforming to rules will seem hypocritical; because it is impersonal, it cannot reflect the romantic's own deepest inclinations.

Underlying the law of the heart are assumptions about the inner self, chief among them that it is unique. Thus individuality makes conformity to law insufferable, since rules number, name, and constrain modes of action and interfere with the free play of energy and originality. In addition there is the sense that the romantic self is potentially full of feelings. Emotional life is mysterious, undefined, and protean. The romantic experience is not unity of sentiment but tumult; longings are variable and boundless. By contrast the preferences utilitarians speak of maximizing are not only cold but unambiguous and sharply defined. The precision and definition of Bentham's legal language reflects his ambition to simplify desires. The romantic law of the heart gives the lie to clarity. Schiller captured the indeterminacy of self-conception perfectly: he called personality "merely the potentiality of a possible infinite expressions."[28]

Because the law of the heart means following not just feelings, but inspired feelings that are evidence of individuality and spontaneity, romantics sometimes associate it with artistic creativity. In Vigny's novel *Stello,* for example, when the would-be poet Stello is asked for signs of his genius, he points to his exquisite sensibility: "I believe firmly that I have been called to a transcendental vocation; the proof is the boundless pity which all men . . . inspire in me, and my constant desire to reach out to them and sustain them with words of sympathy and love . . . while it lives in me, my whole soul lights up . . . and then it is that the golden phoenix of Illusion settles on my lips, and sings." To which the sober Dr. Noir replies, "All that proves nothing but a good heart."[29] Vigny knew that emotionalism and longing for self-expression were not poetic genius. For most followers of the law of the heart, though, a good heart is enough. Freedom means uninhibited obedience to its impulses, particularly tender sentiments of pity, fellow-feeling, and love.

Of course, among personality's "possible infinite expressions" are many that are not benign. The dynamic of inwardness and emergence may produce the dark, dirty, dangerous, and primitive. Envy and loathing may erupt from deep within. After all, unbridled negativity abhors instrumentalism and legalism just as much as pity. The initially tender picture of the law of the heart is marred in other ways. Where impulse is everything, the impulses of two hearts may conflict, and unlike interests sentiments cannot be compromised. No argument can make one heart's sincere feelings more valid than another's, or show why benevolence should take precedence over cruelty. Still, as an alternative to instrumental man, the law of the heart usually suggests sympathy and love. These are the truly personal sentiments associated with marriage and other intimate relations—perhaps unrealistically, as envy, cruelty, and brutality have a secure place in private as well as public life. In fact, one of the reasons for wanting impersonal government is to restrict personal inclinations to private life.

Tender feelings may not be the only feelings, but even they reveal the profound inadequacies of the law of the heart. For when romantics seek expression in friendship or love their utter self-absorption becomes apparent. The law of the heart is incapable of intimacy because it cannot accommodate the hearts of others. Just as the law of the heart cannot provide a source of moral norms and social bonds, it cannot support personal relations. Not only is society insufficiently present in romantic sensibilities, intimate connections are elusive too.[30]

"Love," Shelley wrote, "is the bond and the sanction which connects not only man with man but with everything that exists"; love is "a fusion of all affinities."[31] The metaphor of fusion contrasts dramatically with the liberal image of contractual relations. Even compared with fraternity, it is manifestly spiritual or erotic rather than solidaristic. In fact, connection with "everything which exists" is no actual connection at all. Fusion supplants relationship. Romantic love rarely resembles Shelley's neo-Platonic idea, with its implication of self-transcendence. The law of the heart does not propose losing oneself in love or finding another self in one's friend. It exploits friendship as an opportunity for self-expression. Relationship is eclipsed here too, because the law of the heart is utterly self-involved.

Apart from hoping their own feelings are powerful, pure, and direct, romantics have little to say that has any bearing on relations with others. With its emphasis on boundlessness and spontaneity, there is nothing in the law of the heart to insure that friendship or love will be continuous, much less committed. The law of the heart certainly does not require consideration of the consequences of feelings for others. Even within the narrow field of intimate relations it is irresponsible. It cannot endure discipline or necessity, not even the necessity of considering the beloved's welfare. If friendship is deemed stronger than social conventions or legal duties, it is not because acts of friendship are due to others or because a good character is one that acts as a friend, but simply because friendship is a spontaneous felt imperative. The law of the heart attends only to its own potential for expression.

Other psychologies of sentiment avoid the romantic's thoroughgoing self-concern and successfully enrich ethics. I am thinking in particular of Carol Gilligan's study *In a Different Voice*, which describes a distinctive kind of moral thinking by women whose feelings compel them to protect a fabric of human relationships. Their impulses are coherent, not boundless. They form an articulated ethic that aims at inclusion, cooperation, and interdependence among people in close relations with one another. The dominant consideration is neither formal justice nor self-expression, but concern for the needs of others. Responsibility entails something in addition to liberal self-control and respect for the rights or liberty of others. It can be expressive: "Responsibility signifies response, an extension rather than a limitation of action . . . seeking the resolution that would be most inclusive of everyone's needs."[32]

Because preservation of delicate personal attachments cannot be accomplished by following rules, the morality of this "different voice" is antilegalistic. But it is not self-absorbed. Its psychological logic fosters attachment, not just a sense of one's own potential for feeling, as the romantic law of the heart does.

This ethic of caring and responsibility—not to, but for others—is not the only one that rejects legalism, appeals to feelings, and still avoids solipsistic self-concern. Altruism, charity, and Rousseau's natural morality of pity do so as well. The law of the heart differs from all of these because it is not principally concerned about conduct toward others at all. The law of the heart and its antilegalism are distinctive less because they appeal to sentiment or irrationalism than because they tend to ignore human ties.

In Hume's moral theory, to take another case for contrast, moral judgments are expressions of feeling. But Hume argues that passions are universal, that constellations of feelings produce predictable conduct, and that a system of "oughts" and rules can be derived from them. This is why promises are kept despite changes in feeling. A focus on feelings, then, is not the key to the law of the heart. Nor is subjectivity, which is perfectly compatible with legalism in morals and politics. Subjectivity holds a central place in social contract theory, for example, in which private desires are said to drive men and women to submit to laws in the first place. Subjectivity appears in liberal theories of revolution too, as when Locke argues that revolution is justified when individuals feel that their trust is betrayed. Each person must estimate his or her own feelings of insecurity and judge whether mistrust runs so deep that revolution is necessary. The "innerness" of the law of the heart its not its distinctive feature, either. The law of the heart is directed against both external laws and Kant's draconian categorical imperative, in which the origin of duty is internal but its imperatives are universal.

What distinguishes the law of the heart is its narcissistic self-absorption. Even Nietzsche's irrationalist ethic is extroverted; it involves a will to power. The romantic law of the heart is unconcerned with legislating for others, or with dominating, leading, or controlling them. The "law" in the law of the heart is purely metaphorical. It invokes the imperative of feelings, not any purpose or rule derived from them. Sentiments command, and they are irresistible.

The Painful Failures of the Law of the Heart

As with romantic militarism, the most severe challenges to the law of the heart do not come from rationalist critics of romanticism. They are conceived instead by romantic sensibilities who come to see that consistent obedience to spontaneous and purely personal feelings is impossible. Perhaps, given the romantic anarchist's self-absorption, only failures perceived from within can chasten and provide impetus for reconciliation with liberalism.

Followers of the law of the heart discover that the sense of "possible infinite expressions" is as inhibiting as any external constraint and that the practical consequence of responding to only irresistible impulses is paralysis. Given their boundless expectations of individuality and spontaneity, any particular feeling or course of conduct will seem pitiably finite. Each potential lover and friend will seem incommensurate to the romantic's protean self. Chateaubriand's character René describes the gap between internal experience and actual possibilities for action: inner experience is liberated, open-ended, insubstantial; real actions are concrete and intractable. "Alas! I am only in search of some unknown good, whose intuition pursues me relentlessly. Am I to blame if everywhere I find limitations, if all that is finite I consider worthless?"[33]

This tension can finally become unbearable and any action inconceivable. What remains is merely the longing to find an object commensurate with one's desires. Romantics may go through the entire dynamic of brilliant expectations, disappointment, and internal revulsion without ever acting in the world. Paralysis may be the result less of actual frustration than of a fevered imagination. Romantic anarchy plays out in feelings, as romantic militarism plays out in willfulness, the tension between an impossibly grandiose sense of self and an insupportably trivial world. Individuality and spontaneity become terrible burdens.

The most compelling literary description of romantic paralysis is Benjamin Constant's Adolphe, whose every feeling and thought of action are accompanied by the immediate conviction that they exclude every other feeling and action, and thereby erase potential itself. Adolphe cannot commit himself wholeheartedly to a married woman because this unconventional love would close certain social avenues to him. Yet he cannot choose a career because no work or social position corresponds to his great expectations: "Just as a miser pictures to himself as he gazes at the wealth he has amassed all the objects this wealth might buy, so I recognized in Ellénore the denial of all the success to which I might have aspired. It was not merely one career which I regretted; as I had tried none, I regretted them all. Never having put my powers to the test, I imagined them unbounded."[34]

In this boundlessness, the follower of the law of the heart bears a certain resemblance to the individual in liberal thought—whether the desirous person of utilitarianism or the moral person of Kantianism. For both Bentham and Kant, future preferences and choices are open and the subject is undefined. Kant describes a disembodied will, pure capacity for choice, as the essence of moral agency; utilitarianism acknowledges an infinite field and infinite objects of desire. Possibility is the very definition of freedom for romantics too, but their experience of possibility is different. In Kantian and utilitarian accounts autonomy is exercised by giving oneself laws and making choices. Consent involves taking on obligations. The notion of the pursuit of happiness recognizes that there is a last desire before willing that occasions or causes action. In these accounts self-definition is not final; by the same token, the separability of a person from his or her moral and instrumental choices is not dismaying. The self may not be fully constituted by its choices, and change is always possible, but this does not make every action seem contingent, undermine integrity, or cause paralysis and feelings of radical discontinuity.

The romantic sensibility abhors definition. Even self-legislation and autonomous choice are cruelly limiting. Something is lost, not exhibited or gained, when infinite possibility gives way to the limitations of actuality. Authenticity cannot survive action or choice. This is what Schiller meant when he spoke of personality as "empty infinity."[35] Hegel's extended discussion of the "beautiful soul" in *The Phenomenology of Mind* is the classic statement of the romantic condition. The beautiful soul "lacks force to externalize itself, the power to make itself a thing and endure existence. It lives in dread of staining the radiance of its inner being by action and existence. And to preserve the purity of its heart, it flees from contact with actuality, and steadfastly perseveres in a state of self-willed impotence . . ."[36]

Another source of paralysis is less subtle than dread of limitation: the law of the heart can fail because sentiments are simply not so

irresistible as they are supposed to be. Romantics may have only ephemeral or confused impulses, or a succession of conflicting feelings, or, worse yet, like Musset's "child of the century" they may be enervated and without feelings at all. Impotence and ennui are common states. Constant's Adolphe confesses: "the power of true feeling is such that it can silence false interpretations and artificial conventions. But I was only a weak, grateful and dominated man; I was sustained by no impulse from the heart."[37]

Paralysis may be inevitable. As soon as attention is paid to the promptings of the heart, they are cast in doubt. The law of the heart is supposed to be naive. When it is adopted by sophisticated sensibilities self-consciously defending spontaneous emotional life against a legalistic culture, it loses its imperative character and brings radical self-doubt. Adolphe wants to submit to the reign of tender feelings and longs to give himself over to love. He begins by feigning love for Ellénore, then believes his sentiment is real. The novel traces Adolphe's incessant uncertainty and almost clinical self-analysis. Its drama arises from the way feeling seems to create its opposite when it is exposed to inspection. Is Adolphe moved by love or indifference, pity or pride? Does he remain with Ellénore out of affection, or self-indulgence, or self-sacrifice? Adolphe's dilemma is not the result of imposture, hypocrisy, or self-deception, either; simply, sincerity is no guarantee of self-certainty. Adolphe's doubt is the inevitable accompaniment of emotional introspection. The law of the heart is self-contradictory— not because it requires the mind to hold two contradictory beliefs, but because its single desire is inherently unrealizable, as willed spontaneity surely is.

These problems—infinite possibility, incommensurateness, weakness, and ennui—indicate something more about the tension between the law of the heart and legalistic culture. Modern legalism assumes the capacity for individual responsibility. In liberal conceptions of justice rights adhere to individuals, and respect for those rights and for law generally is the discipline liberal society imposes on its mature and rational members. Legalism also assumes, with considerably less argument, that a sense of personal responsibility is a real psychological experience. The unreliability of the law of the heart may make the romantic anarchist incapable of having this experience.

Responsibility assumes an acting "I" who acknowledges authorship of conduct. This may be inconceivable to romantic sensibilities who comprehend feelings in terms of inspiration and action in terms of self-expression rather than intention, cause, and consequence, or who are paralyzed from acting altogether. The romantic soul cannot be held accountable for his or her feelings; responsibility loses significance when spontaneity is the ideal. Impulsiveness implies purely episodic behavior, which eclipses responsibility further. And if obedience to a chaotic succession of powerful emotional imperatives is experienced as an enormous personal transformation, the romantic may be unable to say "I murdered" or "I loved" in the past tense at all, because it is not the same "I" that acts and recalls. Romantic anarchy implies an absence of personal history.

Critics of the autonomous self of Kantian or utilitarian thought sometimes attribute to it the same discontinuous identity: because a person's choices are contingent and often reversible, the argument goes, there is no essential, integral self. Yet there is a difference between moral autonomy and romanticism. The difficulty of discovering rational proof for the existence of a unified ego has troubled philosophers since Hume. But Hume observed that, despite radical philosophical doubt, identity is a commonplace experience. Identity may not be the work of reason, but nevertheless it exists: "scepticism can be thought, not lived." Rousseau confessed to a myriad of conflicting feelings and contradictory actions, but was able to speak of a "sentiment intérieur," a sense of the "moi qui existe." The idea of an abstract person separable from his or her contingent choices is a construct assumed for specific purposes in philosophy and attributed to men and women by liberal thinkers for political purposes. Most people do not think of themselves as "radically situated" in this way. For romantic followers of the law of the heart, however, spontaneity and diffuseness are real, felt experiences. They may not awaken from the philosopher's dream.

The disquieting failings of law of the heart are most evident when all the conditions for its satisfaction seem to be met—when irresistible passions are freely expressed and inner imperatives triumph over duty and convention. Then the romantic learns that to be satisfying, freedom and expressivity require more than release from external constraints and internal inhibitions. For feelings can turn out to be shackles, and sentiments can be stern masters. Their imperatives can be as binding as those of need, or force, or law. Love especially produces dependency, awareness of the need for another, and with that the impulse to possess and dominate the lover. *Adolphe* shows that lovers thrown back on themselves seem less like free spirits and more like Hobbesian individuals—solitary beings in a raw conflict of power that ends only with death.[38] Constraints and necessities multiply if love inspires love in return, because then not even romantic sensibilities can avoid paying attention to someone else's feelings. None of this was expected to result from obeying the law of the heart. Adolphe rails against being bound by feelings just as he had against being bound by social rules. To be truly free, he realizes, means to be no longer loved and a stranger to all the world.

The Relief of Legalism

When Adolphe recognizes that feelings as well as laws are severe constraints, he suggests a potential course back to liberal legalism. Romantic anarchy begins by pronouncing impersonality unbearable, but obedience to the law of the heart results in the distress of unbridled sentiment and failed intimacy. From this chastened perspective, legalism can be seen as relief from intolerable emotionalism and self-absorption. Following rules may be experienced as self-protection rather than as bowing to external constraint. It can seem like welcome insulation from self-scrutiny and self-doubt as well as from the emotional demands of others, a buffer against the painful failings of the law of the heart. Whereas traditional liberal legalism is a protection against other people's personal feelings, romanticism recasts legalism as protection against one's own. Cold rules offer relief to overheated sensibilities. In legal and market relations, the institutional apparatus of liberal society is there for individuals to use when being strangers is just what they want.

Legalism can also save romantics from hypocrisy. It requires mutual recognition of rights, and liberalism imposes the additional discipline of mutual respect. However, respect is for one another as formal, rights-bearing persons. Neither politics nor economics in liberal society requires sympathy or friendship, or even recognition of one another as substantive equals. Character, religion, taste, and so on lie outside the bounds of what we respect one another for, and they can be safely ignored. For certain designated purposes of law and exchange, men and women act "as if" they respected one another, but it is understood that nothing personal is meant by obedience to impersonal rules. Respect for others' rights does not express one's own true feelings, and it says nothing at all about one's feelings for others. Because it does not require a show of emotion, respect for rights is not an invitation to hypocrisy.

There is no logical or psychological compulsion for romantic anarchists to resign themselves to legalism or to make even this partial peace with life regulated by rules, but given the failures of the law of the heart, it is not surprising that liberalism has particular appeal for some romantic sensibilities. Even so, the relief that romantics may find in the rule of law may not be enough. Sensibilities disturbed by following the law of the heart may still be unwilling to deny the impulses that turned them against legalism in the first place or to abandon the priority of individuality and spontaneity.

One obvious means of accommodation is to relegate the law of the heart to private life. This relation between romanticism and liberalism is encouraged by the traditional distinction between public and private spheres. The conceptual apparatus is in place to set romantic expressivism safely beyond the reach of government and of social relations regulated by rules. Certain forms of romantic expressivism can even be cast as First Amendment freedoms. Freedom of association protects a society of friends as well as a political group; community can be based on emotional attachment as well as shared belief. Or, romantic yearning for infinity can be seen as religious; romanticism has been described as "spilt religion." Even if the sensitive soul's affinity to religious longing has nothing to do with churches or conscience, it might be said to fall within the general constitutional class of privileged activities that preserve the sacrosanct inner life.[39]

Romantic sensibilities find it difficult to reconcile themselves to liberalism by exploiting rights in this way. Even if self-expression takes the form of following the law of the heart and not of defiance, just considering action in terms of what is permissible and protected by law detracts from individuality and spontaneity. If expression is described in terms of actions tolerated or even encouraged by liberalism, it loses meaning and value—which is why romantics do not speak of self-expression as a right. Legalism and expressivism are opposed. The law of the heart's power increases in proportion to the demands of duty and the restrictions of rules, just as legalism is impossibly arid unless it is seen as the counterforce to personality and arbitrariness. Romantics are more likely to consider expressivism and rule-following as mutually compensatory than complementary. They might recognize impersonal legalism as the background against which the experience of purely personal emotions is heightened, but it would be unacceptable for liberalism to legitimate the law of the heart by identifying its expressions with traditional rights and liberties. Like religious dissenters before them, romantics would denounce the "haughty name toleration." For romantics, liberalism must be recast so that individuality and spontaneity are rationales for the separation of public and private spheres, rather than the reverse.

Instead of translating individuality and spontaneity into distinct liberties, they could be described as indifferent, and simply left alone. De facto tolerance will not do, either, though. It is not enough for spontaneity to thrive as an unintended consequence of personal liberty; expressivity must have priority over other values. Schiller wanted deference to individuality to be the declared purpose of government: the state must respect not only the objective and generic, but also the subjective and specific character of individuals.[40]

Traditional liberal individualism does not recognize the subjective and specific. Whether it signifies possessiveness, desirousness, or moral agency, and whether its connotations are favorable or unfavorable— as in atomism, egotism, or "individualisme"—individualism always draws attention to the common and invariant characteristics of persons.[41] This is especially true of recent liberal thought, which emphasizes the respect owed to every individual.[42] Even when individualism is associated with spontaneous activity, there is no trace of the affective or original, the imaginative or unexpected. In liberal thought, spontaneity arises solely in connection with the marketplace and refers to uncoordinated action. Precisely because individual economic motivations are common and consistent, rational and efficient, economists can discover general laws of the marketplace. The "spontaneous" market is predicated on average human behavior.[43]

Romantics would separate "individualism of uniqueness" from the traditional "individualism of singleness."[44] They would replace individualism with individuality, a distinction that appears in liberal thought with J. S. Mill's observation that individualism was triumphant at the same time that individuality was in danger of becoming extinct. For romantics, individuality is everything. Friedrich Schlegel explained: "it is just his individuality that is the primary and eternal element in man. To make a cult of the formation and development of this individuality would be a kind of divine egotism."[45] That is precisely what some romantics would have liberalism do, which is why reconciliation to the liberal private sphere requires more than tolerance or consideration of self-expression as one activity among others protected by a general framework of liberty.

If individuality and spontaneity are to take precedence in liberal thought, the traditional distinction between public and private spheres must be rethought. Private life must be seen as a preserve for "divine egotism" as well as for the conventional pursuit of happiness. It must be recast as a realm of inwardness, detachment, and self-absorption. The private sphere must be valued for its personal uses as well as its public, political uses such as defense against tyranny. This reconstruction is possible because it is not only romantics who are motivated to recast private life (and sometimes public life as well). The traditional liberal distinction between public and private spheres has undergone shifts from within, too. As the senses of privatism in philosophy and law multiply, liberalism opens up to romanticism. At the margins where private life shades into privacy and reasons for privacy lose their baldly instrumental cast, romanticism and liberalism begin to come together.

PART II

Liberalism and Romanticism
at the Margins:
The Uses of Private Life

CHAPTER 3

The Penumbra of Privacy

What is the relation between the personal and the expressive, which lie at the heart of romanticism, and individual liberty, which is crucial to liberalism? What is the relation between romantic detachment and liberal private life? The romantic is always on the verge of extreme privatization, of slipping into inwardness and self-absorption. The romantic sensibility eschews ordinary connections. Whether its ethos is militant or anarchic, it resists the conventional engagements and constraints of both public and private spheres. Detachment from mundane existence is associated with self-development, self-expression, and artistic creation, although it also has darker associations such as paralysis and hatred of the world. In classical liberal thought, by contrast, "private" refers to society, not personal retreat, and society is a domain of free rational activity rather than expressive license. Liberalism protects this sphere by restricting the exercise of government power and by enumerating civil liberties. Pure romanticism and conventional liberalism are separated not only by their notions of private life, but also by their motivations for designating a privileged private sphere. The fear of political authority and official coercion that motivates liberals to limit government is plainly secondary to romantics, for whom privatization is a condition for individuality and self-expression.

Since the nineteenth century, and increasingly in contemporary political thought, those contrasts between the romantic and liberal positions have grown less sharp. Juxtaposing romantic and liberal ideas underscores their dynamic interaction as well as their differences. As liberal rationales for private life have expanded and multiplied, sometimes appropriating romantic perspectives, the notion of a private life has emerged as a critical idea on the margin.

Classical Liberalism: Society versus Government

Until the nineteenth century the liberal distinction between public and private was simple and served a simple political purpose: to circumscribe government. "Public" referred to state officials and to the exercise of power by force, after the fashion of historical tyrannies. "Private" referred to the activities of men and women in society, from which government should be excluded or admitted only with vigilance.[1] Society encompassed institutions such as property and markets, families and universities, as well as a full range of voluntary associations: churches, parties, clubs, scientific societies, neighborhood groups, and so on.

We commonly think of boundaries as protecting society from government, forgetting that they were intended to work both ways. Erecting an independent public sphere was as important as protecting private liberty. Secular and later democratic authority was possible because religious faith had been expelled from the realm of government and religious establishments strictly relegated to private life. The designation of a distinctive public sphere was intended to control the influence of private associations, making impartiality or at least the regular adjustment of interests possible. In addition, Locke and Madison insisted that the public sphere should limit not only the political power of religious groups but also the power private groups exercised over their own members.

The idea was that no public or private association should absorb its members entirely. Madison saw pluralism as a defense against permanent division of society into majority and minority, insiders and outsiders; if diverse associations must compete with one another for members, no one group can make a total or exclusive claim on individuals. The liberal separation between public and private spheres, and endorsement of pluralism within them, encourages both access to groups in which one has a "voice" and the possibility of "exit" from them as equally important parts of freedom of association.[2] Private society offers opportunities to make commitments, but also ways to limit, divide, multiply, and end them. All memberships are partial, which sometimes causes communitarians to complain that under liberalism such membership is insufficiently gripping.

Another feature of the traditional liberal separation of spheres that is often attacked by liberalism's communitarian critics is that private citizens are not responsible for public affairs. In social contract theory, individuals create government to avoid the inconvenience of having to execute justice themselves. Public authorities defend citizens against hostile foreigners, secure their civil interests, and make and enforce laws, leaving them free to pursue private happiness. Representative government authorizes others to govern; private citizens may choose to be politically passive.[3] Participation is voluntary, apathy is permissable, and public activity—when necessary or desirable—is intermittent, rather than permanent and continuous. Moreover citizens have no official connection with one another and bear no responsibility for the actions democratic officials perform on their behalf. Anglo-American liberal theory tends to speak of "public servants" and "private citizens," often (though not always) regarding citizens "first and most simply as the recipient of certain benefits that the state, and no other social or political organization, provides."[4] Nor are private citizens accountable for the consequences of their own conduct in society so long as it remains within the law. The secret ballot protects citizens against undue influence or corruption, but also reinforces a general principle of unaccountability, whereby people do not have to give reasons for acting the way they do. The liberal "claims not merely a private capacity—an area of action in which he is not responsible to the state for what he does so long as he respects certain minimal rights of others; he claims further that this is the residual category, that the onus is on anyone who claims he is accountable."[5]

This boundary between spheres does not imply that private life is radically apolitical or antisocial. Private life means life in civil society, not some presocial state of nature or antisocial condition of isolation and detachment.[6] Liberation from traditional ascriptive attachments does not indicate naked individualism or anomie. Individualism and the pursuit of private happiness are perfectly consistent with interconnection and group membership. Private liberty provides escape from the surveillance and interference of public officials, multiplying possibilities for private associations and combinations. Private civil society is not a vacuum, but comprises an array of "partial publics." Hobbes and Locke assert that liberty increases the number and kinds of secondary associations people form, including many that draw them into politics. Far from inviting apathy, private liberty is supposed to encourage public discussion and the formation of groups that give individuals access to wider social contexts and to government. These groups are potentially constructive political forces that can affect the formation of policy. They are also bulwarks against Bonapartism, mass politics, and totalitarianism. A central theme of liberal political thought is the reciprocal relation between private independence and the pluralist sources of self-government. The great strength of conventional liberalism is its powerful *public* rationales for private liberty.[7]

This is evident in discussions of the First Amendment to the U. S. Constitution, and nothing points up the connection between individual rights and their civil rationales better than justifications for freedom of speech. The strongest political arguments for freedom of speech are negative: suspicion of government's purposes and doubt of its capacity to regulate speech even if there were agreement that certain forms of speech should be controlled. However, liberalism also defends freedom of speech positively by pointing to its beneficial consequences for society. Historically protected speech has been political speech (or speech liable to arouse political censorship and persecution) and every catalogue of preferred freedoms still gives it first place. Public discussion is the favored way of counteracting misgovernment, partiality, and error.

Liberal thought does not assign priority to self-expression as romantics do. Speech, even when it is not political, has social significance; it is rational dialogue and exchange. The prevailing defense of free speech today assumes that speech is communication, potentially harmful but privileged out of concern for listeners as well as speakers. Precisely because speech is not considered to be a self-regarding activity, attempts to extend its privilege to the almost limitless range of expressive conduct—spectacle, demonstration, protest, personal appearance, exhibitions of anger, and so on—turn on whether the expression is sufficiently communicative and not on whether it is authentic or sincere. Not all speech conforms to the ideal of rational dialogue, but expression incapable of restatement in propositional form may not count as communication.[8] In addition to libel and blasphemy, pure self-expression, arrant emotionalism, raving, obscenity, visions, and so on may be excluded from First Amendment protection. Emotive as well as cognitive acts are privileged only if they count as communication and provide information about the intensity of feelings on an issue of public concern. The argument that speech is an end in itself, "the fountainhead of all expression of the individual personality," departs from traditional reasoning. It is a sign of liberalism's permeability to romantic ideas. It marks the intrusion of the romantic notion of the personal into the liberal private sphere whose traditional definition was simply "not-government."[9]

Collapsing Public and Private Spheres

The traditional distinction between public and private as between government and society is a useful shorthand: we speak of private property and private enterprise, private charity and private schools. However, other powerful connotations of public and private have emerged within liberalism. Classical liberal thought is concerned with conflicts between government and society, between obligations imposed by public authority and those imposed by membership in secondary associations. Increasingly, however, liberals have acknowledged that tension also exists between personal inclinations on the one hand and the demands of both government and secondary associations on the other. This division between the individual and any organized group is as important as the division between society and government. From this perspective the individual stands alone—apart from the state and apart from all partial publics; Michael Walzer calls people in liberal society "twice alienated."[10] Public becomes an inclusive category that refers not only to officials but also to cooperation in the workplace, combinations based on the cash nexus, neighborliness, voluntary associations, and so on. Private refers to interior life, to purely personal spaces, activities, and intimate relationships. The identification of private with personal and individual has become so automatic that recently one philosopher felt compelled to remind his readers that a "private" relation or activity is not necessarily an intimate one, and that a group or institution may claim that it is private in relation to the wider community.[11]

The conflict is no longer between official and unofficial obligations but between the demands of life in society and the felt imperatives of individuality and personal life. With this, liberal privacy begins to converge with romantic notions of detachment. The reasons for liberalism's shift in this direction are complex, of course, and a sampling of them can only suggest the forces at work.

For one thing, as government more closely responds to and even reflects social groups, the boundary between public authority and private society becomes indistinct. Politicizing tendencies in democracy combine with pluralism to blur the separation of society and government.[12] For another, government is not the only threat to independence: "The function of Liberalism may be rather to protect the individual against the power of the association than to protect the right of association against the restriction of the law," L. T. Hobhouse writes.[13] Preventing private associations such as churches or kinship and status groups from exercising unrestrained authority over individuals was one reason for creating public authority in the first place, so this peril is nothing new. What is new is the threat to liberty from a growing array of voluntary associations and the dependencies they create: "They are likely to play a prominent role in the life of individual members, sometimes a more dominant one than the government itself. In fact, and this is the core of the problem, voluntary associations in our society tend to become, for all practical purposes, private governments."[14] Courts in the United States have recognized the quasi-public character of some private groups, extending civil liberties such as freedom of speech to members of educational institutions, professional associations, and labor unions.[15]

Another reason that contemporary liberal theorists describe both government and society as public and separate from genuine private life is that they share methods of social control. Locke's definition of the magistrate as one whose power consists exclusively in the use of outward force is obsolete. His purpose was to determine the proper bounds of ecclesiastical and political authority. Churchmen could not employ worldly punishments, but only exhort and excommunicate. By arguing that force cannot coerce true belief, Locke set the bounds of government action too. The successful separation of church and state opened the way for liberals to admit (often in response to criticism by socialists) that society as well as government can be coercive and create inescapable dependencies, because the ability of people to earn a living is shaped by economic forces beyond their control.[16] An even more important source of the sense that public constraint permeates every sphere is the fact that government and secondary associations wield similar instruments of social control: influence, persuasion, scientific management, and inducement, as well as ideologies of therapy, service, and rehabilitation. Most obvious, legalism and bureaucracy mark both government and society.

Finally, liberal theorists have an interest in resistance to social conformity, characterizing it as a kind of tyranny. Individuals need protection against group pressures to conform much as they need protection against the state.[17] Classical liberals thought that pressure from religious associations would be restrained if government were secular and minority rights guaranteed. They also pointed to the market and the marketplace of ideas as powerful forces for differentiation and independence; traditional pluralism saw groups as various, dispersed, and therefore benign. Neither liberalism of rights nor pluralist liberalism anticipated that every social context could be experienced as intrusive or that pluralism would be experienced as homogenization. Neither imagined that liberal society would be seen as a monolithic force: "liberalism . . . fatally misunderstood the crushing power of social conformity. It is usually asserted that, from the beginning, liberalism had urged the liberation of men from all kinds of authority, religious, political, social, and intellectual: *écrasez l'infâme de l'autorité!* This, however, is only partially correct and, in the case of society's authority, quite misleading."[18] As Sheldon Wolin's remarks indicate, groups and spheres collapse into a society that presents a uniform face.

The perception of society as mass society informed J. S. Mill's famous attack on the tyranny of the majority, of course, as well as his reservations about commercial society generally. Whereas Madison made the orthodox case against the tyranny of both majorities and minorities, *On Liberty* defends individuality against the forces of social conformity. The charge of uniformity has become a commonplace, even in constitutional scholarship, as when Laurence Tribe insists that "the more human activity and human personality are shaped by the forces and pressures of homogenization spawned by mass industry and the mass media . . . the less sense it makes to spin out special limits and duties for *government* in its dealings with individual persons and groups."[19]

Perceptions of liberal society as uniform are frequently distorted, but the distortion itself is interesting because it is resonant with romantic claims that society is monolithically bourgeois, philistine, or legalistic. This sense of being surrounded by demanding, controlling, intrusive publics, and the reactions of revulsion and fear for individuality, are familiar features of romanticism. They are the reverse of another distorted perception shared by romantics and some critics of liberalism—that liberal society is hopelessly fragmented and atomistic, and that individuals in such a society are fragmented too. Whether real social complexity is masked by an exaggerated picture of conformity or magnified so that it appears as an irrational splintering that splinters individuals as well, the true private self is lost. In one case it is homogenized; in the other it is dissolved.

As it reassesses the conventional distinction between public and private, liberalism echoes romantic concerns and sometimes romantic responses as well. Complaints of ubiquitous legalism and philistinism may lead to the conclusion that social forces are inescapable except through personal detachment. Liberals begin to reinterpret private life as a retreat for spirits in conflict with the demands of organized political and social life. Social groups are not tyrannies, but they exhibit a public face and cannot be represented as scenes of personal liberty, as they were in classical liberal thought. Tribe's distinction between government coercion and the "passive, incremental coercion that shapes all of life and for which no one bears precise responsibility" is crucial for political theory, but it may not correspond to personal experience. From here it is a short step to the romantic lament that every association is impersonal, and to the romantic inclination to preserve individuality and self-expression by withdrawing, standing aloof, or turning within. The condition in which external reality seems crushing and inner reality alone seems unconstrictive brings to mind Emerson's notion of the "infinitude of the private man." The emphasis has shifted from a concrete, institutionalized private sphere to privatism.

Changes in the way the family is seen illustrate this shift nicely. Traditional liberal thought describes the family as an institution for transferring property or for inculcating social values and roles.[20] As such, the family is a premier element of private life, meaning life in civil society. Increasingly, however, the family becomes the realm of privacy and personal retreat. Its role is compensatory, not complementary. It appears idyllically as a haven not only from government but from partial publics as well.[21] Finally, even the family can seem like a cold public of which one is an unwilling member, so that "except at the margins, personal life is not usefully conceived as a private affair."[22] The family may be experienced this way because the social service state and the "helping professions" intrude upon it. Or men and women bring habits from other social contexts home, so that the family is managed after the manner of a small organization, participated in like a small democratic community, or worse still transformed into a scene of combat and competition mirroring a brutal world outside.[23] Neither nature nor tradition can insure that family relations will be satisfyingly intimate or expressive, or follow the law of the heart.

With the spread of this view of the family, the personal and private have been dissociated from virtually every institutional setting. The result is a dramatic collapse of the traditional liberal distinction between public and private as between government and society. Private refers only to oneself, to the personal, whereas public refers to every formal association with others except for intimate relations like friendship or love. Truly private relations—personal, expressive, and affective—are exclusive and require the privacy that "creates the moral capital which we spend in friendship and love."[24] The focus shifts from protecting society from government (or government from society) to protecting personal affairs from impersonal, organized others. The defense of a privileged private sphere is supplemented or even replaced by concern for privacy proper.

This shift emerges plainly in legal trends in areas as diverse as the right against self-incrimination and prayer in schools. Exemption from self-incrimination, a privilege designed to protect individuals from official persecution and error, has become a symbol of a new moral attitude government should take: "the respect for the individual that privacy entails."[25] In U. S. Supreme Court decisions about prayer in schools, traditional concerns about control of belief by public authorities are supplemented by a new concern for invasion of privacy. At stake here is the liberty *not* to express one's attitudes or opinions, including the liberty not to have to identify oneself as a dissenter. There are reasons besides fear of punishment or intolerance that individuals do not want to make information about themselves public.

What follows shows how the idea of privacy enters the legal sphere as a right. By itself, however, jurisprudence does not indicate fully how liberal theory has moved to address the claims of romanticism. The legal right of privacy is a formal articulation of deeper, more speculative shifts in thinking that are based on new justifications for privacy, in which liberal autonomy and romantic individuality start to come together.

The Right of Privacy

Privacy first emerges as a distinct right in tort law in cases of unwanted publicity, to prevent persons from obtaining information about private citizens (even when they do not disseminate it), and as the basis for protection of a physical zone against surveillance.[26] The classic liberal issue, though, is protection against government intrusion, and the classic constitutional cases are "search and seizure" cases. The right originates in English and Colonial opposition to general warrants to enter premises and search for broad categories of material.[27] Recent exclusionary rules of evidence echo this original political rationale: "security of one's privacy against arbitrary intrusion by the police" extends to illegally seized evidence and makes it inadmissable in court.[28] The invention of electronic surveillance produced a shift away from the historical emphasis on property and on physical areas of privacy, so that now privacy is said to protect people, not places. A person is protected if he or she has exhibited an actual (subjective) expectation of privacy that society recognizes as reasonable.[29]

The notion of expectations of privacy may appear to invite a broader consideration of the right to be let alone and its relation to autonomy, or personality, or even longings for detachment. But in practice the expectations that society recognizes as reasonable are firmly tied to the historical language of the Fourth Amendment, which guarantees protection only against unreasonable search and seizure. The right to privacy is limited to quite specific places and situations, and arguments about search and seizure are indifferent to whether the information seized is personal or intimate. Search and seizure cases, like others involving official collection and use of information about citizens, concern due process more than substantive rights. Privacy is part of the general defense against classic abuses of authority, arbitrariness, and political persecution.

The U. S. Supreme Court case *Griswold v. Connecticut* (1965) in which the Court overturned a state statute prohibiting the use of contraceptives is the most controversial enunciation of a constitutional right of privacy.[30] The justices were not in agreement about the constitutional sources of the right, but for many of them the case turned on a nonexplicit, fundamental right older than the state and any specific constitutional guarantee—the independent right of marital privacy.[31] The right of privacy protects "an association that promotes a way of life . . . a harmony in living," and the *Griswold* decision upholds the privileged status of marriage as a social institution "clearly pressed into the substance of our social life."[32] Privacy is an element of liberty, and liberty is grounded in suprapersonal norms: a way of life upheld by "the conscience of the community," "the living ideals of the nation," the teachings of history and even civilization itself. *Griswold*'s ethos is conservative, not individualistic and expressive. The erratic history of courts' extending the right of privacy in sexual matters to unmarried adults without clear justification, or refusing to consider the question of homosexuals, indicates the tenuousness of the right apart from marriage. *Griswold* is not a celebration of intimacy in general and does not grant claims against social values in the name of private affections. It does not invoke the law of the heart or other doctrines of sacrosanct personal relations.

Justice Douglas's lead opinion in *Griswold* states that the Fourteenth Amendment incorporates the Bill of Rights, which goes beyond its specific guarantees and protects a "zone of privacy" in an enlarged sense. "Specific guarantees in the Bill of Rights have penumbras, formed by emanations from those guarantees that help to give them life and substance."[33] Douglas's reasoning seems expansive: privacy emanates from the totality of the constitutional scheme and tradition. In practice, however, constitutional cases based on the "penumbra of privacy" have so far afforded protection to only a limited range of activities, mostly concerning marriage and childbearing. Judicial opinions have not produced a general defense of privacy as the necessary condition for individuals to pursue a broad range of self-chosen ends, nor have they linked privacy to individuality or self-expression.

The right of privacy is ambiguous, its constitutional justification in dispute. Still, it is sufficiently powerful to be used to advance other claims. Arguments against noise and air pollution, for example, rely not only on considerations of economic cost or public health but also on the normative force inherent in the idea that they are personally intrusive violations of privacy.[34] Appeals to privacy, although they may not be decisive for policy making, do suggest, as *Griswold* with its emphasis on marriage and tradition does not, the connection between the inviolability of privacy and inviolate personality. Reflections on this broader relationship have turned in particular to two ideas outside jurisprudence: self-development and autonomy.

With its romantic resonances, the notion of self-development propels liberal thought beyond the view that privacy protects only traditionally sacrosanct relations like the family or rational activities of the sort enthroned in the Bill of Rights. Such justifications of privacy are instrumental, whereas Humboldt argues that cultivating individuality is the ultimate end of human life. This vein of romanticism in liberal thought runs through Justice Brandeis's argument that the end of government is to make men free to develop themselves—not their intellects only, but their emotions as well.[35] This expands the meaning and value of privacy. It becomes the condition for affective and aesthetic expression. Privacy is necessary to personality, and jurisprudential discussions sometimes link privacy to "deeper concerns of personhood."[36]

The notion of autonomy has been more influential in impelling liberalism beyond orthodox preoccupations with liberty to a distinct appreciation of privacy. Several lines of thought have gone into the view that autonomy is the essence of morality, and that both liberty and the "right to be let alone" rest on the obligation not to restrict another's choice of his or her own ends. For Kant, self-determination means choosing rightly in accord with the categorical imperative. Other philosophers such as Mill are less exacting; for them, what is at stake is not making the right choice but the capacity to choose ends. Autonomy involves developing and exercising faculties of choice, which requires an institutional setting that provides mobility and opportunity for choice among diverse alternatives. It also requires a minimum zone of inviolable personal freedom: "if it is overstepped, the individual will find himself in an area too narrow for even that minimum development of his natural faculties which alone makes it possible to pursue, and even to conceive, the various ends which men hold good or right or sacred."[37]

Conventional liberalism provides only a very general understanding of how broad this area of liberty should be, however; there are few well-developed ideas about what sort of intrusion by what sort of public inevitably frustrates self-direction—just as there are few comprehensive arguments about what sort of public welfare assistance is necessary to permit unfettered choice of ends by individuals. But it is clear that autonomy justifies both personal liberty and privacy: "if we thought that our every word and deed were public, fear of disapproval or more tangible retaliation might keep us from doing or saying things which we would do or say if we could be sure of keeping them to ourselves or within a circle of those who we know approve or tolerate our tastes."[38] Privacy and the general principle of negative liberty are both conditions for autonomy, but the two are not identical. Privacy emerges as an independent good.

What does privacy add to liberty as a condition for autonomy? Lack of privacy is a specific kind of hindrance to choice. Stanley Benn underscores this point: "respect for someone as a person, as a chooser, implie[s] respect for him as one engaged on a kind of self-creative enterprise, which could be disrupted, distorted, or frustrated even by so limited an intrusion as watching."[39] The absence of privacy is degrading as well as constraining, suggesting a more complicated connection between privacy and autonomy than first appears. Privacy is inseparable from autonomy because autonomy involves more than just selecting freely from among various plans by estimating the likelihood that a course of action will satisfy one's desires or correspond to one's values.[40] Autonomy also means that individuals determine their own desires and values, and that inclinations and ends are acknowledged by individuals as their own. It is one thing to attribute autonomy to someone's actions, and another to experience oneself as autonomous. Privacy is crucial to this experience.

Autonomy is the rationale for privacy but it no longer simply means moral agency. It appears as a self-creative enterprise that embraces personality. It may not be clear just what personality entails, but clearly autonomy goes beyond rational moral agency: "when facts about me that I prefer to keep secret are disclosed by another, I have been denied control over my life, my choices and my personality."[41] Control over information about oneself "must be understood as a basic part of the right to shape the 'self' that one presents to the world, and on the basis of which the world in turn shapes one's existence."[42]

Incorporating privacy into a general theory of liberty or describing it as one condition among others for autonomy leaves the traditional conceptual apparatus of liberalism undisturbed. Carl Friedrich's rationale for privacy is another example of the way privacy can be assimilated to conventional liberal thought. Friedrich's preoccupation is with insuring the strength of liberal democracy, so he insists that "only an individual free to shape his own life and that of his immediate human relations is capable of fulfilling the vital function of a citizen in a democratic community, and thus privacy becomes the corollary of democracy." This is the voice of political realism, and Friedrich admits to having no interest at all in "the private aspect of this privacy, individualistic and libertarian."[43] His reasoning is alien to another way of thinking about privacy more consonant with romantic inclinations, in which "the right to privacy . . . is essentially the right not to participate in the collective life—the right to shut out the community."[44]

In practice, of course, privacy may result less from rights or from the restraint inspired by respect for autonomy than from social structure. Liberal pluralist society is diverse; an individual's associations, tastes, and affections are unlikely to be fully known by anyone else. Mobility and heterogeneity make it possible for aspects of personality and behavior to emerge, disappear, and be forgotten. Society's many spheres and "life worlds" may give life its private aura more than privacy does.[45] However, the importance of autonomy in justifying privacy and of the self-restraint privacy requires in our dealings with others should not be underestimated. In liberal thought, privacy is plainly something more than an unintended consequence of social complexity.

So long as protection against coercion and moral autonomy are the ends in view, liberalism has little difficulty accommodating privacy. Privacy is one element in "a network of values that includes such notions as personal rights, civil liberties, the sanctity of the individual personality, personal relations, and the like."[46] It is essentially a condition for free rational activity. Elusive notions of personality and expressiveness are on the verge of being admitted to discussion, but they remain marginal. However, liberalism has gone farther still in the direction of romanticism by admitting tendencies to genuine privatization, in which privacy means detachment and detachment is clearly associated with individuality.

From Activity to Detachment

In traditional liberal thought privacy, like liberty, is a matter of nonintervention, of not being prevented from doing what you want to do. This formula works well when activity is at stake, but in other formulations privacy can mean retreat, not being required to do what you do not want to do. It signifies withdrawal, inwardness, even quiescence. It does not concern activity or choice but preservation of personality itself, especially emotional integrity. Liberalism has always attended to noninterference with activity, and justifications for noninterference extend beyond a fixed set of rational activities to include autonomy and self-development. The liberal private sphere may even evoke a privileged domain of ebullient self-expression, answering certain romantic longings. It is also possible, however, to defend privacy without reference to its positive activities—liberal or romantic. Privacy can be associated with darker, self-protective aspects of individuality, with retreat and withdrawal inward.

Classical liberalism is not attuned to the need for personal detachment, in part because it does not recognize the emotional intrusiveness of public life. It portrays government as potentially arbitrary and a source of political persecution, but as indifferent to feelings. Liberal government is a convenience, a guarantor of civil peace rather than a *patria* to be served or loved. Liberalism also ignores the emotional demands of public life because it identifies political power with physical force and assumes that laws backed by force are unable to compel people to act from conviction or with passion.[47] Locke's argument for religious toleration rests on the assumption that government is unable to affect inner life. Belief depends on subjective disposition. State coercion can force participation in religious ceremonies but not true belief, so orthodoxy and persecution are futile.

Some liberals have been troubled by this justification for limited government. They question its propositions about the mind and its assumptions about the inefficacy of political power. They argue for a separate private sphere not because of the intrinsic incapacities of authority but because of its ability to intrude effectively. Governments can and often do change people's motives, call upon their affections, or influence their deepest inclinations. For this reason, government must be limited, and it follows that government (and society) should tolerate detachment. Wilhelm von Humboldt's romantic argument for religious toleration along these lines offers a clear contrast to Locke's: the reason to refrain from enforcing religious orthodoxy is that government does invade the inner self and can affect belief.

Humboldt rejects both the theological perspective, which sees religion as the way to salvation, and Locke's perspective, which sees the church as a voluntary association. For Humboldt, religion is a purely personal need, a peculiar "want or necessity of the soul" for those who long to pass out of themselves and seek perfection in a personified ideal.[48] Anyone who feels this impulse will be susceptible to official religion, indeed to the forceful promises and demands of any religious group. Humboldt also knows that this longing is not universal; it is felt only by "religious natures." For those without it, pressure to believe or to affect belief is a crushing imposition. The danger comes less from public interference with private activity than from public efforts to excite some feeling or state of mind. The difference is between impeding free expression of belief and evoking affirmation of belief that is not spontaneous—a romantic concern.

Humboldt makes personal emotional needs the reason for limiting government. Only if "wholly subjective" feelings can arise and be met spontaneously, if persons are left to themselves in matters of sentiment and yearning as well as conduct, is individuality possible. Privacy is the condition for "the highest and most harmonious development of [the individual's] powers into a complete and consistent whole." He transforms the standard liberal account of privacy: instead of leaving people alone to do what they want to do, Humboldt would leave them alone so that they do not have to do anything they are not inspired to do, by the law of the heart or some other expressive impulse.

The most vehement defender of the private as self-protective retreat is Benjamin Constant. During the French Revolution, the despotism latent in democracy was revealed as government commanded private citizens to become public citizens who were not permitted to withhold allegiance or enthusiasm. Disengagement was not tolerated. Revolutionary government, Constant warned, requires not only obedience to the laws but also obedience to the most intrusive commands, those directed at feelings. Popular government demands expressions of loyalty and commitment of an intensity that earlier liberal theorists had not imagined. Citizenship competes with private relations, drawing energy and emotions away from personal affairs and setting up awful conflicts between political and personal loyalties. The worst tyranny is the kind that exercises authority over feelings.

Constant responds by insisting on protection from demands that strike at the heart. They are especially powerful when they come not from distant despots but from the people as a whole, as they do in modern states. "To be deprived of my liberty at the hands of my family or friends or fellow citizens is to be deprived of it just as effectively," Isaiah Berlin wrote in defense of privacy.[49] For Constant too the most effective invasions of private life occur when government concerns itself with personality, sentiments, or moral improvement. Nothing is more common than the abuse of enthusiasm and the exploitation of longings. Constant seeks security in formal liberal legalism, with its morality of rule-following that ignores motives and attends to action. He also considers commercial society safer than civic republicanism because it engages interests rather than affections. True privacy means detachment and the possibility of purely personal relations, introspection, self-involvement, and even perfect passivity.

Constant's rationale for a private sphere is unorthodox. Pluralist liberalism, liberalism based on autonomy and rights, and utilitarianism all put interests at the center of their theories of limited government and private self-direction. They assume that no one else can truly know one's own interests, pleasures, or pains, or successfully dictate one's happiness.[50] Humboldt and Constant shift the emphasis away from cognition and interests; subjective interests give way to an interest in subjectivity. They want protection against the demands of public life in order to forestall the collapse of individuality. At stake is personality, guarding energy and personal desire against claims on them by any public. Humboldt and Constant provide a purely private rationale for privacy. Among modern liberals, the most influential heir to this position is Isaiah Berlin.

The Negative Sources of "Negative Liberty"

In contemporary liberal thought autonomy is the leading rationale for privacy; detachment, if it is recognized at all, is considered as a condition and preparation for rational activity and choice. Sir Isaiah Berlin warns against this reasoning in "Two Concepts of Liberty." Arguments for private life based on moral autonomy or self-mastery, and arguments like Friedrich's about the sort of character necessary for democracy, are fatally ambiguous. To think of privacy instrumentally, as leading to better selves and better societies, is to misunderstand the true inviolability of private life.

Berlin begins with the same object in mind as classical liberals: limiting the sphere of action by public authorities. He argues in traditional liberal terms, using metaphors of boundaries, zones, and spheres to describe a preserve whose invasion is the very definition of despotism. His chief concern is to set out the conditions for personal liberty. Yet the argument as a whole is unconventional because Berlin does not rest the privileged status of privacy on its providing a context for the pursuit of traditional liberal ends such as happiness or self-direction. The liberty he describes allows for these but does not exist for the sake of rational action or autonomy at all. Instead, Berlin lauds "the sense of privacy itself" as something "sacred in its own right." Privacy is a "fundamental need." The private sphere is "inviolable" and "sacred."

"Negative liberty" is freedom not only from coercion, then, but also from any external demand that impinges on personal life. Berlin is alert to intrusions on the inner self, such as claims on beliefs or affections. He is especially sensitive to painful conflicts of value. Engagement can be perilous to personality, and privacy suggests detachment. Although rights may be indispensable to a defense of privacy in practice, Berlin does not invoke the traditional liberalism of rights, with its ethos of activity and exercise. There is no hidden social or moral agenda in his defense of privatism. Apathy too deserves to be called liberty, he insists. So do sanctuary, retreat, "dropping the mask," self-enclosure, and a spate of other formulas that refer to liberty and privacy without implying action, choice, or moral aspiration. For Berlin, detachment does not necessarily signal an active, positive state of private searching for the good life; it can mean indifference and unconcern, quiescence and passivity. The defining characteristic of liberalism is the belief that "a man might, without losing face, or incurring contempt, or a diminution of his human essence, withdraw from public life altogether, and pursue private ends, live in a room of his own, in the company of personal friends." Because negative liberty suggests the absence of something, usually obstacles, its critics disregard the fact that private liberty usually involves a plenitude of social norms, resources, associations. Berlin's negative liberty is truly negative. It acknowledges sources in distress and the longing for disengagement. Berlin does not think negativity is adequate by itself; he is critical of stoic self-sufficiency and detachment. But he gives this aspect of privacy its due.[51]

Berlin's case for negative liberty is powerful precisely because it does not depend on logical arguments about the nature and limits of authority, on a catalogue of privileged activities, on rights, or on a theory of autonomy. Its power is the evocative association of privacy with fear for personal life. Indeed fear is a striking element of Berlin's essay; "negative liberty" has negative roots. The conception of what it is to be a "normal human being" should include inviolable frontiers, whose trespass is considered "inhuman" and "insane." Interference where noninterference is the rule should be a matter of "horror" and "revulsion." Berlin's charged language is a reminder that for some sensibilities distrust can be so pervasive and scepticism so acute that the defense of privacy takes on enormous affective force. If privacy is experienced as a desperate personal need, its violation is intolerable. Like Humboldt and Constant, Berlin is fearful that lack of privacy and intrusion on the tenuous inner self might obliterate it entirely.

Berlin is not a romantic sensibility; unlike Constant he is not preoccupied chiefly with feelings. However, he indicates the possibility of a real opening to romanticism within liberalism. In his work, detachment is inspired by suspicion of external claims. He can countenance the thought that men and women may feel a genuine revulsion at public life. For Berlin, it is not only the political principle of limited government that informs privacy, but also the sense that privacy is a fundamental personal need.

As the idea of privacy focuses increasingly on personal motives for withdrawal, its justification becomes more complicated and more tenuous. Classical liberals are able to make strong political arguments for limited government and strong moral arguments for a zone of privacy. By contrast, Humboldt, Constant, and Berlin appeal to longings for detachment. Their justifications for privacy reflect romantic concern for individuality and the fear that external demands will be crippling unless self-protective privatization is possible. A further difficulty with justifying detachment is its negative flavor. Public rationales for private life, such as classical liberalism gives, and positive personal rationales for private life, such as autonomy or self-development or creative self-expression, ensure that privacy will be attractive: "Privacy, like alienation, loneliness, ostracism, and isolation is a condition of being-apart-from-others. However, alienation is suffered, loneliness is dreaded, ostracism and isolation are borne with resignation or panic, while privacy is sought after."[52] Detachment may be sought after in quite another spirit, however. It may have dark sources and signify quiescence and self-absorption. Accommodating this dark side of private life is a separate matter entirely.

The Dark Side of Private Life: The Dynamic of Inwardness and Emergence

Motives for withdrawal include uncertainty, fear, and loathing. For romantic followers of the law of the heart, for example, detachment can be associated with melancholy, paralysis, and anxious introspection. It can suggest a kind of self-absorption that differs dramatically from ordinary egoism and the private pursuit of happiness. Liberalism—the doctrine of comfort, security, and happiness—may have to recognize and accommodate negative forms of disengagement. This is difficult, because when privacy shows its other face it challenges basic liberal assumptions. Some critics of liberalism ignore Constant's warnings and insist that politics and society must try to engage, excite, and "embed" citizens—provide them with community and feelings of belonging. "No political association committed solely to happiness, or committed solely to the pursuit of happiness, can maintain much of a grip on a man who is wretched," Walzer observes.[53] Disengagement need not be suicidally extreme to present a problem, though. Morbidity is not the only attitude opposed to the bustle of civil society. It is threatening enough if private life consists of passivity, or preoccupation with the immoral and irrational, or even imaginative introspection.

Confronted with a darker vision of inwardness and detachment, liberals are pulled in two directions. Some theorists make a special effort to foster and protect traditional elements of private life that provide men and women with a reason for living and connect them with others—religion, the family, or romantic love. They apply the same protective attitude to aesthetic turns inward. For example, if inwardness is conceived as the home of imagination and imagination is redemptive, then retirement can appear as beneficial, and privacy and the freedom to withdraw take on fresh importance. When J. S. Mill recounts his own depression, he describes withdrawal and immersion in poetry as restorative. Retirement and turning within were antidotes to an excess of rational activity. Detachment energized him, awakened new sympathies, and ultimately returned him from depression to public affairs.

However, detachment can also seem a prelude to experiences that are dangerously irrational, dark, or dirty. Everything emotional, arbitrary, and unconciliatory that liberalism expelled from politics and social life threatens to reemerge, undermining the discipline of liberalism. The traditional liberal fear is that passions will be let loose in politics, producing (or being exploited by) despotism, fanaticism, and terror. Romantic individuality and expressivism suggest other dangers, such as a disruptive form of privatization, total and obsessive, that deprives civil society of energy and undermines the claims of legalism. Or, in another grim scenario, inwardness is followed by the eruption of impulses and imagination in romantic anarchy or in a subversive counterculture.

These fears can be glimpsed in arguments for the censorship of pornography. The usual case for censorship claims that pornography has long-range effects on moral standards or that it is a direct cause of criminal or antisocial conduct. The relevant argument in this context, however, is that preoccupation with the gratification of sensual desires results in withdrawal from normal social concerns. "A people devoted exclusively to the satisfaction of sensual appetites is not, strictly speaking, a citizen body at all. It is a collection of private individuals, each concerned with his private gratification."[54] Of course, liberal civil society was recognized from the start as a desirable alternative to a citizen body; it was intended as an arena for private gratification. Yet it does not take concern for civic virtue to make the relation between obscenity and privatization suspect. Eroticism epitomizes the disengaged and purely personal. It removes men and women from regular connections with others. Unlike other obsessions such as rampant acquisitiveness, it is not in any ordinary sense self-interested. Eroticized private life may be self-expressive and pursued under conditions of strict privacy, but it is introverted and "such introversion is far from healthy, liberal self-interests."[55]

The same reasoning may explain liberal ambivalence toward "high culture" when its ethos is darkly self-expressive. In "The Fate of Pleasure: Wordsworth to Dostoevsky" Lionel Trilling discusses the instinct for "unpleasure" (Freud's death instinct) that seems to him to dominate modernist culture: "the ideal of pleasure has exhausted itself, almost as if it had been actually realized and had issued in satiety and ennui. In its place, or, at least, beside it, there is developing—conceivably at the behest of literature!—an ideal of the experience of those psychic energies which are linked with unpleasure and which are directed toward self-definition and self-affirmation."[56] Trilling describes a nihilistic culture of unpleasure that is peculiarly subversive. But all culture may seem like counterculture if it erodes natural bases of support for productivity, the discipline of legalism, or motivations for the rational adjustment of interests.[57]

Imagery for this dynamic of inwardness and emergence was invented by literary romantics. Northrop Frye explains that in response to the failed hopes of the French Revolution poets created an entirely new framework of imagery whose metaphors lead inside and downward rather than outside and upward, with heaven and creative power assigned a place deep within the self.[58] In this new vision, the outside world yields in importance and priority to the "mind's internal heaven."[59] M. H. Abrams draws the same historical connection between the interior/exterior orientation of imagery and reaction to the French Revolution.[60] As revolutionary fervor is followed by political disillusionment, romantics transfer revolution from the social to the mental world. Inwardness and detachment are not purely escapist or self-protective, though; they are "inherently revolutionary." Abrams means that retreat re-empowers men and women, who discover in themselves purely personal resources to respirit a disenchanted world. Inwardness is followed by emergence.

From the first, the romantic dynamic of inwardness and emergence has had a dark side. The journey within and the way back may be ferocious, ugly, or nihilistic. After all, if revolution and natural forces are identified with the imagination and internalized, the violent and demonic are absorbed along with the divine spark. Frye observes that Wordsworth's serene landscape "is a veil dropped over the naked nature of screaming rabbits and gasping stags, the nature red in tooth and claw" that would preoccupy later generations.[61] Among political philosophers, Nietzsche insists that when both spiritual certainties and social reality are repulsive, men must either admit that "the world unveiled is but a tomb" or create beauty and greatness for themselves. For this, they must fix a "horizon" onto the chaos, guided by nothing but raw self-certainty.[62] I mention Nietzsche here as further proof that the salutary vision of detachment and redemption through imagination or the law of the heart is only part of a larger pattern of inwardness and emergence, which includes pure energy, will to power, eroticism, and the chaotic unconscious. "We all carry within us our places of exile, our crimes and our ravages," Camus warned, "but our task is not to unleash them on the world; it is to fight them in ourselves and others."[63]

Liberalism cannot entirely prevent disengagement or the return of the repressed. Benjamin Constant is one of the few liberals able to endure this idea. He is willing to place narcissism and nihilism at the center of his argument for private life. For him, the inner self is not the domain of only benevolent or creative impulses. Inner sensitivity means turbulence; inner depths contain uncertainty, misery, and purposelessness, not just an excited sense of possibility. In fact, Constant turns the existence of the dark side of personal life into an argument in defense of liberalism. The question for him is not whether people will withdraw and turn inward and whether impulses will then be expressed (they will), but whether passionate expression is available for political exploitation. Liberalism offers security against this. Separation of spheres and guarantees of undisturbed privacy can set bounds to narcissism and nihilism. The personal can be excluded from the formal, impersonal domain of society and contained in private. Constant does not imagine some optimal balance or harmony between public and private spheres; privacy simply limits liability by containing the worst eruptions. He also thinks the existence of dark personal forces can be liberalizing: the stronger impulses are, and the more firmly they are projected onto intimate personal relations, the stronger the motivations to resist both public repression and public manipulation of these urges. Romantic expressivism may be negative rather than positive, but in either case it arms men and women with powerful reasons for defending privacy.

The dark side of private life can play the same dual role in liberalism that positive notions of self-expression do—as justification for separate spheres, and as motivation for guarding their frontiers. The difference is that when liberalism acknowledges dark psychic life as a fact of life, the justification for separate spheres shifts from benevolent protection of individuality and self-expression to their safe containment.

Hannah Arendt and the Communitarian Reaction

When liberalism accentuates privacy, and in particular when it appropriates romantic notions of individuality and expressivity, there is reaction from liberals who want to refocus attention on "healthy liberal self-interest" and from antiliberals who are unhappy with privatism per se. In the case of Hannah Arendt, reaction takes the form of longing to resurrect a wholly public existence. Athenian public life meant republicanism—genuine citizen participation in the affairs of the political community—and private life was depreciated as the realm of women, children, and slaves, the arena of necessity, reproduction, and labor. Arendt adopts this ancient distinction between public citizenship and the private household when she describes private life as deprived of that essentially free and essentially human activity—political activity.[64]

She knows, of course, that in modern society labor and welfare are not despised and "private" does not signify emptiness and loss: "Not only would we not agree with the Greeks that a life spent in the privacy of 'one's own' [*idion*], outside the world of the common, is 'idiotic' by definition . . . we call private today a sphere of intimacy . . . whose peculiar manifoldness and variety were certainly unknown to any period prior to the modern age."[65] Yet Arendt tends to ignore the manifoldness of private life. For her, civil society and membership in partial publics are privatizing so long as they are based on narrow self-interest and not on exchanges of opinion about the shared ends of the community. In her political vision the possessive individualist's interest in property is just as detached from the genuine public life of democratic participation as Christian otherworldliness; romantic self-absorption is as privatized as stoic detachment. For Arendt, Mill is indistinguishable from Epictetus.

Arendt has a political reason for identifying Mill with Epictetus. In *The Origins of Totalitarianism* she describes totalitarianism as a result of the isolation of men and women in mass society and of the loss of politics. Historians do not all agree on her interpretation, and political theorists do not all agree that radical privatization is the logical outcome of establishing a private sphere. Nonetheless the connection Arendt draws between atomistic individualism and despotism explains her identification of liberal private life with extreme danger. It also explains why she traces the idea of private life back to the stoics and the Roman Empire, while a historian such as Jakob Burkhardt, who sees private life as a rich and various arena of powerful individuality, traces privacy to the Renaissance.[66]

Arendt is certainly wrong in suggesting that stoics, romantics, and liberal private citizens are similarly withdrawn and antipolitical. She is wrong in her seeming indifference to the various meanings of "private" and to the fact that private life is not the same experience in liberal states that it is in modern regimes of terror. Still, the attractions of detachment make her sharp division between political engagement and radical privatism psychologically, if not politically, relevant. For some sensibilities, romantics in particular, the private life does evoke inwardness, aloofness, and utter separation.

There is good reason to look at extreme forms of individual withdrawal, such as historical stoicism and Christian otherworldliness, which I call "antipolitics." Just as romantic categories are a way of seeing liberalism more clearly, "antipolitics" provides a standpoint from which to estimate romanticism's tendency to inwardness and disengagement. By confronting romantic retreat with more extreme forms of detachment, it is easier to understand why romanticism can come home to liberalism.

CHAPTER 4

Beyond Liberalism and Romanticism: Antipolitics and the Spirit of Detachment

The most radical form of privatism involves complete disengagement from the external world and retirement within, and the distinctions between public and private spheres that provide material for variations in liberal thought are eclipsed. The only meaningful distinction is between the coercive world without and the compensatory world of withdrawal within. I call this position "antipolitics," and I use its picture of detachment as a measure of the limits of romanticism. Romantic self-absorption may seem threatening to liberalism, but it is not really extreme: it can be accommodated by the sorts of privacy liberalism provides. With antipolitics there is no peace to be made.

Antipolitics is a rare but recurrent phenomenon in the history of thought, distinct from ordinary social criticism and from even the most radical movements for reform. Every political order has its dissenters, among them some who express their disgust in global terms. But what passes for wholesale rejection of public life is usually opposition to a specific society by advocates of an alternative ideal, or, it is the moral outrage of disaffected citizens charging governors with the betrayal of some original shared ideal. Antipolitical opposition to politics and society is more profound: it asserts that life in the world has neither meaning nor value. Its sweeping negativity superficially resembles romantic anarchy's opposition to the entire social ethos of rules and romantic militarism's loathing of prosaic peace, but the origins of romanticism and antipolitics are different; certainly, the ways they resolve their world-hatred are different.

Stoicism and Christian otherworldliness, as early versions of antipolitics, point to its origin under despotism. Radical detachment is inspired by radical insecurity. It is a response to the fragility and unsafety of public life.[1] It springs from the conviction that to act in the world is to expose oneself to suffering and dependence. For antipolitical souls, alternative political or social ideals are unimaginable. There is no alleviation of insecurity through reform, and no possibility of positive accommodation. Resignation, martyrdom, and suicide are the only conceivable courses.

In this chapter I talk about stoicism, Christian otherworldliness, and the modern eruption of something that looks like antipolitics among romantic sensibilities. Although liberalism gives a privileged place to private life, liberal justifications for privacy—autonomy, personal liberty, and even self-development—are worlds apart from rationales for pure self-containment; Mill is not Epictetus. It is less clear that romanticism is also remote from antipolitics. In their disgust with the available forms of public and private life romantic sensibilities sometimes imitate stoic or otherworldly stances, but they cannot endure genuine detachment. Romantic expressivism involves a dynamic of inwardness and emergence, not inwardness alone. Despite inclinations to withdraw from prosaic society romantics are not quietist and are never resigned.

Radical Detachment

The political world in which stoicism makes its appearance is despotic and devoid of safety and order. Marcus Aurelius evokes a state of affairs in Rome in which not even Caesar's friends can escape constant threats of death, exile, calumny, or poverty. No one is above contempt or without fear. It is simply not possible to protect "your poor body, your little property, your little estimation." Stoic philosophers translate this sense of victimhood into a cosmology, finding a lack of freedom and safety in a universe that is all flux and flow, without first cause and without aim. Human actions are not amenable to choice or to purposive control. Even imperial conduct depends on circumstances, has unintended consequences, and is vulnerable to the reactions of others and to revolutions of fortune.

The stoic universe is a determined universe, but stoicism is not teleological, as Greek thought and modern historical determinism are.[2] People can know the necessity of generation and death but not their beginning or purpose; hence stoic images of the universe as a wheel and of time as a stream sweeping everything away: "Of human life the time is a point, and the substance is in a flux, and the perception dull, and the composition of the whole body subject to putrefaction, and the soul a whirl, and fortune hard to divine, and fame a thing devoid of judgment. And, to say all in a word, everything which belongs to the body is a stream, and what belongs to the soul is a dream and a vapour, and life is a warfare and a stranger's sojourn, and after-fame is oblivion."[3] The stoic maxim "Live according to nature" is one possible response to this vision, although it is less a positive philosophical doctrine, and still less a practical code of conduct, than a counsel of despair. It prescribes resignation: nothing exists that is not meant to be, and happiness is sighing, "Let it be so."

The works of Tertullian, writing on Christian martyrdom in Roman Africa in the early third century, also show the connection between disengagement and radical insecurity. At every moment Christians face the possibility of imprisonment, torture, and death. Even when persecution is not imperial policy, Christians find themselves at the mercy of mobs. It is not surprising that for Tertullian "public" means popular hatred and "political" connotes bloodshed and the executioner. The Christian is a sojourner on earth, an alien among strangers and foes. His origin, dwelling place, hope, recompense, and honor are all above.[4] "Freedom of the world is not real," Tertullian writes, "it is the slavery of man."[5]

Freedom means just one thing to antipolitical souls: escape from victimhood. Because every attachment exposes men and women to suffering, the only conceivable peace is utter detachment. Absolute privatism is represented by scenes of isolation—the stoic's study or the martyr's dungeon. The early Christian hermit chose physical remoteness in the wilderness, on a pillar, or in a cave; hermeticism is antiworldliness hardened into a fixed principle of escape inward.[6] Retirement to the territory within, however, rather than physical solitude is what matters, and antipolitics is compatible with psychological detachment in the midst of society. Perfect self-containment is the ideal, and its object is entirely practical: Epictetus set out "to study how a man can rid his life of lamentation and groaning."[7]

The difference between this self-containment and modern autonomy or independence separates antipolitics from liberal private life. Liberal theory accepts that shared public life and values do not have a very strong hold on private citizens. Its justification for public authority is security and legal order, the preservation of a sphere of private liberty in which men and women are left alone to "cultivate their gardens." In liberal thought, independence means pursuit of happiness. In antipolitical thought, by contrast, privatism is a condition of uncaring and unconcern. Liberal independence prescribes self-interest; antipolitics prescribes disinterest. The difference is between an ideal of perfect self-mastery and self-containment and the more modest and moderate liberal ideal of calculating self-control.

The same contrast holds if autonomy replaces the pursuit of happiness as the essence of independence in liberal thought. Autonomy signifies freedom from divine and hereditary obligations, freedom to choose a plan of life and to consent to duties. Stoic self-mastery has no more to do with choosing ends than it does with the successful satisfaction of desires. Stoic independence means escape from unrealizable desire and from the illusion of choice. It is self-abnegation, *apatheia*. "Wipe out imagination, check desire, extinguish appetite," Marcus Aurelius advised, following Epictetus: "abolish the acropolis within us and cast out the tyrants."[8] They would substitute an interior world of calm for an outer one of dominion, vulnerability, sorrow, and pain.

Hegel's description of stoic retreat as "the varied activity of life, with all its individualization and complication" contracted into "pure process of thought" needs refining.[9] For not all thought is quietist. Separation of the life of action from the life of the mind does not always mean resignation: the *vita contemplativa* of the Platonic philosopher is an eroticized quest for truth. For the stoic, however, the life of the mind is not action in thought. The stoic *daimon* does not aspire or inspire. It does not hope that the philosopher can return from a tour of contemplation with knowledge of the form of the ideal city.[10] The stoic ideal is personal tranquillity. There is nothing to be discovered or done; the only thing to achieve is resignation.

Antipolitics is quietist, then. Consider one of its chief images: the stoic retirement of statesmen, soldiers, and poets from the court to the countryside. Pastoralism has a long history as a mode of social criticism in European thought. The country estate appears, as in Rousseau, as an agricultural and patriarchal ideal, an alternative social order to court and civil society. For the stoics, however, the estate was not a community; family and property are sources of dependence and upset like any other. The real retreat is to the mind, "this little territory of thy own."[11] Quietism also lies behind the stoics' attempt to distinguish detachment from the solitude of the misanthrope, who withdraws from public life to demonstrate his contempt and loathing. Misanthropy is really a public act; it is critical and exhibitionist, and the misanthrope is "a piece rent asunder from the State, who tears his own soul." In antipolitical detachment inner disposition and the absence of passion and pain are what matters. Detachment does not bear the burden of moral condemnation.

Quietism and the Longing for Death

The stoic explanation for why human agency is insignificant and why quietism is the object of their detachment lies in cosmic determinism. For early Christians, the matter is even simpler: God is the only Prometheus, man does not share his powers, and there is nothing new or more to be done. Quietism means submission to nature, history, and providence. World-hatred has no outlet in political thought or action—not resistance to the powers that be, not construction of new communities, certainly not aggressive pursuit of happiness or heroic defiance. Romantic anarchy is negative, too; it repudiates the ethos of rule-following. But romanticism invokes compensatory norms like the law of the heart. Its inwardness is a search for resources. Its impetus is expressive. Quietism distinguishes antipolitics from romanticism, as well as from other cases where inwardness translates into moral condemnation or political action—utopianism, say, or political fanaticism, which resolve to force the external world to conform to some fixed idea.

Precisely because there is no hope for reform by human agency, the territory within the self must coexist with the external world as it is. The task is delicate. On the one hand, self-containment means renouncing the common motives for action—self-interest and idealism. On the other hand, quietism demands a degree of conformity to the requirements of public utility in order to avoid the appearance of rebelliousness or complicity in harm to others. Thus antipolitics is compatible with political obedience. Tertullian referred to Saint Paul's "powers that be," and Marcus Aurelius worked out a famous "household arrangement" with politics.[12] Missing is any positive disposition to citizenship, obedience, or rule. "Servitude is the fate of palaces," Seneca wrote, and Marcus Aurelius yearned for retirement. For the stoics, office is the "discipline of the world" that must be endured. At best, it is "relief from other thoughts."[13]

It is not surprising that the stoic notion of duty has been called an "empty ought." "Citizen of the world" refers to an abstract conception that transcends the particulars of history and political action. By situating rights and duties in some "highest city," stoics place in doubt the significance of actual cities. Epictetus's formulation is properly negative: you do not belong only to the little nook into which your poor body was born.[14] Acquiescence in the discipline of the world could not be further from the positive value assigned to political participation by the Greeks or Cicero, but it is equally remote from a liberalism in which the private citizen's political irresponsibility is perfectly respectable and instrumental because it is recommended by the separation of public and private spheres and enables immersion in the business of civil society.

The practical requirements of quietism are even more severe for Christians, who must live among the profane. Faith requires vigilant separation from non-Christians because social intercourse can excite forbidden passions. Public arenas, offices, assemblies, and trade expose Christians to pagan ceremonies and force them to see idols and join in (or just smell) sacrifices. Even philosophy can be dangerous: Tertullian is famous for his rejection of learning: "What is Athens to Jerusalem?" His directives make the very routine of life a self-imposed martyrdom.[15] Yet avoiding the appearance of political rebellion is one of Tertullian's main purposes; his "Apology" to the provincial governor is designed to answer the charge of treason. He insists that he does not "recognize the kingdom of this world" but at the same time assures the authorities that his detachment is benign and that Christians "have no need to combine because no concern is more foreign to them than public affairs and the state."[16] Christians assemble secretly in churches of twos and threes to read sacred writings and await redemption. Their love is mutual comfort for those enduring calamity, not the *agape* that would bind together a new Christian society. Visits to kiss the chains of imprisoned martyrs do not indicate the existence of a community, because community must await the coming City of Saints, the "new heaven, new earth" of Tertullian's millennial hopes.[17]

What makes such quietism possible is self-mastery, which depends in turn on a particular disposition toward death. Desires lose their compulsion and despotism holds no terror if people are aware that they can depart this life at any moment. Life is a play in which every player can decide to make an exit, to "play no longer." Voluntary death through martyrdom or suicide is the ultimate expression of self-possession and independence. It is the only available free choice, and it is a reasonable one for the miserable. Quietism prohibits disobedience, but not the ultimate exile and expatriation.

When stoics call themselves men and not citizens, they mean merely mortal. Man is "a poor soul bearing a corpse." In liberal thought, mortality inspires a quest for personal security and political order; but fear of violent death—of a life solitary, poor, nasty, brutish, and short—lacks constructive political force for those who define life as a passage to death and death as a "mere nothing." Tertullian's subject is the daily choice Christians must make between paganism and true faith and between flight and persecution. He does not waver: choose martyrdom. If Christians must starve, faith calls for renunciation; if the whole human race dies out, the end is near anyway.[18]

This attitude toward death makes resignation possible and distinguishes it from apathy, complacence, accommodation, or making peace. When this resignation falters, the face of antipolitics becomes murderous. Tertullian's vision of the apocalypse is a stunning example that mirrors his experience of public life as sheer destructive power and reminds us that antipolitics has its origin in victimhood. Tertullian imagines a "warfare of the living God"; his spectacle of the Last Judgment is a perfect replica of persecution, with monarchs groaning in darkness, provincial governors and other pagans tossing in the flames, and God as executioner.

One reason antipolitics appeals to some romantic sensibilities is its hatred of the world. After all, romantics describe civil society as not only prosaic but unbearably coercive. They see themselves as sensitive souls, mortified victims; recall Adolphe's self-pity, Julien Sorel's desperate attempts to wrest recognition from a cold, uncaring society, or Vigny's martyred soldiers and poets. The elitist ethos of antipolitics also appeals to some romantics. It depends on an appreciation of introspection, and appears as a sophisticated stance that is the product of advanced culture.[19] However, although romantics may see themselves as martyrs and try to emulate stoic or antiworldly turns inward, they are always unsuccessful. Quietism and absolute privatism are impossible for them because their object is self-expression, not self-abnegation.

The "Unhappy Consciousness" and the "Beautiful Soul"

Hegel was the first to understand the significance for modern political thought of what I have called antipolitics. He sees stoicism and early Christianity as related expressions of the "unhappy consciousness," which rejected the Roman political world.[20] He also sees antipolitics reincarnated in contemporary romanticism, in the detachment of the "beautiful soul" from modern society. By identifying romanticism with antipolitics, Hegel suggests that, like its ancient counterparts, the romantic sensibility is indifferent to every division between public and private except the one between the world without and the world within. At the same time, Hegel identifies what separates romanticism from antipolitics.

The misery of the "unhappy consciousness" was caused by the Roman state, which designated everyone a Roman citizen, turning citizenship into a purely legal status—bearer of property rights. Public relations became cold, formal, and contractual.[21] Force became the only available political bond, and the inevitable historical result was the "crushing destiny" of Roman imperial power.[22] In Hegel's account, the Roman lives in a joyless state, feeling only its pressure.[23] Everything urges the "severance of mind from world, soul from circumstance, human inwardness from external condition."[24] Hegel calls the unhappy consciousness "politics in exile."[25]

Hegel's interest is more than just antiquarian. He sees antipolitical flight from the empire as the start of a recurrent pattern in European history, a pattern of retreat from a dispirited world of utility and force. Whenever actuality is hollow and unstable, individuals take refuge within. Whenever contemporary manners do not satisfy better men so that they cannot find their duties there, they will try to find harmony in an ideal inner life.[26] Hegel sees imperial Rome as the paradigm of the modern legalistic state, in which once again personhood is nothing more than a legal right and all that remains of public life is an economic aggregate.[27] Hegel's discussion is echoed in Hannah Arendt's writings, which do not discriminate among stoic escape, romantic withdrawal, and liberal privacy.

Hegel was also careful to point out, however, that there are different modes of withdrawal, with entirely different consequences for political culture. Not every flight inward results in the lasting conviction that freedom is found only in detachment. He traces a double history of subjectivism since Rome.[28] In one thread of this history, inwardness is associated with religious conscience, which manifests itself externally in the splintering of Protestant sects. Here, inwardness is followed by emergence and creation of a distinctive political culture of religious rights and liberty and ultimately liberal constitutionalism. Its history begins with the inner voice of conscience and culminates in the French Revolution.[29] The second thread of Hegel's history links the ancient "unhappy consciousness" to his romantic contemporaries.[30] The true modern counterpart of stoic and otherworldly detachment is the irrationalism of the romantic "beautiful soul," which is expressed most purely in the flights of Jacobi, Novalis, and Schleiermacher into intuitive religion.[31] Finding nothing but restriction in the world, the romantic conceives of freedom as a state of mind, as awareness of pure possibility. The beautiful soul is drawn "into the inmost retreats of its being" in the hope that truth will arise spontaneously from emotional inspiration.[32] Hegel's description brings to mind the romantic follower of the law of the heart and recalls accounts of romantic retreat inward following the disappointment of the French Revolution, in which "militancy of overt political action has been transformed into the paradox of spiritual quietism . . . a wise passivism."[33] However, for Hegel, the "beautiful soul" is not quietist.

Hegel knows that identification of romanticism with the "unhappy consciousness" is imperfect. The romantic heart is a "spiritual hothouse"; romanticism is inseparable from a diffuse and unrelieved state of longing. Nothing contrasts more sharply with stoic *apatheia* or with Christian self-certainty, in which salvation is the sole object of desire and is never in doubt. Failures of the law of the heart demonstrate that the romantic's sense of inner power and infinite possibility often sours, turning into dread of impotence, exhaustion, and self-hatred. Romantics experience inaction as enervation and ennui, not resignation. Paralysis is a failure of action and of will, not their transcendence, and it is unaccompanied by personal peace.

In *René*, Chateaubriand's romantic character withdraws to the wilderness of America after the fashion of the beautiful soul in retreat. The missionary Father Souël explains to René that the belief that we are sufficient to ourselves is presumptuous unless we live with God or at peace with ourselves. The saints retired from society in order to subdue their passions, the priest reminds him, whereas René refines his in solitude. Romantic self-absorption does not discover calm within because inwardness is supposed to compensate for the dullness of actuality, with its lack of charm and of opportunity for exhibiting individuality. Besides, inwardness is an element of romantic expressivism, and René is the epitome of the beautiful soul's "frenzy of self-conceit."[34]

These different forms of withdrawal result in part from different political contexts. Antipolitical self-containment provides relief from despotism. Stoic doctrine is the product of a statesman and a slave; Christian martyrdom that of the persecuted. Although romantics describe civil society as insufferably coercive and "too much with us," their actual experience contradicts this. The necessity they confront is social convention, utility, or prosaic materialism, not the crushing destiny of despotic power. Sometimes romantics do feel crushed, and turn to privatism as relief from the intrusive emotional demands of intense political life; but when they do, they are pursuing authentic personal feelings, not uncaring and unconcern. In fact romantics' sense of victimization arises most often because something is lacking rather than because something is being actively forced on them.[35] The typical romantic lament is lack of opportunity for expressing individuality, through heroism or spontaneous personal attachments. Thus Musset feels condemned by the end of the Napoleonic Wars to idleness, inaction, and ennui; and Chateaubriand's René longs for a real misfortune to give him a reason for his suffering.[36] Typically the romantic does not have to ward off a world that pursues and torments him. Instead, he is a proud and sensitive soul unappreciated by society. Romantic self-absorption is less an escape from the demands of philistinism than the uneasy condition of feeling ignored and left alone. Romantic sensibilities may look back to antipolitics for models of detachment, but in the spirit of admiration for a dignity and self-containment unavailable to them.

Antipolitical detachment is a response to the insecurity of subjection; perhaps it is also inspired by modern regimes of terror. Liberalism does not inspire this extreme; instead it produces romantic opposition, which is more complicated but can be reconciled to it. One possible exception is the romantic sensibility's response to the democratic face of liberalism. To the extent that popular sovereignty implicates every citizen in government, the claim that the state is intrusive and personally injurious has some basis in political reality. Thoreau flirted with antipolitics: *Walden* and "Civil Disobedience" announce that freedom and personal purity require noncomplicity. They can be seen as recipes for detachment. Not even Thoreau could maintain quietism as a way of life, however. Besides, detachment loses both its original temptation and its dramatic force if democracy is not Jacobin but liberal and instead of imposing obligations or demanding loyalties leaves Thoreau alone.

Nevertheless, romantic sensibilities see themselves as victims of a despotic world and imagine that freedom lies in detachment. This aspiration to detachment distinguishes the romantic pose from the general social condition of anomie. Anomie is an objective condition marked by weak institutions and the insufficient presence of society in individuals. Romantic privatism, on the other hand, is a deliberate self-distancing from a world "too much with us." Disengagement is elected. Stoicism and otherworldliness become appealing when romantics work themselves up to such a pitch that they see themselves as martyrs. This happens when they exaggerate and personalize their discontents—arid legalism, prosaic commercial peace, and so on— into a powerful vision of the sensitive soul persecuted by philistines.

Philistinism: Despotism for Romantics

For romantic sensibilities philistinism is more than an offensive attribute of a specific group or class. It characterizes their contemporaries, indeed civilization as a whole. Society seems an oppressive, blind, and uniform mass that delights in the ordinary and is a stranger to individuality and creativity. Because philistines are everywhere, victimhood is inescapable. There is no appeal from a vulgar patron to a more tasteful public, and no possibility of solidarity with a party, group, or social class.

Ordinarily social critics use the term "philistine" more narrowly, to attack a dominant social group by challenging its aesthetic orthodoxy.[37] Although taste is at issue, the real concern is political. Rousseau attacked official taste because it stood for the moral decay of a stratified society. His philistines were the aristocratic patrons of art in the ancien régime, members of the privileged world of Parisian polite society. Rousseau's concern was inequality, not art, and certainly not wounded romantic sensibilities.[38]

The charge of philistinism came into its own as an instrument of social criticism when Matthew Arnold identified it with the bourgeoisie. His catalogue of philistine traits includes materialism and a pinched notion of reality that considers only immediate usefulness. Philistines are uncultured, guided by conventional formulas rather than emotion or virtue, and incapable of apprehending greatness. The "stout main body" of philistines are industrialists who are perversely indifferent to beauty.[39] The bourgeoisie's interest in art, where it exists at all, is purely acquisitive or snobbish. Art may be treated as currency rather than acquired as property, in which case it is a means of purchasing status or self-esteem. Cultivation, once a noble ideal of human perfection inseparable from self-discipline, later a matter of good taste— of enjoying all good art in the proper order of merit—has finally been reduced to a frivolous personal accomplishment.[40] Other social critics

attack the bourgeoisie for assigning art and creativity a crude instrumental value, such as diversion from labor.[41] Art is literally a pastime
("as if you could kill time without injuring eternity").[42] The bourgeois
philistines are also accused of intruding their values into the process
of artistic creation, so that society looks upon art as a commodity
produced for profit.[43]

Philistinism becomes shorthand for a wide variety of criticisms of
the middle class, and the same aversions are voiced by socialists and
political conservatives, cultural radicals and romantic sensibilities. In
most accounts the offended critic does not confront the philistines
alone but is allied with the dominant class's other victims—with the
nobility or the democratic citizenry, with peasants or workers (fellow
creators in some views), or with social elements such as revolutionary
parties, Jews, or homosexuals.[44] For romantics, however, philistinism
is a monolithic and pervasive despotism that each faces alone.

Because romantics ignore differences among social groups and see
society as a uniform mass, they have a sense of a real physical force
arrayed against them that recalls the personal insecurity that turned
the subjects of political despotism inward. This vision of society as
the "masses" also draws attention to the elitist strain in romanticism.[45]
"Society is a republic. When an individual strives to rise, the collective
masses press him back through ridicule and abuse . . . every sovereignty, intellectual as well as material, is hated by it," Heine wrote.[46]
In Mill's *On Liberty* the significant social division is not between the
educated few and the ignorant many, as it is in *Representative Government,* but between the extraordinary individual and all the rest.
The public is "always a mass, that is to say, a collective mediocrity,"
and Mill wants readers to "form a conception of the vastness of all
that is implied in the words, growth of the middle class."[47] This feeling
is not restricted to British and European romantics who had both an
aristocratic tradition and a tradition of social revolution to fuel the
rhetoric of victimization. Emerson made the same point in typically
American terms: "neither the caucus, nor the newspaper, nor the
Congress, nor the mob, nor the guillotine, nor fire, nor all together
can avail to outlaw, cut out, burn, or destroy the offense of superiority
in persons."[48]

Mill portrays middle-class philistinism as a sort of tyranny, but
takes a reformer's view. He studies the development of this social
mass (it depends upon "the natural laws of the progress of wealth,
upon the diffusion of reading, and the increase of the faculties of
human intercourse") and explores moral and institutional corrections

for it.[49] Romantic sensibilities do not analyze philistinism. After all, acute feelings of victimization and powerlessness do not encourage careful discrimination among social groups or comparative analyses of institutional arrangements. For romantics, the bourgeoisie appears the same as the people; the people is indistinguishable from the masses; and every government regardless of its constitutional organization appears as the servant of the masses.[50]

It is not surprising that this sense of victimhood should make detachment an ideal or suggest stoic and otherworldly models; what is striking is the cold eye romantic sensibilities cast on their own exaggerated representations of insecurity and on the possibility of quietist withdrawal. As it does in the cases of militarism and anarchy, romantic disillusion with radical privatism arises from within.

Romanticism and the Stoic Ideal

One literary work captures the progression of romantic attitudes toward stoic resignation, from attraction to disillusion. Alfred de Vigny's *Stello*, composed of a dialogue and a trio of stories about tormented artists, is the classic account of romanticism's harking back to antipolitical origins and of the unbridgeable gap between the two. Vigny's work is an exemplary account of romantic victimhood because its subject is not the fate of artists only. Stello himself is just a would-be poet; the proofs he offers Dr. Noir of his artistic nature are his exquisite feelings, not literary creations. Vigny uses this character to show that all romantic sensibilities suffer paralysis and depression when they are thrown back on themselves. For them, detachment is unlivable.

Vigny sees the poet's heart as the last refuge of genuine public ideals in a disenchanted world. The aspiring poet Stello is prompted by his heart to write on behalf of a sublime form of government; when art proves unable to realize political ideals Stello sinks into a morbid depression. To be cured of his misery and artistic paralysis Stello must learn that it is impossible for creative men to serve public ends. In a disenchanted world there is no common subject matter for art to mirror or express. Even if, through sheer genius, artists could create new myths, there would be no receptive audience for them. Artists would have to create a public and a public taste as well. Every therapeutic regimen, including phrenology, is employed against Stello's "bump of the Marvellous," the sanctuary of his painful idealism. Finally the sceptic Dr. Noir effects a cure by disillusion.

Dr. Noir's medicine consists of retelling the tragic careers of the poets Nicholas-Joseph-Laurent Gilbert, Thomas Chatterton, and André Chenier. These are tales of martyrdom that teach Stello that poets belong to "a tribe which the earthly powers execrate." Monarchy imperils artists by the arbitrariness of its patronage, bourgeois society by its materialism, and republicanism by its demand for ideological purity. "The first is afraid of us, the second scorns us as useless, the third one hates us and tries to pull us down, as if we were the aristocrats."[51] Dr. Noir's advice to Stello to withdraw from public life repeats the classic Rousseauian warning that artists are liable to serve the sinister interests of rulers: "Need raised thrones, the sciences and the arts have strengthened them."[52] That art may be used as an instrument of political oppression is secondary to romantics, however; their main concern is the personal trials of the sensitive *poète maudit*. Dr. Noir recommends resignation and retreat within.

When Mill reviews Vigny's writings for the *Edinburgh Review* he accepts this description of the career of the romantic sensibility without question. A world made by and for harder types will always be a vale of tears for "poetic natures."[53] However, Mill accuses Vigny of promoting self-dramatization. His characters are ill-regulated personalities who suffer more from pride than from persecution. If they want worldly recognition and rewards, they should enter society as businessmen or statesmen. Otherwise, Mill argues pragmatically, they should withdraw and gracefully accept that poetry is naturally a soliloquy.

In fact, detachment is just what Dr. Noir urges on Stello. The novel is not sentimental but stoical. "Let the Caesars play their role" and "pity them," Dr. Noir tells Stello. The last hope of dignity lies in the freedom of a detached life. Vigny recorded Epictetus in his journal: "independence is only in the mind." But Vigny does not have a sanguine view of retreat. Unlike Mill, he does not think that self-distancing is the ideal condition for expressivism. Vigny's lesson is harsh: if the "bump of the marvellous" is destroyed and with it all political idealism, if no beauty remains in "the gloom of this shadowy world," there is no hope. The only certainty and sure relief is death. Doubt and pain are the human destiny and in the end all endeavor comes to "nothing more than a question and a sigh"—"Why?" and "Alas!"[54]

Vigny knows that radical withdrawal is devastating for romantic sensibilities who long to exhibit individuality. For stoic resignation turns poetry into prose—only "Why?" and "Alas!" are needed to express victimhood. Dr. Noir brings Stello to resignation and turns his extraordinary misery into bearable unhappiness by substituting head for heart, reason for imagination. Stello's cure is really a transformation. For an expressive romantic sensibility, it would be not only self-defeating but also impossible. Stello's education is designed to show that quietism is just a dream, in the same way that the extraordinary education Rousseau designs for Émile shows that complete independence is a myth. Vigny could not have made it clearer that quietism is unavailable to romantic dispositions because they cannot be free of longing and because they retain some confidence in human agency.

Another Form of Privatism: Aesthetic Self-Distancing

The miserable Stello could adopt stoic quietism only by abandoning the romantic promise of an expressive self, which most romantic sensibilities cannot resign themselves to do. It may be possible, however, to accept estrangement from philistine society and still manage to preserve the ideal of creativity. Certain aesthetic ideas propose to combine detachment with expressive individuality. Rather than retreating for self-protection, as the "unhappy consciousness" does, these aesthetic romantics grant a positive value to detachment. Aloofness from the public in every form becomes a virtue and an artistic necessity.

Consider the implications for art of the romantic's monolithic view of philistinism. Art is conceived as soliloquy and the audience is left to eavesdrop on the nightingale who sings for himself alone. Images of the solitary creator have become commonplace, as has the idea of artists' dedicating work to an exclusive audience of friends or writing for that one true community, the timeless republic of letters.[55] Independence from the external world lies behind theories of the process of creation as well: idealists theories in which art mirrors a transcendent reality; notions of inspiration in which receptivity depends upon detachment; and claims for the hallucinatory origin of images or for the oracular power of poets as priests of "an unapprehended inspiration, the mirrors of gigantic shadows which futurity casts upon the present."[56] Flaubert calls aloofness monstrous but also judges it absolutely necessary for creativity: "you will only be able to describe wine, love, women, and fame if you are neither a drinker, neither a lover, a husband, nor a soldier."[57]

The conviction that expressivism requires distancing extends beyond romanticism as a historical movement in art and, indeed beyond aesthetic theory altogether. The association of aloofness with creativity has been incorporated into more general claims on behalf of detachment. The psychiatric theory of "creative loneliness" is one example.[58] In political theory even the fiercest resistance to privatism can be overcome, as when Hannah Arendt exempts artistic creation from her call for committed republicanism: "in order to be in a position to add constantly new things to the already existing world, [the artist] must be isolated from the public, must be sheltered and concealed from it."[59]

Under these conditions expressivity is characterized by an articulated rejection of the social responsibilities of art or self-expression that recalls the self-absorption, even solipsism, of the romantic law of the heart.[60] The aesthetic doctrine of "art for art's sake," which makes the extreme case for dissociation, is an amalgam of several propositions. One is that the value of a work of art lies solely in its existence as a beautiful object, apart from its effects. Another has it that art does not assert anything about external reality but only mirrors moods or exhibits purely formal qualities, so that it cannot be judged true or false.[61] These ideas have made their way into modernist accounts of art works as "heterocosms"—self-contained and self-referential worlds—and into explanations of the observer's relation to a work of art as a "text," an autonomous construction that is subject exclusively to standards of aesthetic coherence.[62] Art refers only to itself; its subject is its own essence and artfulness; it does not extend beyond its own surfaces and techniques. "Art for art's sake" is a tenable aesthetic theory, but the idea that a work of art is perfectly autonomous owes as much to philosophy (namely, to Kant's notion of the disinterested character of beauty) as it does to the belief that expression or image-making requires detachment.

Whereas "art for art's sake" separates art and life, the doctrine of aestheticism prescribes their fusion and demonstrates what it can mean to combine detachment and expressivism. Aestheticism involves cultivating certain exquisite sensations and tastes, but more importantly bringing artistic criteria to bear on every experience. By submitting every action and relation to this imperative aestheticism privatizes experience, or at least does not respect the conventional division among pluralist spheres with distinct attitudes, obligations, and norms. At its most demanding aestheticism subordinates conventional duties to the single imperative of revealing beauty, as in Ruskin's example: "does a man die at your feet, your business is not to help him but to note the colour of his lips."[63] Like stoicism and

Christian otherworldliness, aestheticism prescribes distancing oneself from mundane affairs; but whereas the "unhappy consciousness" finds freedom in pure inwardness, the aesthete finds it in consecration to "la religion de la beauté."[64]

The heart of aestheticism is detachment, but it is activist rather than quietist. Aestheticism raids the world for images. It fabricates art and personal styles that are impressionist, moodily expressionistic, cryptic, or surreal.[65] The aesthete withdraws from a reality that is without charm to a realm of appearance he or she knows is purely fictitious. "We have Art in order not to perish of Truth," Nietzsche wrote.[66] The advantages of aesthetic detachment over stoic quietism are plain. Vigny's triumph of head over heart meant subduing the poet in Stello and relegating him to silence, but aestheticism invites exquisite sensitivity and fine expressivity. Thus it effects a delicate balance between arid aloofness and creative involvement; there is connection to the world, but its fruit is purely personal aesthetic appreciation or invention of a fictitious rose-colored world. It does not recognize external demands.

In the end aestheticism remains marginal to romanticism. Its object is not to free the authentic self, as it is for romantic militants or anarchists, but to preserve distance and restraint. As a form of self-expression aestheticism is severely limited; the aesthete eschews sincerity and emotional intimacy in favor of irony and imaginative inauthenticity.[67] Heroic individuality is replaced by a discreet sensibility. The oddly ascetic cast of aestheticism goes against romanticism too. The romantic self is extravagant, expansive, rich, deep, and full of potential; it is unlikely to find fulfillment in the pleasure that comes from noting the color of a corpse's lips.

Aestheticism does not offer any obvious way back to liberalism, either, perhaps because its defiance is so subtle that it is compatible with personal liberty, with cultivating one's own garden. On the other hand, aestheticism offers little incentive for genuine reconciliation to civil society. For romantic sensibilities like Vigny aloofness is barren and paralysing, and self-expression loses its charm when it loses its power to attach us to the world, much less reform it. The best response to disenchantment is to endure private life stoically, which is certainly better than the agony and self-hatred of the *poète maudit*. Vigny suggests reasons—sober, resigned, and self-protective as they are—for making peace with a society that leaves men and women alone.

For some chastened romantics, however, making peace with liberalism goes beyond this stern resignation. Resources exist for a genuine reconciliation with reconstructed liberal thought, and in some reconstructions aesthetic delight plays a part. Unlike aestheticism it involves engagement with liberal society, attachment and excitation, not aloofness. In the following chapters I describe ways to bring romanticism home to liberalism, beginning with heroic individuality, which incorporates expansiveness and expressionism into a new vision of liberal democracy.

PART III

Bringing Romanticism Home

CHAPTER 5

Heroic Individualism
and the Spectacle
of Diversity

Heroic individualism, shifting involvements, and communitarianism
are the three faces of "another liberalism." They share a source in
the frustration of romantic longings for individuality, spontaneity,
and self-expression. And they are all made possible because romantics
become chastened and seek reasons for reconciliation. What distinguishes them is the particular oppositional stance that precedes each
one and the particular elements of liberalism each draws on to make
its peace.

Heroic individualism is the romantic pose at its most militant and
self-assertive. Its resources for reconstruction are the revolutionary
elements of liberalism—self-government, consent, and independence.
I have already shown that open-ended liberal notions of liberation
appeal to certain romantic sensibilities who cannot abide prosaic peace
and long for action commensurate with the dignity and intensity of
desires. Heroic individualism finds a complement to revolutionary
political action in continual, personal declarations of independence.

Reconciliation is not simple, though. Liberal individualism is typically calculating, or accommodating, or it rests on rights; it is not
heroic. Even when individualism becomes politicized and liberalism
supports popular revolution or civil disobedience, the end in view is
securing conditions for the regular pursuit of private happiness. Reconciliation requires finding opportunities for continuous self-assertion
within liberalism. For its part, romantic militancy is an activist, exhibitionist stance, but hardly that of a democratic citizen, and disenchanted romantic militants may prefer detachment to mundane
existence. The writings of Henry David Thoreau suggest how a gen-

uine integration of heroic individualism and liberal democracy could look and feel. He captures the affective impetus behind this reconstruction. And he reconciles heroic individualism not only to private liberty but to the public life of liberal democracy as well.

Thoreau has often been treated as an exemplar of democratic individualism. He is the conscientious liberal citizen exercising his right of resistance, and his name is invoked to lend moral authority to disagreements with the state. Thoreau has also served as a model of romanticism. He is the sensitive soul repulsed by philistinism, who declares his loathing and seeks personal peace by withdrawing from the world.[1] He has been called "the guru of getting away from it all."[2]

There are two Thoreau legends; he can be described as either liberal or romantic with justice. My point is that he embodies a dynamic relation between the two in which every description of Thoreau as a romantic sensibility evokes his embodiment of liberal principles, and every description of him as a political activist evokes thoughts of the sensitive soul turned within. The author of *Walden* introduces himself as a quietist withdrawn from social affairs, immersed in nature or in inspired acts of literary creation, but it soon becomes clear that Thoreau's hut at Walden Pond and *Walden* itself are designed to be provocative. His privatization is exhibitionistic, a public act calculated to engage others. Similarly, "Civil Disobedience," which presents a strong liberal case for government by consent, is also an appeal for standing aloof from public concerns. Its socially conscious author emerges as a self-absorbed romantic soul.

My discussion of Thoreau reflects this shift back and forth from activism to detachment, from public to private, each moment rich with both liberal and romantic resonances. Analyzing Thoreau this way I do not find ambiguity or painful self-division but instead a complex fusion of romantic and liberal—genuine reconciliation. Thoreau gives heroic individualism a place in liberal thought, and his example encourages us to pursue other visions of liberalism as a scene of heroic self-display.

From Activism to Detachment

Although Thoreau starts from the radical, activist, democratic side of liberalism, which emphasizes revolutionism and independence, his intense politicization eventually shades into detachment. The peculiarity of his vision is not immediately evident because his work conforms in many respects to conventional political thought. This is especially true of "Civil Disobedience," which on first reading is an impassioned restatement of the fundamental liberal principle of consent. Lockeian government is based on the consent of the people, who reserve a residual right of revolution if authority oversteps its bounds. Thomas Paine's *Common Sense* democratizes and radicalizes this idea to make revolution more than a rare last resort in the face of tyranny. Because consent to government must be renewed by each generation and each generation must initiate its own political experiment, unconstrained by the past, the "birthday of the new world" is always at hand. Thoreau moves beyond Paine by transferring the notion of consent from "the people" to men and women personally and individually. No one is bound by particular acts of government or particular obligations unless he or she consents to them, and anyone can withdraw consent at any time, without waiting for the concurrence of popular judgment.

Thoreau points up the opportunities for inspired action created by consent theory but recognizes its limitations in practice. Individuals may be sovereign, but apart from moments of revolution it is not clear how this sovereignty is exercised or given up. "I do not wish to be regarded as a member of any incorporated society which I have not joined," he insists; but he also knows that in modern society occasions for consent are few and marks of membership are ambiguous. He is unable to name all the societies he has never joined.[3] Has someone native to a nation consented to citizenship? Does owning property or paying taxes constitute a stake in or an obligation to society, and if so, why? In a liberal society dedicated to the private pursuit of happiness, what sorts of political participation, if any, define membership? Even more problematic, how does one dissolve the union between self and state once it is decided that consent should be withdrawn? Only one thing is clear: "the only obligation which I have a right to assume is to do at any time what I think right."

Disobedience is one way to withdraw consent. Still faithful to the fundamentals of liberal thought, Thoreau directs attention to the close connections between liberalism and civil disobedience and to the power of liberal ideas to inspire resistance, even if this power is only latent. For example, because consent is the sole source of legitimacy for liberal authority, liberal theorists define tyranny subjectively as a loss of trust rather than objectively as misgovernment.[4] Thoreau also recalls that ideals such as individualism and democracy have an inherent antiauthoritarian bias, and he observes that although the pretext of democracy is one cause of civil disobedience it is also what makes it possible to conceive of "civil" disobedience in the first place. Samuel Huntington accounts for the chronic instability of American politics in precisely these terms. According to Huntington, most political ideologies legitimate established political institutions, but the American creed of individualism, liberty, democracy, and equality has the opposite effect on institutions that are inevitably hierarchical, coercive, and authoritarian. Liberal democracy actually excites a recurrent revolutionary politics of "creedal passion."[5]

"Civil Disobedience" is evidently at home with the politics of "creedal passion." Like Huntington's enthusiastic reformers Thoreau sees political authority as a fall from first principles: "this American government,—what is it but a tradition, though a recent one, endeavoring to transmit itself unimpaired to posterity, but each instant losing some of its integrity?"[6] Agitated and denunciatory, Thoreau's favorite charge is hypocrisy. Yet he does not precisely fit Huntington's description of the political idealist. Thoreau is not historically minded, for one thing; conscience, not original promises, is the real measure of political failure. More to the point, Thoreau separates himself from the actual politics of creedal passion. In radical politics there is always a gap between imagination and attainment, but for Thoreau the vast distances between possibility and outcome are vivid. He cannot endure the frustration of intermediate steps and compromise. He dismisses the organized activity of reform altogether: "improvement is slow"; abolitionist leaders "sit down with their hands in their pockets," postpone, hesitate, and wait. For the true reformer, "the information floating in the atmosphere of society is . . . evanescent and unserviceable." Money is irrelevant too, since all great enterprises are self-supporting.[7] The true reformer becomes "one perfect institution in himself."[8]

There is a strong current of self-containment here. Thoreau declares his independence by himself and looks for the effects of reform on himself. "It is not so important that many should be as good as you, as that there be some absolute goodness somewhere."[9] He is obsessed with one type of action, "a life of exposure"—exhibiting himself and thereby relentlessly exposing the failings of others. The pose of the dissenting democratic citizen shades into romantic militancy. Individualism begins to look like individuality and like the romantic heroism that is more concerned with self-assertion than with estimating political consequences. Thoreau stands alone, committed only to "giving a strong dose of myself."

Classical liberalism has a heroic aura of its own: enlightenment demands self-emancipation, and liberty is the work of independent spirits able to resist authority and find their own way out of prejudice. As with Locke and Kant, individualism is for the strong. The difference is that in orthodox liberalism it is reserved for revolutionary situations. The struggle for intellectual independence may be ongoing, but liberalism mitigates its heroic ethos by anticipating that general benefits will flow from personal liberation and that eventually independence will be general. Enlightenment and liberty promise progress and the greatest happiness of the greatest number. In conventional liberal thought we are at least potentially linked, even though we are independent. Thoreau's declaration of independence is devoid of this ethic of utility, potential equality, and mutual respect.

Perhaps "Civil Disobedience" will conform more consistently to the essential outlines of liberalism if it is read from a slightly different perspective, as a moral defense of the claims of conscience. Historically, religious toleration and the privilege of conscientious objection have been granted to members of organized churches; but Thoreau is not a member. When he says that he will do only what he thinks right, he speaks "absolutely, and as a private man."[10] In liberal thought the right of conscience can extend to individuals personally, of course, but Thoreau seems to set himself outside this category as well. His conscience is a purely personal voice that does not necessarily speak consistently or in terms of rules. Perhaps that is why Thoreau never actually offers a moral refutation of slavery; he determines to withdraw his support from government because his inner voice commands it. Personal inspiration takes priority over reason, and conscience is more like the law of the heart than like rectitude. Thoreau's concern is authenticity, not obedience to general moral norms or social consciousness. "If one listens to the faintest but constant suggestions of his genius, which are certainly true, he sees not to what extremes, or even insanity, it may lead him; and yet that way, as he grows more resolute and faithful, his road lies."[11]

This openness to irrationality marks Thoreau's distance from Kantian conscience. For Kant, being persuaded that one is right does not determine the morality of an action. Morality is a matter of adopting a universal maxim discoverable by reason; conscience is the result of conforming one's will to the categorical imperative. There is a further difference: Kantian moral absolutes refer to the unconditional, but Thoreau's absolute is psychological. He experiences conscience as imperative, uncompromising, and extreme. It is no wonder that he considered the title "fanatic" the greatest compliment.

Perhaps conscientious objection, unlike civil disobedience that aims at political reform, is inward-oriented and concerned mainly to avoid personal complicity in evil.[12] In a liberal democracy, conscience seeks exemption from certain obligations. Thoreau extravagantly declares himself altogether free of responsibility for the smooth working of their machinery. "It is not a man's duty to devote himself to the eradication of any, even the most enormous wrong . . . but it is his duty to wash his hands of it."[13] The conscientious objector's exemption from certain duties has a recognized place in liberal thought. So does political irresponsibility; it is the normal condition of private citizens. Passivity is accepted too, though it has sources in cynicism or complacency. However, these do not amount to the deliberate stance of detachment that "washing one's hands" seems to prescribe. For Thoreau, life with principle does not require constant attention to government's unfaithfulness to principle. Not even a public matter as compelling as slavery has a continuous hold on his attention, nor should it: "I do not think it is quite sane for one to spend his whole life in talking or writing about this matter, unless he is continuously inspired, and I have not done so. A man may have other affairs to attend to."[14]

What began for Thoreau as civil disobedience within the framework of liberalism culminates in an ethos of retreat within. It is less principle that governs the heroic individualist than genius, and when inspiration fails, rather than returning to the hopeless banality of business as usual the romantic retires to await fresh internal imperatives.

Fear of complicity in the evil of slavery is only one of Thoreau's motives for disengagement. It is more accurate to say that like other romantic sensibilities Thoreau withdrew from what he experienced as the despotism of philistinism. Descriptions of his contemporaries reflect revulsion and self-distancing: they are trivial and complacent, acquisitive and without creativity, "wooden" and lacking in energy. His neighbors have "either much flesh, or much office, or much coarseness of some kind . . ."[15] John Brown is one of only a half a dozen men who truly died; the rest simply "run down like clocks."[16] For Thoreau, those commonly deemed good citizens and neighbors "command no more respect than men of straw, or a lump of dirt. They have the same sort of worth only as horses and dogs."[17]

The whole critical agenda of romanticism is contained in these attacks. They show that Thoreau does not simply challenge liberalism from within—by pointing to a falling-off from original shared values such as consent. They reveal a deeper disagreement. "Civil Disobedience" is not just an indictment of liberalism for its failed promise but also an assault on every government and all laws. Like other romantic sensibilities, Thoreau casts aside conventional political distinctions. He refuses to distinguish democracy, at least as it exists, from other forms of government, and he identifies government in general with a militarized empire. He calls the American state Leviathan and its citizens subjects. "Majority rule is the result of submission to greater strength." In an escalation of loathing, he calls government a demonic force, a monster, "a semi-human tiger or ox, stalking over the earth with its heart taken out and the top of its brain shot away."[18] Thoreau hoped "only to live safely on the outskirts of *this* provisional army."[19]

Thoreau also writes as a romantic antilegalist. He opposes the Fugitive Slave Law. He attacks the American legal system as a whole, associating legalism with gross imperialism. He has little patience with popular enthusiasm for constitutionalism: "seen from a lower point of view, the Constitution, with all its faults, is very good; the law and the courts are very respectable," but seen from what he calls the highest perspective, "who shall say what they are, or that they are worth looking at or thinking of at all?"[20] Because his neighbors labor to acquire comforts, they require the protection of laws. He will not have to rely on the state's protection because he declines its advantages. Without property or family, Thoreau lacks the common excuses for conforming to the law. His ideal is self-containment.

"I was not born to be forced" is the authentic voice of romantic anarchy. Thoreau rejects every organization, not just government; no group or voluntary association—no antislavery society, school, or university—has a claim on his loyalty or obedience.[21] His conviction that social institutions are uniformly coercive leads Thoreau to call excessive attention to black slavery "frivolous" and to speak of "so many keen and subtle masters that enslave both North and South."[22] "Our foe is the all but universal woodenness of both head and heart, the want of vitality in man, which is the effect of our vice; and hence are begotten fear, superstition, bigotry, persecution, and slavery of all kinds."[23] Stanley Cavell interprets this as an expression of Thoreau's philosophical idealism, of the Platonic assumption that "the state of society and state of our minds are stamped upon one another."[24] However, it is hard to see Thoreau's identification of his own victimization with slavery as shorthand metaphysics. Rather, it is a characteristically romantic substitution of hyperbole for social analysis.[25] The expression "slavery of all kinds" is first of all a charge of hypocrisy against his contemporaries for claiming to be free themselves. It is also an expression of disgust and powerlessness that evokes romantic martyrdom.

Thoreau's disclaimers are, in fact, superfluous. He was not required by either hereditary class or republican ideology to be responsible for the "smooth working" of any machinery. As a private citizen he came up against government only once a year, in the person of the tax collector. By European standards mid-nineteenth-century America was devoid of absolutism, bureaucracy, and restrictive social conventions. Henry James would itemize all the things America did not have: no class, no status, no established church, no monarchy, no aristocracy, no guilds and closed professions, no nobility of sword or robe, no high culture, no polite society. Nonetheless Thoreau's protests cease to be remarkable if we think of romantic anarchists, for whom exquisite sensitivity to limitation is a point of pride and for whom the nobility of stoic withdrawal is compelling. Like them Thoreau sees society as at once crushingly powerful and beneath consideration: "what is called politics is comparatively something so superficial and inhuman, that, practically, I have never fairly recognized that it concerns me at all."[26]

It is worth noting that part of Thoreau's continuing appeal lies in the way he captures the feeling that the outside world of politics and society is crushing and monolithic, idiotic and inescapable. The specific causes of this feeling change over time, of course, but both Henry Miller and Stanley Hyman consider Thoreau prophetic for seeing the political world as mad, government as incompetent to control the diabolical forces loosed among men, and the "problem of power" as incomprehensible. For these authors, we are all helpless in the face of the threat of nuclear war. They find solace in Thoreau's writings and recommend following his lead—by which they mean his example of disengagement and falling back on inner resources.[27]

That is in part the picture Thoreau presents. "It is not many moments that I live under a government, even in this world. If a man is thought-free, fancy-free, imagination-free . . . unwise rulers or reformers cannot fatally interrupt him."[28] Like Vigny, Thoreau flirts with quietism: "You must live within yourself, and depend upon yourself . . . and not have many affairs."[29] Inner life is the realm of freedom. Both Walden Pond and the Concord jail are a "far country." Freedom of imagination "not-in-this-world" is farther still. Civil disobedience may be a principled position, but Thoreau insists that he did not come into the world chiefly to make it a good place to live in—only to live in it. "I have other affairs to attend to."[30] Because his affairs have nothing to do with private business as usual, attending to them requires genuine detachment. "I have my horizon . . . my own sun and moon and stars, and a little world all to myself."[31]

Romantic abhorrence of philistine society has brought Thoreau a long way from engaged citizenship. His detachment has a second source: the heroic individualist's ambivalence toward the democratic aspects of liberalism. Strong democracy—participatory and egalitarian—does not accommodate elitism. The romantic sense of grandiosity and infinite possibility demands special recognition. Romantics often rage against the democratic ethos, and Thoreau does. But unlike many European romantics, including Vigny, he is thoroughly imbued with liberal democratic principles. He cannot pronounce his superiority and bemoan his victimization without ambivalence: he does not feel altogether at home in liberal democracy, but also does not feel perfectly free to attack it. By detaching himself from society he can be grandiose safely. Depoliticizing his separateness makes his heroic longings tolerable. Romanticism is a less direct challenge to democracy if it means retirement to nature or contemplative withdrawal.

However, like other romantics enamored of quietist retreat, Thoreau found it unendurable. There is nothing sanguine in his observation that "from the desperate city you go into the desperate country, and have to console yourself with the bravery of minks and muskrats."[32] Unless it is part of a constructive dynamic of inwardness and emergence, detachment is negative and escapist. It is bound to frustrate romantic longings for self-expression, which is why there is another side to Thoreau's complicated response to liberalism.

Thoreau's movement from concerned citizenship to detachment continually reverses itself, from inwardness to emergence and heroic self-assertion. And as Thoreau shifts back and forth from activism to detachment, he recasts liberal democracy to encompass heroic individualism.

Uncommonly Good Neighbors

Thoreau's account of being a good neighbor illustrates his fusion of detachment from and engagement with civil society. It captures what he takes from liberalism for the reconstruction of political thought, what he brings to it from romanticism, and how he joins the two. First, Thoreau methodically strips from the idea of neighborliness its moral and sentimental associations of familiarity and attachment, common purpose and mutual obligation. The principle of "Love thy neighbor" is eclipsed. Instead, "neighbor" indicates the bare minimum of human connectedness, physical proximity to others. It evokes private life and absence of community.

Neighbors are strangers: "We dream of foreign countries, of other times and races of men placing them at a distance in history or space [but] we discover often, this distance and strangeness in our midst, between us and our nearest neighbors. *They* are our Austrias and Chinas, and South Sea Islands."[33] Estrangement is not all; like many classical liberals, Thoreau is misanthropic. His neighbors are selfish and snobbish, cruel and disloyal. In a liberal democracy personal relations such as friendship are just as inconceivable as genuine political community is. Civil society does nothing to transform men and women; it rewards their worst traits, so that "we have had to agree on a certain set of rules, called etiquette and politeness, to make . . . frequent meetings tolerable and that we need not come to open war."[34] Neighborliness involves only literal coexistence.

Thoreau's answer to what a society of radically separate, self-interested men and women would look like is an array of neighboring lives, with a bare minimum of mutual aid and the mechanical workings of government cranking along outside—and that is all. His description of good neighbors is as impersonal in its way as any marketplace or legalistic order. Neighborliness means minding your own business, an extreme idea but one not after all incomprehensible to liberals committed to cultivating one's own garden. This is a scenario for romantic privatism; but it is also a standard description of liberal society, in which men and women lack shared values and cannot know one another's minds.

"Mind your own business" is an ambiguous demand, though, and the originality of Thoreau's vision of neighborliness—in particular his injection of romantic militancy—hinges on its interpretation. It suggests privacy, but paradoxically for Thoreau minding your own business also suggests political and expressive aspects of public life. Thoreau's experiment in neighborliness at Walden Pond was a public, even exhibitionist, act that exemplifies a "life of exposure." It has something of "épater le bourgeoisie" in Thoreau's conspicuous idleness, the constant affront of his hut situated close to the town road, and his jeremiads. Thoreau's main business in the woods, composing *Walden,* was ultimately directed toward his Concord neighbors. He did not want to be left alone entirely and he certainly did not want to leave others be. He was militant, not quietist.

What stands out in his writings, and in *Walden* especially, is Thoreau's use of paradox to shock and insult. Paradox has been called the literary mode perfectly suited to the transcendentalist task of separating appearance from reality (Emerson said Thoreau's paradoxes were the "habit of a realist"). It is also part of Thoreau's "literary redemption of language."[35] Most of all, as an attack on common understanding and as a way of withholding consent from shared meanings, paradox is the literary expression of Thoreau's militancy. It proceeds by inversion and disorientation, undermining argument, persuasion, and common sense. The same aggression is apparent in Thoreau's technique of "ontological assassination." Questioning the usefulness and truth of current ideas is not enough; Thoreau positively denies their status as noncontradictions. Accepted notions are not just wrong, they *are not*. Philanthropy is injury; killing is benefaction; "there is absolutely no common sense, it is common nonsense."[36]

Thus minding your own business does not mean simple detachment or peaceful coexistence. One's own business requires intrusiveness, shock, and affront to others. Neighbors are irritants to one another. They impose themselves on one another's consciousness. The struggles that exist in standard liberal accounts of civil society are caused by scarcity, competition for property, or religious differences. Thoreau's vision of conflict, however, arises among individualists and is associated with self-display. At stake in these conflicts is heroic self-affirmation.

This vision of society evokes a mortal struggle for self-preservation, except that literal survival is replaced by the survival of individuality: "I perceive, that when an acorn and a chestnut fall side by side, the one does not remain inert to make way for the other, but both obey their own laws, and spring and grow and flourish as best they can, till one, perchance, overshadows the other. If a plant cannot live according to its nature, it dies; and so a man."[37] This struggle is for self-expansion. It requires irritants, which is why Thoreau calls the true friend an enemy.[38] Thoreau takes one standard picture of private life, in which individuals are atomistic, egoistic, and lacking any official connection with one another, and recasts it in a heroic mold. Next to this sort of conflict liberal competition seems benign.

That society is in a condition of potential war among masterless men is hardly original with Thoreau; Hobbes insisted that a Leviathan state was necessary to prevent it. Unlike Hobbes, however, Thoreau has no patience with weakness and is not concerned to calm people's fears and make them secure. Life is for heroic spirits and thrives on discord. The peaceful coexistence of neighbors is no existence at all. Thoreau is no isolate, even if he is self-contained. He acknowledges social or personal relations, but only in his terms of antagonism rather than mutual utility or respect. Neighborliness becomes public agon.

Thoreau was a student of Homer, and ancient heroism provides some of the strongest imagery for his conception of self-assertion. A hero's actions spring from personal destiny inexorably working itself out. A hero is not prudent; he does not calculate consequences or reason. He is not a moral man. Like a force of nature—a meteor, volcano, or vital seed—the hero is unselfconscious. "I do not mean to prescribe rules to strong and valiant natures, who will mind their own affairs . . . not knowing how they live." Thoreau made this point more than once in *Walden:* the woodchopper, the "true Homeric man" who was his visitor at Walden Pond "suggested that there might be men of genius in the lowest grades of life . . . who take their own view always, or do not pretend to see at all."[39] Thoreau's heroism is divorced from both ancient civic virtue and aristocratic service because for him, as for all romantic militants, the point of heroism is sheer self-assertion and not conformity to the ethos of a collective political culture. Homeric imagery serves Thoreau because its heroism is unreflective. Self-affirmation is spontaneous, "beyond good and evil," and impulses to self-assertion take priority over social consciousness. In the epic battle of the ants in *Walden* heroic and naturalist images come together. It does not matter that Thoreau can discern neither the cause of the insect war nor which party is victorious (or ought to be); heroic self-assertion has no economic or evolutionary purpose.[40] Conflict is gratuitous.[41]

Leon Edel accuses Thoreau of never having "thought through to the end the meaning of personal freedom when it is gained at the expense of others."[42] It is true that Thoreau is not a systematic libertarian, but there is no reason to assume he is thoughtless. His vision of good neighbors does not pretend to be harmonious. It is an anomic and amoral Nietzschean vision, and there is good reason to think he would have accepted the consequences of personal freedom gained at the expense of others. By making self-assertion the overriding good, Thoreau recreates libertarian liberalism in a self-consciously heroic key.

Heroic Self-Assertion and Democratic Liberalism

Heroic individuality is a mythic conception of the person, not an eternal truth about human nature; but conventional liberal individualism is not a complete or factual account of human nature or psychology either. The rational, autonomous person who figures in conventional liberal thought is a powerful fiction that serves a specific theory of politics. It is how we must think about ourselves if we are to act the part of agents bearing and respecting rights. The discipline of legalism depends upon this self-conception. Thoreau's alternative is to think of oneself as heroic. Then it becomes possible to imagine a liberal democracy in which romantic sensibilities feel at home.

The American War of Independence failed to realize respect for individuals, and Thoreau likes to imagine a state that would "treat the individual with respect as a neighbor; which even would not think it inconsistent with its own repose, if a few were to live aloof from it, not meddling with it, nor embraced by it."[43] He is able to reconcile himself to liberal democracy because America is a "comparatively free country"; it does allow individuals to stand aloof. And heroic types are particular beneficiaries of this liberty. They are not asked to feel like members but are free to think of themselves as irrevocably apart. They can be neighbors, not citizens, and can reject the national embrace. Thoreau confesses that he can abide the cranking of the mechanism of government so long as he does not have to assist in its smooth workings or admit to its advantages too often. The first connection between Thoreau's heroic ideal and a new vision of liberalism is the promise of private liberty, being left alone.

By itself, however, this is not enough to explain liberalism's appeal for heroic individualists. Thoreau does not want to be left alone in peace. His militancy means boycotting politics as usual, resisting social conventions, flouting pragmatic business, and denouncing the "haughty name" toleration. Because he wants freedom to irritate and meddle, and occasions for declaring his independence, he recasts private life, giving neighborliness a revolutionary aura and experimental character. He does this by reclaiming the elements of liberalism that invite radical independence. In classical liberal thought, it is political arrangements that are without inherent sanctity and acquire only the meaning we invest them with, conditionally and for only as long as it suits us. Thoreau extends this idea to private society: traditionalism has no more place in private life than it does in government. For true individualists there are no inherited social norms, only accidents of proximity or inner imperatives. Genuine liberty means independence from every apparent necessity.

Thoreau, like the stoics and Rousseau, defines independence as self-containment, a balance between needs and capacities. He is alert to the false needs created by social convention and to the inadequacy of accepted notions of welfare. But unlike the stoics, he never thought balance should be achieved by contracting needs. *Apatheia* is inconceivable, as are restrictions of personal powers. For Thoreau, the individual is typically romantic and boundless. Private liberty involves striving to discern one's own true necessities, not resignation, comfort, welfare, or repose.

Thoreau recasts liberalism: the state can leave individualists alone, and a private life of neighborliness can serve as a scene of self-assertion. More important, Thoreau reclaims the public life of democratic liberalism. The beautiful soul may express itself in the privacy of nature or among neighbors, but public self-display is something else. Thoreau refuses to choose between militant antiliberalism and detachment. Instead, by identifying heroic self-assertion as the epitome of freedom and saying that democracy invites individuals to "cast their whole influence," he brings heroism and romantic elitism into liberal democracy.

Making peace with the public face of liberalism is more difficult than reconciliation to private liberty. Liberalism traditionally restricts inspired public action to revolution; once resistance secures constitutional government, politics loses its dramatic appeal. Some limited commitment to public affairs is necessary in order to restrain governors. Apathy is dangerous. But vigilance and democratic participation are prudent rather than inspired. Ordinary politics involves negotiating and persuading, adjusting and compromising. The public sphere is not an arena for romantic expressivism, much less heroic self-display. Thoreau, however, imagines public life as life in public, a life of exhibitionism. And he imagines democracy as a scene for "giving a strong dose of myself."

The formal institutions of liberal democracy do not offer opportunities for heroic self-affirmation. Like modern-day political scientists, Thoreau observes that the available forms of participation do not appear to rational individuals as worth the expense of time and effort. Voting is a confession of passivity, not power; for Thoreau it is also evidence of political hypocrisy: "All voting is a sort of gaming, like chequers or backgammon, with a slight moral tinge to it."[44] This analogy is an accusation of vulgarity as well as of false promises, of course, and Thoreau makes his case for "casting one's whole influence" as part of a full-blown criticism of culture that dissociates individuality from ordinary political affairs. That does not diminish his claim that individuality requires public exposure and that liberal democracy calls it up, though. Thoreau's account of life is manifestly politicized, even if it has no use for traditional institutional politics. It posits conflict among separate individualists who impose themselves on one another. And it interprets liberal democracy as an invitation to heroic self-assertion.

In Thoreau's vision public life is served indirectly, as a result of self-concern. Men and women are bound to aim too low if they always address specific issues, even issues such as slavery or constitutionalism. They must attend to themselves. Then democracy is transformed into a scene of continuous declarations of independence, a spectacle of heroic self-display. Ancient and modern civic republicanism are concerned with self-development because they hold that regimes mirror their citizens, whereas conventional liberalism asserts that good government and civil liberty do not require good characters—a race of devils will do. The most liberalism requires is the disposition to legalistic behavior and a modicum of tolerance and impartiality. Thoreau revives the notion of politics as a mirror of citizenry, but his citizens are romantic individualists rather than any specific historical or moral type.

Thoreau's politics is thus personal and expressive, but not dangerously seductive. Heroic individualists are not a threat to liberal democracy because in giving a strong dose of themselves they exhibit power rather than exercise or institutionalize it. They are disinclined to govern or lead, much less blindly obey. They do not excite erotic attachments or arouse collective passions. The individualist's motive is self-affirmation, not self-abnegation through identification with a group or subordination to a cult of personality. Nothing could be farther from the irrationality and mass mobilization that afflict personal politics in many democracies and that are sometimes erroneously identified as the essence of romantic political thought.

Thus Thoreau's account of democracy as exhibition of individuality conforms to the needs of even the most aloof romantic. Self-display does not demand respect for others, and the independent spirit does not need to act as leader, educator, or legislator. By itself self-expression is an inspiration to others, a public education in the meaning of liberty. Heroic types are exemplary. Thoreau believes that genuine individuality is rare, but admits that it is impossible alone. It requires resistance and contest. He can imagine a plentitude of expansive selves, an infinite number and type of individualists, in democracy as in nature. Heroic expressivism is extraordinary but not exclusive. Perhaps that is why Thoreau's language is elusive; it is never quite clear whom he speaks for or to, and he uses the pronouns "I," "we," and "they" interchangeably. The effect is at once distanced and democratic.

Stanley Cavell's apt characterization of *Walden* as "a political education for isolation" applies to Thoreau's political vision as a whole. It is an education in isolation because individuals remain at a distance from one another, and because this lesson in minding one's own business could only be taught by a self-absorbed sensibility familiar with the attractions of detachment. It is a political education because it attends to personal freedom, takes political revolution as its model for personal independence, and prefers self-assertion in a democracy to withdrawal.

It is possible to move beyond Thoreau's "political education for isolation." Romantics can reclaim the democratic face of liberalism in a more obviously democratic spirit: more generous, more engaging, and less militant. Heroic individualism can be toned down without losing its aura of expansive self-expression.

Liberalism as a Spectacle of Diversity

For Thoreau liberalism is an invitation to heroic self-affirmation. But the militant character of self-assertion can be taken away without discarding its romantic ethos. Individuality can become delightful rather than provocative, enjoyed in company with others rather than self-contained. The result is a vision of liberalism as a wonderful spectacle of diversity. Heroic individualists come together in a lavish display. This vision of liberal democracy affords special aesthetic gratifications and even holds out the promise of solidarity.

Literary romantics first described the power of particularity and diversity in connection with nature. Nature is a chaotic plenitude that cannot be approached through scientific laws but must be grasped immediately, in appreciation of variety rather than regularity. Romanticism calls this display of individuation "sublime." It is terrible and energetic, not useful, tame, or harmonious.[45] To imagine oneself in a natural setting diminishes one to just an atom in a whirling universe of particles, but it is also exhilarating. It points to the wonderful correspondence between external nature and the romantic's inner sense of boundlessness and infinite possibility. It also confirms that men and women are unique creations themselves and participants in the spectacle. Thoreau uses natural forces in this way, as images for capturing "one's own nature" and for the imperative of self-assertion. Natural imagery suggests that individuality is not a quality of genius only but exists everywhere.

Parallel to this romantic naturalism is aesthetic delight in the chaotic display of individualism in democratic society. Here too plenitude excites and attracts. The romantic perspective on liberal pluralism sees particular men and women instead of the usual pluralism of organized groups. Apprehended through romantic eyes, the familiar is made new by "freshness of sensation, moments of illumination."[46] Masses dissolve into a dazzle of personalities, each of them heroic. Even when the setting is Trenton, New Jersey, rather than the Alps, the spectacle of liberal democracy can be as affecting as the spectacle of nature: "Here at last," Whitman wrote, "is something in the doings of man that corresponds with the broadcast doings of day and night. Here is not merely a nation but a teeming nation of nations. Here is action untied from strings necessarily blind to particulars and details, magnificently moving in vast masses. Here is the hospitality which forever indicates heroes."[47]

In the classic "human comedy" the spectacle is moralistic: virtue and vice are on display. Hegel's picture of plenitude comes to mind here too: history appears as "a vast picture of changes and transactions; of infinitely manifold forms of peoples, states, individuals, in unresting succession. Everything that can enter into and interest the soul of man—all our sensibility to goodness, beauty, and greatness—is called into play."[48] But Hegel searches for reason in the spectacle of history: the romantic vision of liberal democracy as spectacle is purely aesthetic.

Liberalism is seldom discussed in connection with the binding power of aesthetic responses. Introducing this spectacle of diversity breaks up the monopoly on aesthetic interpretations of politics usually granted to conservatives. Historically aesthetic and emotional attachment to a political order have been the provenance of opponents of liberalism, for whom solidarity is produced by veneration and habit supported by the magnificent rituals of court and church, pomp and circumstance, and "all the pleasing illusions which made power gentle and obedience liberal." Burke was horrified by the disenchanted world of the French Revolution, which demonstrates that fragmentation and violent disorder are the only conceivable outcomes when people act out of self-interest and have nothing to soften and beautify their "naked, shivering natures."[49]

Shedding of traditional plumage is not necessarily pitiful or horrifying, however. In the spectacle of diversity, the plain face of liberal democracy takes on its own enchantment. Masses are disaggregated, individualism does not remain abstract, and men and women emerge heroic, clothed in all their concreteness. This vision of democracy as display clearly corresponds to Thoreau's impulse to "give a strong dose of myself." Missing is Thoreau's preference for irritation and resistance. Militancy has given way to charm, and self-containment to luxurious company.

The exemplary voice of liberalism as aesthetic display is Walt Whitman. In the face of civil war, he looks to the spectacle of diversity as the most hopeful source of national union. Only immediate affective and aesthetic forces are sufficiently strong to bind men and women to liberal democracy: "For not only is it not enough that the new blood, new frame of democracy shall be vivified and held together merely by political means, superficial suffrage, legislation, etc., but it is clear to me that unless it goes deeper, gets at least as firm and as warm a hold in men's hearts, emotions, and beliefs, as, in their days, feudalism or ecclesiasticism, and inaugurates its own perennial sources, welling from the center forever, its strength will be defective, its growth doubtful, and its main charm wanting."[50] In Whitman's eyes the democratic "En-masse" is dissolved into vast artistic contrasts. For him the perennial source of union is appreciation of individuality; union begins with "independent separatism." Individualism is not necessarily cold. It can be a force for adhesiveness and love: "There is, in our sanest hours, a consciousness, a thought that rises, independent, lifted out from all else, calm, like the stars, shining eternal. This is the thought of identity—yours for you, whoever you are, as mine for me. Miracle of miracles."[51] "The fervid and tremendous Idea," the binding national idea, is diversity.[52]

Theories of nationalism ordinarily attribute unity to cultural, linguistic, or historical similarities, or to shared exigencies.[53] Resistance to Napoleon inspired Wordsworth's exultant description of a militant people fighting for liberty, for example. Herder's orthodox romantic account of nationalism sees language and art as expressions of a people's collective spirit. The assumption that unity can be achieved only through likeness has always posed a problem for liberal thought, which assumes a religious, ethnic, and cultural pluralism that creates conditions for partial membership at best. As a result, in American political thought national identity is a matter of allegiance to a common political ideology. Contemporary theorists affirm the existence of a "collective conscience," shared moral meanings, or latent community. In place of a neutral, purely procedural political theory liberalism seems to them to offer a substantive philosophy of the good life that provides material for national identity and reasons for strong commitment. This line of argument is problematic, however, because what is fundamental and what is dispensable in liberal political thought is frequently contested. More important, neither political nor moral consensus are the same as affective identification with others. Certainly consensus opposes Thoreau's vision of liberal democracy as an invitation to radical individuality.

The spectacle of diversity is an alternative source of liberal unity that celebrates differences rather than managing them. Whether its aesthetic impact affects people immediately or through the intermediary of the artist's vision, the spectacle of diversity has power to engage and attach. It excites delight and feelings of belonging. It is also a source of self-love: diversity makes us conscious of our uniqueness, for when everything that I am not is out there for me to see, my own individuality is brought home to me. Diversity gives romantic sensibilities a special affection for the national stew.

George Kateb calls the ethos of diversity "impersonal individuality".[54] He means that it lacks ordinary egoism and narrow self-interest. The problem for romantics is that it also lacks the element of striving that is a constant of romanticism. Responses to democratic display as beautiful or sublime are aesthetically satisfying; they do not leave a residue of longing or desire for reform because beauty cannot be improved. There is no place here for the romantic's troubling suspicion that genius, the law of the heart, and even individuality may not exist without cultivation, or that the expressive self stands at the end of a circuitous journey. The spectacle of diversity corresponds better to this aspect of romanticism when it is seen as a condition for self-development. Where there is plenitude and exhibitionism, individuals "complete" one another. Liberalism appears here in yet another guise, as a complementarity of excellences.

Liberalism as a Complementarity of Excellences

The idea of complementarity of excellences appears most often in discussions of friendship. Because we seek in our friends the qualities that we lack, difference among individuals is the condition for bonds of sympathy and comradery. Friendship with others promises not only intimacy but also self-perfection, for "in joining with them, we participate in some measure in their nature and thus feel less incomplete."[55] Diversity results in both self-fulfillment and attachment. This account has a discernible connection to liberalism.[56] Self-fulfillment is impossible without a heterogeneous society and without free access to a spectacular array of individual qualities; men and women must be at liberty to find their complements. However, nothing suggests that solidarity extends beyond friendship to society as a whole. This version of friendship as a complementarity of excellences provides a justification of liberalism but not a description of it.

It is possible, however, to respond to liberal democracy as a whole on this basis. For the anarchist Herbert Read, democracy is not a form of government at all but "a free association of creative personalities; it is individualism, varieties, and organic differentiation."[57] More recently, Samuel Beer has portrayed liberal democracy as nothing less than an inclusive complementarity of excellences.[58]

His terms are borrowed from Emile Durkheim's writings on the division of labor and social solidarity, which analyze the centrifugal tendencies of individualism that lead to anomie. Collective belief in individualism, in a "cult of personality," is incapable of arousing passionate attachment to society as a whole.[59] Fortunately collective beliefs are not the only source of solidarity; "collective" and "social" are not synonymous.[60] Organic solidarity in modern society is derived from the division of labor, which uses difference and mutual dependence to create a new kind of exchange among individuals. It produces a higher form of unity than uniformity or collective belief. Instead of attaching themselves to transcendent entities like the state that they can grasp only as abstractions, men and women in the division of labor have feelings of belonging that are lively and concrete. In differentiation Durkheim finds a solution to the dilemma of how to be "at once more individual and more solidary."[61]

Samuel Beer mutes and softens Durkheim's ideas and applies them to liberal democracy. Whereas Durkheim sees solidarity based on differences as a condition for social functioning, Beer sees it as a condition for personal fulfillment; and whereas Durkheim discusses the organized division of labor in the economy, Beer discusses the unorganized appearance of differentiation in activities of every kind. In Beer's account, men and women of diverse habits and occupations each exhibit particular personal qualities—discipline, say, or grace. Unselfconsciously, in the ordinary course of affairs, they exchange these "gifts of humane powers." In economic exchange something given up is lost, but in this social exchange people keep what they give to one another. "The parties do not have something more, they have become something else."[62] Becoming something else is the point. Diversity is the condition for self-realization, and liberalism becomes a complementarity of excellences. The novelty of Beer's vision is that exchange is general and social, not restricted to a circle of friends.

Other liberal theorists have recognized the importance of liberty and variety for an empowered sense of self. One of J. S. Mill's chief arguments for toleration, for example, is that it encourages diversity, which multiplies choices and provides opportunities for exercising and developing mental and moral powers. Other visions are less didactic. For John Rawls, complementarity of excellences cannot exist without dedication not only to liberty but also to the distribution of other goods. In Beer's picture, complementarity is the spontaneous gift of humane powers; for Rawls it must be brought into existence by justice. Only with a public commitment to justice can social relations promise self-realization: "It is through social union founded upon the needs and potentialities of its members that each person can participate in the total sum of the realized natural assets of the others . . . Only in social union is the individual complete."[63]

Rather than emphasizing justice or morally pleasing mutuality, Beer's vision captures the romantic response to liberalism experienced as a spectacle of heroic individualism and speaks directly to the romantic desire for exhibitionism and self-cultivation. Beer recasts liberalism by transforming the romantic passion for individuality into a force for solidarity. Liberalism does not have to depend exclusively on utility for its hold on men and women. Romantic sources of union are available: "the thrust for self-fulfillment can lead the way in social development as powerfully as the compulsions of the struggle for existence."[64]

Heroic Individualism and the Reconstruction of Liberal Political Thought

Thoreau suggests new reasons for making peace with liberalism: it invites individuality and declarations of independence pierce both public and private spheres. The spectacle of diversity and the complementarity of excellences also contribute to this recasting. Many of liberalism's essential elements remain—individualism, liberty, tolerance—but they are apprehended in a fresh way, and valued for new reasons. They no longer rest on a defense of rational liberty, but on satisfying romantic longings.

There is something lost in these new visions, though. Aesthetic delight supersedes reasoning about justice. Revelling in one another is not the same as dealing fairly, respecting rights, or promoting the general welfare. In conventional liberalism, the alternative to formal hierarchy is equality or mutuality; the spectacle of diversity may be just as opposed to hierarchy, but uniqueness stands outside the political spectrum of equality. Furthermore, the causes of diversity are placed beyond scrutiny, along with differences themselves.[65] Thoreau considers individuality a fact of nature; for him the origin of differences among individuals is not suspect.

Liberalism's institutional apparatus also disappears from view in these reworkings. The spectacle of diversity and complementarity of excellences work outside institutions; the effects of individuality have nothing to do with constitutionalism, markets, or pluralist groups. Like the heroic individualism from which they spring these extravagant visions erase social contexts and constraints. They are variations on the theme of abstract individualism, taken literally as it was never meant to be taken. Heroic individualists, severed from all contexts, float in an atmosphere populated only by a host of other heroic types. Nothing suggests how self-assertion, or solidarity, or self-development have come into being or how they will be sustained. As plenitude inspires a sense of personal uniqueness and an appreciation of liberalism as spectacle, liberalism loses its sobriety and balance.

In a second type of reconstructed liberalism, reconciliation extends to the institutional elements of liberalism. Constitutionalism, legal formalism, and political representation no longer appear cold and restrictive to romantic sensibilities. Romanticism does not give up its sense of a boundless self but rather finds a way to accommodate it to those actualities. Pluralism, for example, is less a way of dividing power than a condition for the cultivation of many-sided personalities. Romanticism makes its peace with the separation of public and private spheres on terms less exploitative and more attuned to the dangers of arrant self-expression.

CHAPTER 6

The New Face of Pluralism: Self-Cultivation and Shifting Involvements

For Thoreau, liberalism is a revolutionary theory. Public and private life, citizenship and neighborliness are dramas of resistance. They are recast to satisfy his longing for heroic self-affirmation. Romantic sensibilities can also be brought home to liberalism if it is conceived less expansively, as a theory of limits and balance. A less-dramatized liberalism that focuses on limited government and boundaries between separate and distinct spheres can accommodate romanticism as well. The most successful reconstructions of liberal thought do not tolerate heroic aloofness from the actualities of liberal institutions but instead make use of the mundane elements of conventional liberalism—legalism, pluralism, and the traditional division between public and private spheres. "Shifting involvements" gives these structures fresh meaning and value as answers to romantic needs.[1]

For Humboldt, Mill, and Constant, who share this vision, public and private life are mutually compensatory. Each sphere provides a corrective for the excesses or deficiencies of the other. If one sphere becomes loathsome or overwhelming, an aspect of the other sphere—public legalism, or private materialism, or retreat into self-absorption—compensates. The existence of differentiated spheres promises not the classical ideal of harmony, which romanticism resists, but relief from extreme instrumentalism or arrant emotionalism. There are good personal reasons for appreciating the traditional topography of liberalism with its boundaries, hedges, and countervailing domains. Humboldt, for example, proposes that a cold legalistic state leaves a protected sphere of private liberty, which for him means freedom for

cultivating originality—"beautiful individuality." J. S. Mill emphasizes the other side, describing public involvement in the business of
representative government as a corrective for the narrow egotism and
philistinism of private society.

When separate spheres are marked by distinct experiences and call
up diverse qualities in individuals, they can appear as arenas for
exciting and exercising personal powers. In some accounts, the spheres
are not so much mutually corrective as luxuriously complementary.
Pluralism provides a plenitude of scenes for self-cultivation, and individuality results from exploiting these opportunities rather than
clinging to one or choosing in a disciplined fashion among them.
Rich, complex personalities result. For Mill, political participation,
private egoism, and detachment are all necessary for self-cultivation.
For Benjamin Constant, private life invites romantic expressivism and
public life offers needed relief from exhausting emotionalism and self-
absorption.

In exuberant visions of shifting involvements, differentiated spheres
call up different powers and pluralism multiplies occasions for cultivating and expressing a fully realized, many-sided self. A more sober
vision, and one that answers to the needs of chastened romanticism,
sees pluralism as a way of limiting liability. Romantic feelings of
boundlessness and infinite possibility are commonly frustrated by a
restrictive external world, but liberal pluralism can eliminate the harsh
necessity for definitive choice. Romantics' inner impulses and the
outside world seem less acutely incommensurate, and they can avoid
the worst frustration and paralysis.

Shifting involvements involves two aspects of pluralism and separation between spheres. One is social complexity; the other is individuals' opportunities and incentives to enjoy it. It is one thing to
give reasons why pluralism and a differentiated social structure with
public and private spheres are politically or personally desirable; it is
another to give reasons why people should divide their experiences
between public and private life and among diverse social contexts.
Social pluralism and the proliferation of associations do not necessarily mean variety for men and women personally. Historically public
and private life have been parcelled out to separate social classes or
sexes. In pluralist societies, membership can be ascriptive or stifling.
Heterogeneous spheres must not only exist; they must be open and
accessible, so that individuals are free to exit as well as enter them
and so that immersion in one context does not exclude others. With
shifting involvements the two faces of pluralism come together and

liberalism meets romantic longings for self-expression, plenitude, and self-development.

Traditional liberal justifications of separate spheres as a means of dispersing power do not speak to these needs. Traditional and romantic rationales are not mutually exclusive, though; in fact, romanticism provides resources for resolving a dilemma that is intractable in standard accounts of separate public and private spheres. Liberal theorists have argued persuasively that both overpoliticization and overprivatization are dangerous threats to liberty. They are less successful in providing an adequate theory of motivation to explain why individuals would give up tending their own gardens to attend to public affairs, or resign the rewards of public life for private society. Romantic notions of self-cultivation and romantic longings for various scenes for self-expression suggest strong motives for shifting involvements.

A Romantic Answer to a Classic Liberal Problem: Shifting Involvements and Self-Cultivation

The idea that public and private spheres are not only separate and distinct but also mutually compensatory is implicit in liberal thought; indeed one way of interpreting the history of liberalism is through changes in the priority given one sphere over the other. Sometimes the emphasis is on the public character of political authority, sometimes on the private character of social and domestic life. The usual interpretation is that government is separated from society in order to strengthen and protect the private sphere. Metaphorical language encourages us to imagine fences, hedges, and frontiers restraining public authority, containing political surveillance, interference, and control. Boundaries also delineate space for the proliferation of social ties and of centers of power independent of the state. In another interpretation the purpose of boundaries is just the reverse: separation of spheres protects public authority from powerful private loyalties and from the competition of "private governments." It requires officials to be impartial toward private interests and conflicting opinions of the good life. And it sets limits to the power private groups can exercise over their own members.

Traditionally the solicitousness liberal theorists show one sphere and their assessment of which sphere is the corrective is explained by political events. If the immediate threat to freedom comes from political authority, liberal theorists will decry antipolitical strategies of disengagement but they will promote another sort of private life— the formation of independent associations—as an antidote to Bonapartism, mass politics and totalitarianism. At other times liberals recall Madison's warning that the threat to liberty comes from private despotism, the power of private groups to interfere with government and with one another and to tyrannize their members. Events have also led political theorists to emphasize the ways in which secondary associations shore up government. Limited government may be desirable but unstable government is not, and "in the absence of effectively self-governing groups, the state not only lacks restraint; it also lacks support."[2]

Conventional liberalism justifies the separation of public and private spheres because it disperses power and promotes liberty. The mutually compensatory nature of public and private life also has direct personal consequences for men and women. When attention is turned from the structure of society to shifting involvements between spheres, a chronic problem in conventional liberal thought emerges: that although a balance between public and private spheres is crucial for political liberty, the impetus individuals have for dividing interest and energy between spheres is unclear.

A recurrent preoccupation of liberal thinkers is determining how individuals immersed in the private pursuit of happiness can be inspired to participate in politics (or even to defend themselves against injustice). Locke, Madison, Tocqueville reflecting on Napoleon, as well as contemporary liberals, warn that the strictly private pursuit of happiness is self-defeating. If there is no duty except to submit to laws, Mill observed, people become "a flock of sheep innocently nibbling the grass side by side."[3] How to get people out of their own gardens is the problem. Participation must be voluntary, and liberal theorists are loath to use any of the means associated with tyranny or with the politics of mass mobilization. They are reluctant to arouse public spirit. They resist appealing directly to loyalty or civic virtue, much less the passion for glory. Madison explains that because the people are not public-spirited and have only a limited capacity to be altruistic he substitutes institutional mechanics for civic virtue as the guarantee of liberty. He is resigned to this thought because he knows that public-spiritedness is dangerous, not just undependable. Competing ideologies of the public good can threaten liberty as severely as religious conflict can. In the same cautious spirit Bentham argues that the "public interest" and the "common good" are dangerous fictions, rhetorical invitations to unanimity associated with both hierarchic and revolutionary governments. To Bentham these phrases signal fanaticism and intolerance. Thus standard liberal arguments for political participation remain narrowly instrumental and indirect. Voting, for instance, is described as a way to advance particular interests or to legitimize a system of government that serves one's interests.

Except when government totally disregards particular interests, however, self-protection has proved a feeble motive for getting men and women to turn from private involvements to public affairs. Reason may demand that "the people" be active and vigilant, but from the individual's perspective a single vote or voice seems negligible. Political passivity may also reflect the perfectly accurate judgment that one's own interests can be advanced better by those more competent.[4] Moreover, politics motivated by private interests within a regular constitutional framework is bound to be unsatisfying, especially to those who imagine passionate public involvement as compensation for the woodenness of prosaic civil society. Ordinary politics is positively revolting to Thoreau, for whom public action must satisfy the romantic impulse to heroic self-affirmation if it is to have as much significance as contemplative withdrawal.

Short of direct political excitation, liberal theory must somehow make egoists altruistic and make impersonal institutions appear as settings for self-expression. Romantic notions of expansive feelings and self-cultivation are alternatives to self-protection on the one hand and civic virtue on the other.

Sentimental Education and Public Life

Mill considers public involvement a corrective to an all-consuming private life. The problem is to justify and inspire participation in public affairs. People in civil society routinely attend to the satisfaction of daily needs, to commercial business, and to their own amusement. They are narrow, materialistic, and without dedication to common goals;[5] they lack sympathy and fellow feeling, "largeness of sentiment." "Giving [them] something to do for the public supplies, in a measure, all of these deficiencies."[6] Public life appears as a compensatory realm of expansive feelings and ideas.

Altruism is nothing heroic. It means impartiality, not grand acts of benevolence or self-sacrifice. It is the inclination to take into consideration the larger national interest.[7] It brings to mind Madison's pragmatic definition of statesmanship as the capacity to subordinate particular short-term advantages to the permanent need for peace and progress.[8] Even so altruism is rare, and the question arises of what could make "mean and slavish" men and women interest themselves in the well-being of all of the members of society.[9] The traditional answer, when arguments from immediate self-interest fail, is self-discipline. Even if this is true, what can encourage men and women to constrain themselves to attend to the general interest?

Mill proposes a motive: if people alternate public involvement with attention to their private welfare, they will cultivate the full range of their powers. The promise is self-development, the cultivation of a many-sided self. The idea of self-cultivation is powerful in part because it is wonderfully resonant. It brings to mind Ben Franklin's admonition that powers should not be wasted but be developed, because they produce happiness and worldly success. It also echoes romantic concern for feelings; in Mill's mind public life is distinguished by its association with large sentiments. Altruism may entail utilitarian calculations of the greatest happiness, but these calculations must be inspired by feelings. Mill gives a purely personal rationale for public life. And when political participation is seen as an occasion for self-cultivation in this way, the standard estimates of the costs and benefits of public involvement change. Mill describes feelings that can be aroused and expressed only in politics; public involvement is affective, not just instrumental. The "free ride" loses its appeal and fear of being inefficacious recedes because the focus is less on political outcomes than on effects on oneself.

Because he is concerned with arousing feelings Mill applies standards besides efficiency and accountability to the institutional arrangements of government. He judges the capacity of institutions to affect individuals internally.[10] At stake is not only development of the rational capacity to calculate the greatest happiness of the greatest number, but more important cultivation of the emotional impetus to perform the calculus in the first place. Nurturing sentiments of sympathy and identification is Mill's chief rationale for expanding representative institutions: for jury trials, local self-government, and participation in democratically organized industrial and philanthropic enterprises. The test of good government is its "tendency . . . to improve or deteriorate the people themselves."[11]

Besides large feelings Mill was also interested in cultivating mental powers and the capacity for choice, in bolstering all the elements of autonomy. But emphasis on autonomy threatens to push his concern for feelings into the background. When Mill speaks of inner culture he means sentimental education. He believes that political institutions can stimulate sympathy as no sophisticated argument on behalf of altruism can. To know that a feeling is a constituent part of happiness does not necessarily bring the feeling itself; experience is necessary.[12] "The food of feeling is action; even domestic affection lives upon voluntary good offices. Let a person have nothing to do for his country, and he will not care for it."[13]

Thus it is wrong to portray Mill as a naive romantic liberator of feelings. The law of the heart assumes a dichotomy between the true self and artificial institutions. Mill does not. He knows that sympathy and other beneficent emotions are not deeply rooted in human nature apart from external influences. Moreover, as romantics learn through cruel experience, the demonstration of feelings is not all that matters. Well-meaning souls are not necessarily liberal. The disposition to impose one's opinions on others is "energetically supported by some of the best and by some of the worst feelings incident to human nature."[14] He has no use for sentimental moralists who find utilitarianism insufferably cold. Because free-floating benevolence and fellow-feeling are at best inefficacious and at worst pernicious, Mill would arouse altruistic sentiments in an institutional setting designed to attach them to liberty and utility.

Mill's rationale for shifting involvements is self-cultivation, and the particular promise he holds out is the experience of larger sentiments that are not excited or expressed in the ordinary course of private life. As a utilitarian Mill might have ignored sentiment and inner culture entirely. As someone sympathetic to romantic impulses he might have been content to criticize the crippling effects of prosaic civil society on emotion and individuality. Instead, he makes utilitarianism and romanticism mutually supportive and rethinks liberalism from the inside out. The same characterization applies to Humboldt's theory of government, only he uses romantic longings for many-sidedness to support the private half of the public/private divide.

Beautiful Individuality and Separate Spheres

Difficulty with motivation also afflicts the conventional liberal account of private life. What satisfactions besides property and prosperity does the private sphere hold out? Liberal theorists often try to divorce the private sphere from an exclusive identification with material interests and claim that if possessive individualism is valued at all it is as much for its pacific political consequences as for its strictly economic benefits. This still makes the desire for security the central reason for private life. It neglects romantic pleasures such as sentimental attachments or aestheticism. These attractions of private life emerge when it is juxtaposed with a formal and uninspiring public life and when separate spheres are presented as a condition for self-cultivation. Humboldt turns romantic individuality into a nonprosaic, noneconomic rationale for limited government and into a compelling motive for privatism.

For Humboldt, the bureaucratic state and the pathetically enervated condition of individuals make the genuine public life of a citizens' community inconceivable. Yet political passivity and immersion in private affairs are not necessarily regrettable if they are conditions for developing "beautiful individuality." Self-cultivation compensates for the loss of political community and for the coldness of the *Rechtsstaat*. Indeed it is only possible under a limited government and with a strict separation between spheres, guaranteeing that private life will be truly private. The range of government action must be limited to things individuals cannot do for themselves such as maintaining external security, preventing mutual harm, and compensating for injuries. Public authority must exercise its power formally and impersonally. The ideal constitution has the least possible positive influence on the character of its citizens: it should "fill their hearts with nothing but the deepest regard for the rights of others, combined with the most enthusiastic love for their own liberty." Humboldt imagines that in the absence of imperatives to be dutiful and public-spirited (imperatives that in any case his contemporaries were unfit to fulfill) people can absorb themselves in the business of self-cultivation. By making itself felt as little and as impersonally as possible the liberal nightwatchman state provides the conditions for uniqueness and originality.[15]

Is self-cultivation a romantic ideal? Like romanticism, it is deliberately antiutilitarian. Economists understand shifting involvements between public and private life instrumentally, as a strategy by which individuals maximize gratification and minimize disappointment. Albert O. Hirschman's sophisticated account of this dynamic in *Shifting Involvements: Private Interest and Public Action* uses a psychology of disappointment to explain cycles of politicization and privatization in a capitalist society with distinct public and private spheres.[16] He criticizes standard consumption theories that do not take into account the actor's evaluation of preferences as a result of experience. According to Hirschman disappointment with consumption and the antipublic ideology of private life produces a pendular swing toward public action and an ideology of service and commitment. Dissatisfaction with the anonymous political institutions of modern liberal democracy produces in turn a rebound to private preoccupations.

Mill's account of self-cultivation invites people disenchanted with private society to turn to public life, and Humboldt describes privatism as compensation for the disappointing absence of public community; but they do not speak of shifting involvements as a strategy for maximizing satisfaction. The language of economic preferences and maximization is inappropriate to self-cultivation, which entails a different relation to oneself than simply knowing what one's preferences are or when one's desires have been sated.

Humboldt's notion of self-cultivation is a romantic ideal. I have discussed how Humboldt substitutes originality for the classical ideal of character and "beautiful individuality" for virtue. Character cannot be cultivated in private, removed from citizenship or other definite social relations, but Humboldt imagines that individuality can. He describes a privileged private sphere in which the only significant group is a close circle of friends. Humboldt respects the institutional apparatus of liberal government; he discusses the Rechtsstaat in detail. But his account of private life is a chimera. He imagines beautiful individualists who regard one another as works of art to be created and loved. He imagines "the true art of social intercourse" flourishing as men grasp "the innermost individuality of one another."[17] Humboldt clings to the idea of *Bildung* at the same time that he exalts privatism, for privatism shades into a vision of aesthetic communal life.[18] Like classical *Bildung,* Humboldt's notion of self-cultivation involves fulfillment and joy with others. It is part of an idealist historical vision. His thoughts about self-cultivation are taken over by romantic longing, which threatens to eclipse his sober conclusions about limited government and separate spheres.

When Mill uses self-cultivation to justify separate spheres and shifting involvements he invokes Humboldt's confidence in the "absolute and essential importance of human development in its richest variety."[19] *The Sphere and Duties of Government* was written in the early 1790s but was not completely published until the 1850s. Mill cited it in his work, recognizing how powerful the idea of self-cultivation could be for liberal thought. Mill is more faithful to the commercial and institutional actualities of private as well as public spheres, however, and unlike Humboldt he does not call on the classical dualism between man and citizen, even to reject it. For him the ethos of self-cultivation is neither classic nor romantic. Mill does not propose a universal ideal of wholeness, but he does not glorify originality or "beautiful individuality" either. His idea of self-cultivation is more modest. He accepts that the personalities of modern men and women are complex; rather than providing beauty or wholeness, shifting involvements guards against one-sidedness. The public life he recommends is compensatory, not redemptive or magnificently self-expressive. Mill's judgment that individuals need to take up public business is historically contingent and based on the limitations of private life in civil society, in particular its failure to provide occasions for large sentiments.[20] The cultivation he prescribes is romantic only to the extent that Mill sees personality as infinitely various and recognizes certain longings for a sense of unlimited possibility. It is not so much Mill's ideal of individuality that is resonant of romanticism as his picture of how the process of self-cultivation transforms the experience of liberalism.

As I have presented it so far, self-cultivation strengthens liberalism by providing fresh rationales for separate spheres and fresh motivations for shifting involvements. It is also possible to reverse the emphasis and to see liberalism instrumentally, as the condition for exciting and exercising personal powers. This raises the question of when shifting involvements becomes more than a practical necessity imposed by the fact of pluralism or a strategy for maximizing satisfaction. When is liberalism experienced as a scene of self-development?

Mill suggests an answer by insisting that only the person whose desires and impulses are his own has character. The concept of autonomy does not do justice to Mill's meaning; he does not stop with independence but explains that a person's desires must be "the expression of his own nature developed and modified by his own culture."[21] In this prescription, "the expression of his own nature" recalls romantic individuality, uniqueness, and self-display; "developed and modified by his own culture" is even more striking. It goes beyond ordinary notions of rational choice to say that unlike consumers in economic theory, men and women do not have fixed desires or tastes. Following Bentham, economists tend to take human beings as they find them and to speak simply of preference and choice. Mill suspected that individuals are never found in a stable state with a comprehensive range of wants. They do not take themselves as they find them.

Mill opposes the Christian ideal of self-denial in *On Liberty* and speaks confidently of the need for pagan self-assertion; but he clearly knows just how problematic self-assertion is. One of his most important insights is the difficulty of knowing or even having impulses of one's own, "expressive of one's nature." Mill recognizes what other utilitarians do not, or choose not to pose as a problem for political thought, when they describe maximizing pleasure as if desires were self-evident and preferences settled. Thus he speaks of desires and impulses "developed and modified by his own culture"; shifting involvements has to do with self-cultivation first and only indirectly with the pursuit of happiness.

The cultivated balance Mill imagines among the elements of a many-sided personality is not simple or dualistic. It encompasses not only public altruism, private egoism, and shifting involvements between public and private spheres, but also withdrawal within. Mill draws the romantic connection between individuality and detachment. Detachment becomes for him the critical condition that transforms shifting involvements from a practical necessity imposed by the fact of pluralism into a romantic project of self-cultivation.

Self-Cultivation and the Necessity of Detachment

In *On Liberty,* liberty appears as a condition not only for satisfying one's desires but also for ascertaining for oneself what they are. Liberty provides opportunities to make mistakes and rectify them, to remember, evaluate, correct, and complete wants in an endless process of education and self-development. Mill's phrase "style of life" indicates these "second order volitions" and signals his understanding that men and women may actively consider the sort of persons they want to be. They can reflect on how they feel about both their desires and their powers. Shifting involvements can have enormous personal significance if it is a means to self-cultivation as well as a setting for exercising autonomous choice. This does not happen automatically, though. Shifting involvements serves self-cultivation only if one has a sense of oneself as a personality with a history of error, disappointment, imagination, and change. It depends on tolerating a romantic sense of indeterminacy and possibility.

Two things stand in the way of the self-knowledge required for personally exploiting liberal pluralism and the separation of spheres. One is that society is overbearing. "Framing the plan of our life to suit our own character" is impossible if men and women never consider what would suit their dispositions or what would allow the best in them to thrive.[22] Instead people "like in crowds; they exercise choice only among things commonly done . . . until by dint of not following their own nature they have no nature to follow." They become incapable of any strong wishes or native pleasures; they are "generally without either opinions or feeling of home growth, or properly their own."[23] Another difficulty is the dangers of rational analysis. It faces those who like Mill *are* independent and capable of reflection and self-probing. In his autobiography Mill describes how he was concerned for the general happiness as well as his own, only to become oppressed by the logical possibility that reform would be completed and that there would be nothing further to perfect or pursue. The very habits of rational analysis that make him fearful of romantic illusion eventually undermine the dream of utilitarianism. Although pursuit of happiness seems to promise boundlessness Mill finds, on examination, finitude. For him analysis leads to dejection.

In the face of excessive socialization and the limitations of rationality, Mill proposes genuine privatization as a personal necessity. If shifting involvements between public and private spheres is a condition for self-cultivation, retreat from both must be possible too. Self-knowledge is an internal affair; so is recovery from depression. Detachment means relief from other things, as it did for the stoics. It is an antidote to the world "too much with us." Mill describes the withdrawal inward that accompanied his own crisis of self-doubt as a salutary period of intermission, at least in retrospect. During this period he was undisturbed by action or ambition. Just as important, his capacity for feeling was refreshed. Feeling overcomes dejection. And feelings enable men and women to use and interpret experience in their own way.

Certainly the most important result of detachment is the discovery of "passive sensibilities." When Mill says that his turn inward produced "a transformation in my opinions and character" he meant that he came to give "its proper place among the prime necessities of human well being, to the internal culture of the individual."[24] The internal culture he speaks of is not purely intellectual. It is more than taking stock of wants and choices, or calling up the moral capacity to choose. Inner culture refers to emotional resources. Thus Mill, like many romantics, associates detachment with personal intimacy and even more closely with immersion in art, poetry in particular. For Mill poetry is soliloquy. It is "feeling, confessing itself to itself in moments of solitude."[25] Poetry delineates "the deeper and more secret workings of the human heart" and provides access to that "quite other world" that artists, with their tender sensibilities, know and make available.[26] Mill found in poetry "the very culture of the feelings, which I was in quest of."[27]

The significance of detachment lies in the possibility of cultivating feelings and being energized by them. The real reward of aestheticism is "the deeper and more varied interest you will feel in life; which will give it tenfold its value, and a value which will last to the end."[28] Poetry shows its readers that every truth, thought, and impression can be invested with the coloring of emotion.[29] It reminds us what it truly means to be "interested."[30] Through detachment and immersion in art Mill finds unlimited sources of pleasure to overcome instrumental reason's depressing revelation of finitude and exhaustion.[31] In this way he recovers from the fear that there is "a flaw in life itself" and becomes confident that life is worth living. "I was no longer hopeless," Mill confesses, "I was not a stock or a stone."[32]

Schiller's great work on aesthetic education offers a systematic account of this process. He attributes to men and women a third capacity in addition to reason and sense—really a state or mode of being—which he calls aesthetic and to which he assigns special power as a corrective. Beauty softens and relaxes natures that are one-sidedly sensuous or critical. It works on those obedient to inclinations and on those morally disciplined and attuned to categorical imperatives. "Through Beauty the sensuous man is led to form and thought: through Beauty the spiritual man is brought back to matter and restored to the world of sense." Art, or "play," is respiriting. It contains no direct moral message and has no concrete political results. Yet it is enabling: it gives people the energy to emerge from inwardness to action in the world. Schiller's aesthetic state is one of "indeterminacy," but indeterminacy is not paralysing. It is associated with feelings of possibility and power, with a sense of having an "unlimited capacity for being determined." It brings consciousness of freedom and opens men and women up to engagements in the world.[33]

Schiller assigns aesthetic indeterminacy a mediating function. It facilitates movement among other modes—rationality, sensuousness, intense emotion—and shifting involvements among spheres. It diminishes the tension of transition from dutiful citizen to consumer, from worker to lover. In Schiller's account we are more complex than standard dualisms such as rational/irrational, man/citizen, interior/exterior suggest. We are constituted for diversity: differentiation is not a falling-off from some original unity, and personal complexity corresponds to pluralist society. Aestheticism helps negotiate this complexity.

Mill's experience leads him to a similar conclusion, though he does not share Schiller's utopianism. Like Schiller he accepts the fact of inner and outer differentiation. His ideal is not simplicity, either: "The feelings of the modern mind are more various, more complex and manifold, than those of the ancients ever were. The modern mind is . . . brooding and self-conscious; and its meditative self-consciousness has discovered depth in the human soul."[34] Mill also assigns a special place to the feeling of indeterminacy. It is the source of energy and of every sort of action. There must be a deep inner pool of affect to sustain interest in the pursuit of truth (which must be "felt"), in the instrumental activities of private life, or in public altruism. Reason is not strong enough to nourish these by itself. Detachment, particularly when it involves aesthetics, alerts us to our capacity for feelings, which underlie "interestedness" of every kind, whether public and altruistic or private and narrowly egoistic. Thus feelings are not substitutes for analysis or utilitarian calculation. Like Humboldt and Schiller, Mill welcomes many-sidedness and variety rather than simplicity and unity. For him too feelings help in cultivating and negotiating complexity. In Mill's own experience the dynamic of inwardness and emergence returned him from detachment and self-absorption to the mundane tasks of liberal society.

Liberalism and the Many-Sided Self

Mill's picture of liberalism and personality is one of plenitude. In the process of self-cultivation things are added, not discarded, lost, or transformed. Public life retains its character as calculation of the greatest happiness, and civil society is left unchanged, providing a legitimate field for selfishness, materialism, industrial progress, and a host of "sympathetic associations." The cultivated self contains romantic elements of infinite striving, boundlessness, dread of finitude, longing for spontaneous affect, but these do not eclipse other capacities; in fact they serve the independent self of conventional liberal thought.

For example, detachment, aestheticism, and emotionalism actually reinforce rationalism. They are particularly important to liberalism because they make scepticism tolerable. Mill is famous for his epistemological defense of scepticism and for his argument that scepticism serves liberty. Scepticism is an irreplaceable force for moderation; it tends to make citizens engaged in public affairs more tolerant and to make businessmen less heartless and obsessive. Uncertainty and doubt are also natural stops to grandiosity. Mill knows, however, that scepticism can be frightening and paralyzing. And he knows that scepticism cannot be made palatable through logical argument alone. Mill was a master of argument; *On Liberty* is a brief for the inescapability of human error and for the way doubt produces progress. But argument alone cannot convince people to endure fear of doubt or the discipline of tolerance. Scepticism *can* be made bearable, however, by periodic emotional relief from the painfulness of doubt, which detachment provides. It offers absorption in pure aesthetic pleasures and in intimate expressive relations. Inner culture discovers resources to take away the terror.

When individuals are many-sided and personally impelled to shifting involvements between spheres, liberalism is strengthened. Romanticism is strengthened too by avoiding the most painful failings of arrant romantic sensibilities. Mill was never a proponent of wild emotionalism or unconstrained self-expression, as some interpreters have claimed.[35] It is true that like romantic sensibilities he associates excessive practical reason with inhibition of feelings ("analytic habits are a perpetual worm at the root . . . of the passions").[36] Mill is also casual about what exactly is lost when affect is inhibited; the list includes "inclination," "spirit," "strong wishes," "native pleasures," "feelings," "strong susceptibilities," "energy," and "the raw material of human nature." Yet his language describes clearly enough a cultivated balance: the inner culture of feelings provides "redress," "correction," "relief," and "compensation."[37] He does not set rational analysis and emotion against each other. "Feeling confessing itself to itself," is not everything. Emotions attach to principles and institutions and make both public and private life interesting to us. Mill gives many elements of romanticism their due without indulging its worst tendency—narcissistic self-absorption.

For some critics of liberalism, however, detachment and self-absorption are not moments in the dynamic of shifting involvements; they are everything. Privatism can seem the sole preserve of humane values, "a saving clause in a bad treaty." Mill does not subscribe to this view; for him self-cultivation requires only a "sojourn" in the "quite other world" we find through retirement within. Privatism is a corrective, not a world to itself. The world it serves, and the necessary setting for full self-development, is pluralist liberal society.

Lionel Trilling has described the degeneration of this view. He too sees immersion in art as a powerful form of self-analysis. He argues that as a method of confronting whether life is personally meaningful, literature "ought to be encountered in solitude, even secrecy."[38] However, from his twentieth-century vantage point Trilling doubts that art can continue to play a part in self-development. For one thing, it is encountered in institutionalized educational settings rather than solitude. More important, disaffected social groups have grown up around art and for them cultivation of exquisite feelings becomes a whole way of life. Trilling describes this counterculture within liberalism as subversive. It undermines traditional institutions and the ordinary habits and discipline of liberalism.

If self-cultivation is linked to shifting involvements, detachment and self-absorption are not threatening. They reinforce engagements in public and private life. Both liberalism and romanticism are stronger for this romanticization of pluralism and separate spheres, as Mill shows. He proposes self-cultivation as a new justification of liberalism, and he explores the benefits to liberalism of inner culture.

Romantic Relief: Another View of Separate Spheres

Whereas Mill excites elements of romanticism to reinforce liberalism, Benjamin Constant looks to liberalism to subdue romanticism. Mill infuses the standard image of a rational autonomous self with affect and aestheticism; he relates the institutional structure of liberal democracy directly to the cultivation of feelings. Constant looks to shifting involvements to curb the dangerous excesses of romantic sensibilities; liberalism's uninspired politics of rights and interests provides relief from arrant emotionalism. Because overheated feelings arise in both public and private contexts, liberalism is a double corrective. Limited government is an antidote to the emotional intensity of a public life that demands spiritedness, loyalty, or ideological purity. Limited involvement in government is also an antidote to a surfeit of privacy, intimacy, and stifling self-absorption.

I have already discussed Constant's argument that modern "revolutionary" despotisms differ from older forms of tyranny because they do not affect their subjects only at intervals and from a distance. They are penetrating. They interfere with our innermost feelings.[39] Despotism "pursues the vanquished into the interior of their existence, it maims them spiritually in order to force them to conform."[40] Constant advocates the bourgeois "spirit of commerce" over the ancient "spirit of conquest" (and over nostalgic romantic yearnings for republicanism and heroic self-assertion) because a legalistic commercial order leaves the inner person alone. Apathy and antipolitical withdrawal are antidotes to this sort of excited tyranny.

Thus a pluralistic society is crucial. A separate private sphere offers other outlets for feelings and self-expression besides politics and war.

Civil society is not a warm community, but it is not an aggregate of isolated, atomistic individuals either.[41] Romantic longings do not have to be frustrated there; the emotional intensity of personal life can compete with the seductions of politics. Constant points in particular to the flourishing of intimate relations between men and women. Private expressivism protects against the political exploitation of romantic feelings. Liberalism is also strengthened because private attachments supply a source of resistance to public demands on our affections. This has not always been possible: "the ancients found more enjoyment in their public existence and less in their private existence; as a result when they sacrificed individual liberty to political liberty they sacrificed less to obtain more."[42] In pluralist societies, however, in which men and women can create expressive personal associations, full-time self-government and preoccupation with the public good can mean only loss.[43] Constant represents intense personal life as both a rationale for limited government and its best guarantee.

If the public sphere is formal and impersonal, the private sphere issues a virtual invitation to a return of the repressed. Private life becomes a scene of spontaneous affect and irrationality, of religious impulses and imagination, of friendship, intimacy, sensitivity, and love. Yet Constant is too much a chastened romantic himself to ignore the dangers of excessive emotionalism, as his devastating diagnosis of the law of the heart in *Adolphe* shows. When Constant opposed "l'arbitraire" he had in mind romanticism as well as political tyranny. In conventional liberal thought arbitrariness refers to inconsistency and self-preference on the part of governors. For Constant, it also refers to romantic enthusiasms and to the radically unstable law of the heart. Like so much of liberal political thought, Constant's defense of pluralism and limited government is based on scepticism; but whereas liberals such as Mill are sensitive to the limits of reason, Constant as a romantic sensibility is attuned to the limitations of feelings and expressivity.

Constant's mistrust of unbridled romanticism causes him to place importance not only on a separate private sphere but also on certain institutional elements of public life, in particular legalism and representative government. Constant does not indulge excessive privatism; no liberal with his fear of despotism would.[44] Private liberty is insecure without a degree of self-government: "the danger of modern liberty is that, absorbed in the enjoyment of our private independence and in the pursuit of our particular interests, we will renounce too easily our right to share in political power."[45] His prescription is shifting involvements between public and private spheres. Representative institutions provide settled procedures for electing and scrutinizing public officials and for defending interests, at the same time ensuring that politics will not become all-consuming. In representative government participation is voluntary and leaves time and energy for other affairs. It is meant to be elective, not expressive. In fact, public involvement is relief from private emotionalism. Constant himself entered public life as a distraction from debilitating self-absorption: "not for happiness—is there any such thing in life?—but as a task, as a chance to fulfill a duty, which is the only way to lift the burden of doubt, memory, and unrest, the eternal lot of our wretched and transitory nature."[46]

Constant is even more resolute on the subject of legalism and impersonal rules, and his arguments for legal formalism are as vehement as anything found in Jeremy Bentham. He prescribes engagement in the ordinary contractual and commercial affairs of civil society to romantics sated with intense feelings. Dealing fairly with strangers can be a welcome escape from the exhaustions of intimacy and self-analysis.[47] Following rules as a reprieve from personal life is a variation on the familiar liberal theme that in a heterogeneous society indifference and impartiality are preconditions for cooperation. Men and women must set aside personal and political feelings to have peaceful and beneficial relations. To this political argument Constant adds a personal one: indifference as a respite from exhausting intensity.

For Constant the peace promised by liberalism is more than just subduing ideological conflict and balancing interests, as in conventional liberal thought. Peace is the calm of regularity. It is relief from the romantic's inner turbulence and terrible ennui. This is a modest claim. Pluralism does not produce wholeness, happiness, or wonderful self-realization. It mirrors inner complication, uncertainty, and real self-division. Yet it offers liberty, and protection against the worst miseries romantics suffer.

Humboldt, Mill, and Constant illustrate how romanticism reinforces the separation of public and private spheres. They each describe a correspondence between external heterogeneity and personal longings. Shifting involvements excites a variety of capacities. Certainly it wards off the frustration of one-sidedness. Humboldt is the most sanguine, with his promise of "beautiful individuality." Mill's cultivated balance is more sober, as is Constant's desire to secure a safe context for expressivity. Each finds a way to get around the paradox of casting a system of limits, boundaries, and balances as home to sensibilities averse to limitation.

A vision of shifting involvements can be distilled from these that suggests reconciliation to limits without promising self-cultivation. Like conventional liberalism it offers security, only not for material interests but for the romantics' sense of infinite possibility. Romantics abhor restriction and are vulnerable to frustration and self-loathing. Shifting involvements becomes a way of limiting liability. It exploits pluralism to protect romantic sensibilities from the shock of finding that inner impulses and the external world are incommensurate. Just as conventional liberalism disperses power, this liberalism disperses risks to the romantic's grandiose sense of self.

Shifting Involvements and Limited Liability

Albert O. Hirschman has studied cycles of mass politicization and privatization in a liberal society with separate public and private spheres. In his analysis shifting involvements serves to limit the vulnerability of the "consumer-citizen," whose expectations are continuously disappointed. Satiation with consumer goods and services motivates the shift from private to public life. The same psychology of disappointment produces a rebound from political activity to private preoccupations. Shifting involvements minimizes unhappiness. Hirschman's study recognizes that liberalism, pluralism, and shifting involvements speak to the dread of frustration, but it does not go far enough either in its description of pluralism or in its appreciation of the psychology of infinite longing.

For Hirschman "wildly exaggerated expectations, total infatuation, and sudden revulsion" characterize shifts between political participation and consumption. This is a curious description; Hirschman's language evokes nothing so much as the instability of personal affections. He could be describing romantic militants or followers of the law of the heart instead of "consumer-citizens" engaged in the ordinary pursuit of happiness. Hirschman's language evokes the romantic experience even where his analysis does not. For his purposes, perhaps, nothing is lost by defining shifting involvements narrowly as a movement between the two poles of consumption and political participation or by identifying private life with consumption and public life with civic spirit. But this analysis fails to capture the romantic response to liberalism. What are its limitations?

Consider first whether Hirschman's distinction between public and private corresponds neatly to that between citizen and consumer, as he suggests. There is no obvious reason for the opposite of public involvement to be consumption. Despite the importance of separate public and private spheres, liberalism is not starkly dualistic. In a heterogeneous society private life encompasses family, entertainment, scientific and intellectual enterprises, a host of organized engagements such as religion, personal relations, and work. Private life also refers to detachment and self-absorption. Liberalism does not limit men and women to a choice between two options. Hirschman identifies private life with consumption because he takes consumption to be the quintessential instrumental activity marked by calculations of cost and benefit. He represents public participation as the exact counterpart of consumption by identifying politics with commitment to an ideology of the common good. Both assumptions are questionable. Consumption can be compulsive rather than calculated; democratic politics can be self-serving rather than passionate and altruistic. More questionable still is Hirschman's characterizations of private and public spheres as respectively instrumental and noninstrumental.

Instrumentalism does not apply peculiarly to private life, nor noninstrumentalism to public involvement. Neither the internal nature of actions nor common understanding determines once and for all and for everyone whether a course of conduct will be experienced as utilitarian or expressive. Certainly for romantics instrumentalism is not restricted to economic affairs but extends to virtually every aspect of public and private life; calculating philistinism is everywhere. On the other hand, virtually any activity can be expressive. Recall Stendhal's Julien Sorel, who exploits each social domain, even the most conventional, to exhibit his grandiose self. Romantics can experience almost any context as a scene of self-affirmation, or self-cultivation, or relief from ennui. Benjamin Constant makes the case for engaging in commerce and embracing legal formalism in just these terms.

The quintessential romantic dilemma arises from fear of losing the sense of infinite possibility. Every course of conduct appears frivolous and incommensurate with inner longings, yet at the same time depressingly definitive. Adolphe preserves his sense of beautiful individuality only by avoiding action altogether. For many romantics the reason for action (or for paralysis) is to protect this feeling of boundlessness. The object is not to test and affirm one's powers, as it was for Thoreau, but to limit the liability of expressing them. Even ordinary public and private life may be bearable if individuals do not have to be identified too closely with any one sphere.

From this perspective shifting involvements is more than just a matter of reevaluating preferences; it is part of the obsessive project of avoiding constraint. Hirschman partly recognizes this psychology when he describes the dynamic of satiation and disappointment. He acknowledges that a stable hierarchy of wants may be neither psychologically possible nor desirable. The men and women he describes "can conceive of *various* states of happiness, are able to transcend one in order to achieve the other, and thus escape from the boredom of permanently operating on the basis of a single, stable set of preferences." For romantic sensibilities, however, shifting involvements is not a sophisticated pursuit of happiness. Its ethos is negative: it wards off threats to the sense of possibility, threats of self-definition and closure.[48]

The idea that shifting involvements can limit liability appears in contemporary feminist writings. For many feminists today liberation means multiplying the spheres open to women; diversity becomes a radical alternative to the restrictions of woman's "proper place." Carol Gilligan describes how women see themselves mainly in the context of personal relations, "depicting their identity *in* the connection of future mother, present wife, adopted child, or past lover." Women assess themselves by a single standard of relationship, "an ethic of nurturance, responsibility, and care."[49] Gilligan documents the painful consequences of this identity when it is exhaustive and there are no alternatives. It inspires self-sacrifice and guilt. It frustrates what she calls mature autonomy. Sometimes the feminist aspiration is freedom for self-cultivation, but sometimes it is a negative, self-protective reaction against limitation. In either case feminist literature reminds us that shifting involvements for personal ends assumes the success of liberal pluralism. It depends on the possibilities created by a complex social structure and on liberty to enter and exit from separate spheres.

Shifting involvements assumes that political and social contexts are "open" and plural affiliations are possible. It requires civil liberties and a cultural climate of diversity. Other social conditions may be relevant as well. Unemployment, for example, tends to eliminate social ties and access to associations. Shifting involvements may require that the family act not as an isolated unit but as an entrée to other social spheres. Liberals have traditionally seen pluralism as a way of dispersing power and providing material opportunities for individuals. Madison, for one, asserts that individuals restricted to one sphere are vulnerable to both public and private despotism, with their accompanying social vices. Romanticism adds to this standard argument. It also helps us to see that liberal thought is permeable not only to positive romantic claims for the way pluralism serves self-cultivation but also to the negative promise of limited liability.

Take for example Judith Shklar's examination of the relation between pluralism and social vices. She shows that in liberal democracies the common vice of snobbery violates patriotic values and directly attacks equality. "Anyone who closes himself off from his fellow men and who lacks a sense of his own and other people's equal rights is now a potential snob."[50] Because pluralism increases the number and kinds of groups that include some people while excluding others, it contributes to the problem; snobbery is the inevitable consequence of diversity, even if it is unintended. Yet pluralism can also provide relief. As groups multiply, everyone "can have some occasion for inclusion and exclusion, which should make it far easier for everyone to bear."[51] Expanding opportunities give everyone some context in which to feel equal or even superior to others, so no one is always and everywhere excluded. The standard account of pluralism as dispersal of power and opportunity leads to Shklar's revisionist picture of pluralism as a bulwark against the injury and self-hatred of permanent exclusion. This ethos of self-protection is not expansive. It is negative, as promises of material opportunity or self-development are not. And it is just a short step to the romantic portrait of pluralism as limited liability.

Romantics are the worst snobs, if snobbery can be said to exist outside indentifiable social cliques. They see the whole world as philistine and idealize aloofness. Of course the "beautiful soul" is also likely to be despised as useless and affected by virtually every social group. Pluralism and shifting involvements can limit the liability of romantic sensibilities to inflict and to suffer snobbery, not so much for the reason Shklar gives, because everyone has one particular circle of his or her own, as because a sense of individuality and spontaneity can be preserved by moving from one circle to another. Shifting involvements wards off complete acceptance and perfect integration in a social group, heightening feelings of personal uniqueness. It guards against definition and disillusion, sustaining the dream of an infinitely versatile self. And dissociation is always possible. This experience of pluralism may seem like alienation, but it satisfies romantic yearnings. Avoiding the crushing sense of restriction is a strong reason for chastened romantics to make peace with liberalism.

Liberal theory recast to emphasize separate spheres and shifting involvements has powerful political and psychological implications. First, it invites personal movement and variety as traditional liberal thought does not. It draws more attention to questions of opportunity than does liberalism as a bourgeois ideology or doctrine of formal rights. This is true whether the romantic notion of possibility is one of ecstatic plenitude or somber self-protection. Humboldt imagines beautiful individuality but Constant and Mill are sceptical. For them, self-cultivation is different from self-perfection; individuality and expressivity do not necessarily promise happiness, or marvelous creativity, or social peace. The notion of limited liability is even more negative; it has its sources in uncertainty and vulnerability. Because romantic self-protection means protecting a sense of possibility, however, it has radical potential. It craves diversity and mobility and inhibits the conservative tendency of liberalism to rest content with existing rights and liberties, groups and spheres.

The second implication of shifting involvements is a correspondence between the romantic sense of self and the external world of liberal pluralism. Thoreau complains that liberal democracy appears insignificant to him because it does not recognize individuals; it does not address him as a conscience or a unique personality. In theories of shifting involvements, however, liberalism mirrors romantic self-conceptions. Romantic sensibilities are many-sided and resist the claims of any one sphere; the external world is similarly complex and differentiated. Romantics can feel at one with liberal society precisely because it is not unified or homogeneous.

Shifting involvements limits liability so that men and women may successfully ward off the painful sense of finitude, but the opposite danger—fluidity and absence of identity—remains. Constraint may be loathsome, but "empty infinity" is fearsome too. The dark side of shifting involvements, like the dark face of liberalism, is atomism and fragmentation. An alternate vision of shifting involvements promises both personal wholeness and a conscious feeling of being at home.

Life-Cycle Theory:
Pluralism and Personal Development

This optimistic vision can be distilled from the psychological literature on the individual life cycle. Even though the focus of this theory is not politics, its vision of personal wholeness captures a certain way of coming to terms with liberalism. The essential outlines of life-cycle theory are familiar: individuals pass through a series of developmental stages, each related to a different sphere—family, peer group, workplace, and so on. Personal development is inseparable from plural contexts and shifting involvements. This cycle encompasses the development not only of powers but of identity—a sense of personal integrity and wholeness.

Psychologists such as Erik Erikson and Daniel Levinson and his colleagues emphasize the logical and lawful elements of personal development. An individual progresses through an empirically identifiable sequence of life phases. The specific character of a stage derives from its developmental tasks, and a period ends when they lose their primacy and new tasks emerge to initiate a new period.[52] For Erikson, for example, the components of a successful resolution of the stages of childhood are basic trust, autonomous will, and initiative. Levinson extends the analysis of life phases and tasks into adulthood.

Romantic resonances are evident in the very idea of a fully realized, expressive personality and in descriptions of the process of development. Consider the way life-cycle theory echoes a theme of literary romanticism—that individuality is the outcome of a circuitous journey. In most organic and pedagogical theories development is conceived undramatically as a gradual evolution of qualities or a formal training of powers. Here, by contrast, each stage has a dramatic contour defined by "phase-specific psychosocial crises"—conflict, fear, recovery, and resolution.[53] Development has the character of a heroic enterprise. Conflict and striving are unavoidable. Developing an identity requires traversing these periods of crisis and self-testing in order; tasks not accomplished in the appropriate phase recur and "demand their due."[54] As a result, shifting involvements is purely personal but not random or impulsive, because different contexts and engagements are intimately related to powerful inner drives. The process of development has an affinity to romantic self-discovery. And the self whose identity is traced in life-cycle theory has an even closer affinity to romanticism.

This is not obvious at first because psychologists often explicitly associate the image of the mature self with conventional liberalism. Concepts such as "life-plan" bring to mind standard discussions of autonomy and choice.[55] The notion of the liberal free agent is present in Erikson's concern for "lawful independence" and for relations with parents, employers, and government that cultivate autonomy.[56] However, the usual liberal emphasis on will and preference is replaced by an emphasis on crisis, energy, affect, and intimate relations. Identity assumes a romantic cast: Erik Erikson defines identity as an "unbroken sense of initiative," as feeling "self-activated" and "in free possession of a certain surplus of energy."

The strongest evidence of romanticism, however, is that infinite possibility and endless variation are core ideas. In life-cycle theory the quintessential romantic complaint against choices that fix and define oneself is recognized and given its due. It is incorporated into the psychological business of particular stages and described as a powerful motivation for shifting involvements. The impulse to hold on to intense feelings of unexhausted potential is not confined to adolescence, but discovered to be a normal aspect of adult life. This longing does not have to mean hopeless paralysis, either: "A man hears the voice of an identity prematurely rejected; of a love lost or not pursued; of a valued interest or relationship given up in acquiescence to parental or other authority; of an internal figure who wants to be an athlete or nomad or artist . . . During the Mid-life Transition he must learn to listen more attentively to these voices."[57]

Possibility and many-sidedness are built into the very idea of identity formation, distinguishing it from notions of eudaimonism, innatism, or self-actualization, with their teleological conceptions of life as the perfection of an essential self.[58] Classical notions of personal harmony and balance imply selection, weighing, and exclusion; by contrast identity is wonderfully inclusive. It rejects simple unity. Life-cycle theory's picture of identity is one of fantastic plenitude, for in the process of development, nothing is ever lost.[59] Nothing past remains alien, discontinuous, or incapable of being integrated into one's self. "Identity formation emerges as an evolving configuration . . . which is gradually established by successive ego syntheses and resyntheses" until at maturation "each period contains all the others."[60] Life-cycle theory proposes something more extravagant than successful socialization, ego development or autonomy: a genuine myth of wholeness.

This myth of wholeness is related directly to pluralism. The notion of ages and stages assumes diverse spheres and shifting involvements; different stages give different social contexts central place. And these social contexts are more than just settings for self-development, as private life is for Humboldt or public life for Mill. Psychological terminology is not always helpful in sorting out the exact relation between personality development and social spheres. Theorists speak of "interpenetration" of self and social world, of "participation in" and "engagement with" institutions. Relationships and roles are said to be "lived out"; the world is said to "impinge on" the self, and so on. What is clear is that pluralist social contexts are ingredients in a developmental process, in "a patterning of self and world."[61] With the claim that heterogeneous spheres are not just scenes of self-cultivation but ingredients of personal development, life-cycle theory proposes a new experience of liberalism. An objective structural correspondence between pluralism and identity-formation converses with a subjective feeling of being at home in a complex and differentiated society.

In this theory plural spheres do not appear external and contingent. They are appropriated. Each stage with its accompanying structures is accepted as necessary to the self one has become and to one's continuing sense of possibility. Each stage and its corresponding social context is recalled as one's own, something to which the individual belongs. When the final assembly of all the converging identity elements is accomplished, the individual can return to the different spheres and earlier life structures, which now feel continuous with his or her past self.[62] Erikson writes: "the possessor of integrity . . . knows that an individual life is the accidental coincidence of but one life cycle with but one segment of history [but] for him all human integrity stands and falls with the one style of integrity of which he partakes."[63] This is a romantic story of movement from differentiation to wholeness, from fragmentation to reconciliation, in which none of the pieces or possibilities is lost.

Conventional liberal theorists rarely take an interest in personal development and when they do it is out of concern for the stability of liberal democracy. Not everyone agrees that liberal government can be run by a race of devils if only it is well organized. This is not to say that society must mirror the character of its citizens; liberalism can disregard the presence or absence of many virtues and vices, attitudes and beliefs. It does mean that liberalism is fragile unless men and women are tolerant, reasonably independent, and disposed to make and obey rules. The conventional question is how liberal society can insure the existence of personalities who value and preserve liberty. I have described part of Mill's answer. Instead of asking how development serves liberalism, however, some theorists ask how liberalism serves personal development. Mill spoke to this point too; he answered that liberalism invites self-cultivation by erecting distinct public and private spheres as well as opportunities for detachment. Life-cycle theory attends in much greater detail not only to the dynamics of personal development but also to the nature of involvements in various spheres.

Of the several ways of recasting pluralism to emphasize shifting involvements, the one I have distilled from psychology claims the most. It promises wholeness, not just limited liability or even self-cultivation, and it aims beyond reconciliation to pluralist spheres to deeper feelings of being at home. This suggests why romantic sensibilities may not be content with justifications of limited government and separate spheres even if the promise is self-cultivation or limited liability. Romantics may want political theory to capture a correspondence between liberalism and identity that is genuinely affective. Then liberalism is recast in a communitarian mold.

CHAPTER 7

Repairing the Communitarian Failings of Liberal Thought

In Humboldt's judgment modern men and women are not whole but fragmented, lacking "perfect oneness of the entire being."[1] Theories of shifting involvements make a virtue of this fragmentation. Heterogeneity is not seen as alienation or a falling-off from some original unity; rather, plural spheres and shifting involvements appear as external complements to internally complex and tumultuous selves, conditions for self-expression and self-cultivation. Heroic individualism solves the problem of fragmentation differently. Thoreau turns his particular perspective into a whole world. In his imagination Concord appears as a microcosm of all nature and America and each person is "one perfect institution in himself." This vision is isolating and solipsistic, however. It lacks the mutual sympathy and solidarity, the belonging to a company of others, that some sensibilities look for to overcome fragmentation.

Aestheticism and life-cycle psychology respond to the problem of unity by making imaginative use of the rich fabric of liberal democracy. The spectacle of diversity brings individualists together in self-display and provides unity from difference; an aesthetic sense of the dramatic or sublime creates coherence. In social psychology, integrity and a sense of wholeness lie at the end of the circuitous journey through stages of personal development. Yet these promises of individual wholeness are inadequate if what is wanted is community.

Political promises to merge the individual in some transcendent unity exploit longings for wholeness. Individuality and spontaneity are qualities of groups, not of beautiful souls personally and individually. Romanticism has sometimes been identified with a group mind or the general will, with excited nationalism or an assertive state personality. It is a common fact of intellectual history that liberalism and community have been considered antithetical. Yet communitarianism poses problems for romantic sensibilities too, because personal liberty and self-expression may be given up and individuality submerged in a higher expressive unity.

The challenge of repairing the communitarian failings of liberal thought is somehow to conceive of community without appealing to examples of all-consuming public spirit such as ancient Greek citizenship or revolutionary republicanism with its Jacobin fervor, without idealizing primitive communities, and without resorting to organicism. Consistent with romantic individuality, communitarians must hold up the "creative, expressive potential of man" and "the infinite quality of personality" as goods served by communal experience.[2] They must imagine community without self-immolation. At the same time they must preserve basic elements of liberal thought. This attempt at recasting liberalism is more dangerous than heroic individualism or shifting involvements because communitarianism is always on the verge of slipping into intolerance, parochialism, and vicious separatism. When it is inspired by romantic impulses and still retains the essential elements of liberalism, though, it joins shifting involvements and heroic individualism as a type of liberalism with which romantics can make their peace.

Liberalism's most adamant critics cannot imagine repairing its communitarian failings. They tend to see dualisms between community and impersonal market relations, solidarity and legal formalism, a rich socially constituted and embedded self and an autonomous chooser maximizing preferences. For these critics liberalism is irreparable. Alasdair MacIntyre, for example, believes that liberalism suffers from irremediable moral disorder; there is no belonging and modern man "is a citizen of nowhere, an internal exile wherever he lives . . . modern liberal society can appear only as a collection of citizens of nowhere who have banded together for their common protection."[3] But communitarians need not be implacable critics of liberalism. They can replace these stark dichotomies with more nuanced interpretations of liberalism that are open to affective, associative impulses. Metaphors of layers and depth indicate shared meanings and latent community beneath surface divisions. Or images of spiralling suggest a theory of history in which falling off from traditional unity to liberal atomistic individualism is followed by some more complex stage, marked by fully realized selves and expressive political unities.[4]

The ethical aspects of traditional communitarian thought—mutuality, reciprocity, or equality—are secondary here. So is defining and distributing goods, which preoccupies socialist theorists of community. The central promise of these reconstructions is that community membership offers personal, affective satisfactions that formal liberal citizenship does not. Commitment to liberal political principles does not provide powerful feelings of belonging. The complaints against conventional liberalism are distinctly romantic, and by now familiar: "Freedom and equality can be cold. People may be free and equal—and strangers. Integration means 'to form into one whole; to complete; to perfect.' That goal embraces and lies beyond freedom and equality."[5] In community, relations are not legalistic; obligations and personal inclinations coincide. In community, the regime appears "lovely" to its members.

Clearly community promises more than consensus or an alternative to a society radically divided by incompatible ideologies or cultural traditions. Contemporary communitarians rarely attempt systematic conceptual distinctions between political unity and community, though; they appeal to intuition or to a few specific examples. Even so what they propose contrasts sharply with traditional communitarianism and with mainstream social science.

The model for community among social scientists today is East Asia. The Japanese sense of place holds particular interest for its practical implications. Whereas Japan's traditional community was once thought to inhibit economic development, now communitarianism in the workplace is seen as a conscious policy and a chief cause of economic productivity.[6] From the point of view of romantic discontents with liberalism this picture of community as a deliberate instrument of market effectiveness is ironic: affect and attachment are supposed to be alternatives to materialism and commercial relations, not their basis and support.

Social scientists have also studied how a market economy and an ideology of individualism can be adjusted to produce public goods. Under the impetus of a "revolution of rising entitlements," the argument goes, government becomes a manager and provider of public needs. Alongside the domestic household, which serves diverse private wants, they project a new "public household." This provides an alternative to viewing liberal government as a "political market" or scene of "corporate grabbiness."[7] However, social scientists do not make a symbol of the public household, or see it as the embodiment of a general will or deep shared meanings; it is not asked to bear the weight of affection and solidarity. For communitarians, by contrast, the idea of a public household resonates with longings for emotional attachment and mutual sympathy and concern. In this spirit Samuel Beer loads as much affect onto national policy as he can: compulsory public education, military conscription, and the progressive income tax could have been inspired only by "a new form of political community with a power to generate public affections and mobilize solidarity beyond anything of which the old regime had been capable."[8] In the same spirit communitarians like to substitute the term membership for citizenship to emphasize that rights and interests do not take priority over feeling at home in a unique, expressive order.

I propose three ways to recast liberalism in a communitarian mold: pluralist communitarianism, latent community, and a community of direct relations. Each type modifies and preserves different elements of liberal thought, just as each is in danger of slipping away from liberalism in its own fashion. Each has its own affinity to romanticism as well. It is not my intention to classify theorists; often the work of a particular author mixes elements from the different types and it would distract from my purpose to try to assign Michael Walzer or Charles Taylor, say, to one category or another, much less to characterize their thought as pure communitarianism. The routes from romantic disaffection to communitarianism are various and complex, and a surprisingly wide array of elements of liberal thought—from pluralism to equal rights to mutual respect—become resources for this work of reconstruction.

Pluralism and Community

Political theorists have historically taken their models of community from societies remote from modern liberal states. Like other philosophers before and after him, there was only one community for Hegel, the Greek polity, which provided free men with a second nature: *Bildung* identified them with the life of the city and perpetuated it. Contemporary theorists often look back to the ancient *polis* or to closed religious communities such as the Puritans or the Jews in medieval Christian Europe. Not all communitarians are nostalgic, though. What I call "pluralist" theorists attribute communitarian qualities to subgroups within liberal society. They point to groups bound by familial relations such as ethnic communities, religious orders, or experimental communities.[9] Legal scholars find signs of community in the "living inner law" of associations.[10] Even the unrelenting critic

Alasdair MacIntyre, who describes liberal society as a collection of strangers, observes that "we still . . . find it difficult to think of families, colleges, and other genuine communities in this way."[11] Theorists may be generous in their findings of community, recognizing many structures within liberal society in which the individual is "a particular member . . . He is at home here, and he knows his place; he reigns in his own company."[12]

These communitarians deny that pluralism and shifting involvements translate into fragmentation and anomie. They also deny accusations that articulated groups and subcommunities have been homogenized. In assessing this criticism it makes a difference whether liberalism is supposed to have completely erased the structures of community life, leaving a vacuum where they once stood, or whether liberal government is supposed merely to have "neutralized" these groups. Impartiality is not the same as destruction. In the most negative view, Charles Taylor's for example, liberalism has swept away old positive structures and partial communities, leaving no resistance to the forces of atomization.[13] Pluralist communitarians insist however that private relations in civil society successfully attach individuals' affections and provide expressive unities to identify with. They claim that membership in certain groups can be experienced as commensurate with the dignity and intensity of desires.

The examples of community cited by pluralist theorists are radically dissimilar, though. These groups, which range from traditional positive structures like ethnic and kinship groups to economic, ideological, and culturally expressive associations of all kinds, suggest altogether different kinds of belonging. Membership in corporate bodies, families, and other conventional structures may not be the result of personal decisions. They may not correspond to personal impulses, let alone arise out of consent. They may be experienced as suffocating rather than embracing. Private despotism is common: many women would be dissatisfied with a designation of the traditional family as the dominant scene of self-cultivation and expression. Yet contemporary theorists frequently number the traditional family among "genuine communities," ignoring domestic tyranny, dependency, and women's enforced privatization. The feminist point of view reminds us that pluralist communitarianism can be limiting rather than liberating if it refers to conventional external structures, especially ones that are coercive and exploitative. "Embeddedness" can mean being stuck. It can certainly work against romantic expressiveness, spontaneity, and the law of the heart.

Communitarianism tells us little about the character of membership if the quality of relationships in voluntary groups and other social structures is not analyzed. Michael Sandel, for example, regrets that people are "dislocated, roots unsettled, traditions undone"; he wants "situated selves."[14] Roots and traditions are not identical to situatedness and attachments, though; the terms suggest distinctly diverse social milieus and psychological states. The sort of attachment he wants is not clear. Dislocated, frustrated selves "at sea in a world where common meanings have lost their force" can be reconciled to tribes or democratic workplaces, traditional nuclear families or circles of friends. Communitarians must show whether their aim can be met by voluntary and perhaps temporary associations formed for limited purposes and capable of attaching only some of our loyalties, or whether it is necessary to be violently gripped by feelings of attachment.

Some of these difficulties are avoided when communitarians reassert both individuality and attachment to others. This is not the case with the classic form of communitarianism sometimes associated with nineteenth-century romantic thought, in which political communities are said to have their own history, spirit, energy, and personality, and self-expression is attributed to a personified group. In attempting to distill communitarianism from liberalism while preserving romantic individuality, the focus shifts from the personified group to the satisfaction of personal longings through membership. The result is a strong argument for liberal pluralism, in which groups are not fixed and traditional but spontaneously created to answer personal needs.

Within both liberalism and romanticism there are good personal and political reasons to replace the idea of groups as expressive associations with the notion of groups as scenes for individual self-expression. One of the things expressed, then, is impulses to attachment—communitarian sentiments. Thus communitarianism becomes an outgrowth of the fundamental liberal freedom of association.

The U. S. Supreme Court case *Village of Belle Terre v. Boraas* indicates how difficult it is to identify a genuine community and to distinguish affective associations of individuals from conventional political entities like neighborhoods, which sometimes claim authority over men and women because of their presumed communitarian character. Belle Terre town zoning ordinances prohibited groups of three or more people unrelated by blood or marriage from sharing the same household. The court upheld these ordinances, which excluded communes, groups of students, and others living in arrangements that do not conform to the traditional family. The reasoning was that by this restriction the community could preserve its character. The Belle Terre case raises more vital questions than the justices attempted to answer. When is a town a center of "value formation and value expression" and when is it just a collection of persons or an accidental overlapping of location?[15] When is an informal group such as a commune, say, more communitarian than a political subdivision? When should private affective associations take precedence over established political subcommunities?

Interpretations of the case suggest that when it comes to weighing First Amendment rights of free association the motives for association should count, and communitarian impulses ought to receive special consideration. Laurence Tribe is sympathetic with communitarian longings. He agrees with liberalism's communitarian critics that public life is fragmented; men and women are "isolated and made vulnerable to the state's distant majorities at the very moment that they are liberated from domination by those closest to them." Yet Tribe disagrees with the court's decision in Belle Terre because in his view hope for community lies less with political subcommunities than with informal private associations. Creative personal attachments facilitate "the emergence of relationships that meet the human need for closeness, trust, and love in ways that may jar some conventional sensibilities but without which there can be no hope of solving the persistent problem of autonomy and community."[16]

From the perspective of pluralist communitarianism, liberalism entails a more dynamic relation between the elements of government and civil society than traditional notions allow. Government does more than regulate or mirror society. It tolerates pluralist groups, and even generates and protects them by giving them special privileges and responsibilities.[17] A broader political unity may be forged from this common interest in the subjective need for association. The conventional pluralist framework of liberalism is preserved here, but recast. Respect for associations because of their basis in objective interests or political opinions, or because of their role in insuring political liberty and stability, is superseded. It is replaced by respect for associations because of their basis in personal longings to escape isolation and ennui and find a company of one's own. Liberalism becomes the political theory of expressive association.

Ambiguities in pluralist visions of communitarianism remain, such as how to discern whether a group is mainly instrumental rather than spontaneous or affective. The communitarian character of a group has to do with the felt experience of members, not its declared purpose or function. However, it may not be necessary to decide this point in practice, because pluralism accommodates a wide range of groups and allows them to stand in abstract relationship to government much as the individual has traditionally done. Pluralist communitarianism preserves the framework of liberal impartiality while harboring expressive, erotic, and playful associations alongside those historically privileged.

Other elements of liberalism are reinforced as well. In the past the idea of a "community of character" posed a dual threat to liberalism—the threat that individuals might be totally immersed in community and unable to escape its surveillance and control, and the threat that minorities might be excluded from the majority community with none of their own to belong to. Communitarianism based on voluntary associations blunts both threats. There is a potentially infinite number and kind of groups, and because they are incorporated within the liberal framework of separate spheres, membership remains partial. Both characteristics insure that from the point of view of personal liberty, communitarianism is benign.

The attraction of pluralism for romantic sensibilities is its variety of possible expressive attachments. Romantics abhor restriction; pluralist communitarianism promises partial membership and the possibility for continuous fresh associations. Because identity is not fixed by a single attachment a sense of openness and unlimited potential is preserved. As one political philosopher writes of groups, "none absorbs him completely, and he doubtless retains a native capacity to be a member of many others that in fact he never is a member of."[18] Pluralist communitarianism is distinguished from shifting involvements by the emphasis on expressive attachments rather than contexts for self-cultivation. Here pluralism speaks to the law of the heart. There are echoes of the spectacle of diversity too: the cult of promethean energy is manifest in the proliferation of "companies of one's own rather than in purely individual self-display."

As an answer to romantic longings and to the problems community poses for liberalism, pluralism also has obvious weaknesses. One is the recurrent danger of confusing pluralism with separatism and slipping from a theory of individual expression back to one of expressive groups. Liberal government does not typically distribute rights and benefits to groups directly. Individuals do not and should not earn their standing as citizens through groups, nor should they lose status and protections that accompany membership in society as a whole when they leave or change groups.[19] When communitarians describe attachments as gripping or constitutive of personality they oppose the basic tenets of liberal pluralism—that groups should not be all-encompassing and that within them members express only certain aspects of their personalities and purposes. They also oppose the romantic sensibility, which seeks intimacy and attachment while at the same time resisting limitation and sharp definition—especially definition in terms of some external collectivity.

The possibility of divided loyalty raises another difficulty for pluralist communitarianism: which connection is primary, the group nourished by powerful personal impulses, or society and state? "Secondary associations" may claim primacy, successfully attaching their members' loyalty, defining their obligations, and providing them elements of self-development and expression. In *Obligations* Michael Walzer shows how pluralism creates the conditions for painful conflicts of loyalty. The worst tension produces the hard politics of confrontation between the authority of the group and the authority of government, as in civil disobedience.

Escape from Abstractness

Given these difficulties with pluralism as an answer to the communitarian failings of liberalism, there must be a further explanation for interest in membership as a compelling form of relation to others. Whether communitarians laud traditional attachments or freely created associations they all "betray a dissatisfaction . . . with personal existence under liberalism."[20] This dissatisfaction is romantic revulsion at coldness and impersonality, instrumentalism and narrow self-interest. Membership is seen as the antidote to arid conceptions of individuals as autonomous legal persons. Membership also implies plenitude and emotional fullness to offset emptiness and ennui. It answers the charge that the values and choices of individuals are "inexplicable starting points," as they are to philosophical critics of autonomy and of the utilitarian self.[21] In all this, community is important less for its own sake—because it is a just, or natural, or an axiomatically good life—than as an escape from abstract personhood.

Communitarian critics of liberalism take the standard notion of abstract persons literally. Instead of recognizing it as a conceptual tool for thinking about politics they see it as a frighteningly accurate description of individuals. Atomism and anomie are said to characterize liberal individualism: "the liberal psychology of human nature is founded on a radical premise no less startling for its familiarity: man is alone. We are born into the world solitary strangers, live our lives as wary aliens, and die in fearful isolation."[22] The opposite assertion, that the self is a social being capable of powerful affections and attachments, may have been an important statement as long as anyone was inclined to neglect it.[23] Few liberal theorists have ever denied it, however. Recall the distance between liberal autonomy and privacy on the one hand and the truly isolating tendencies of romantic anarchism on the other, or the distance between either of these and genuine antipolitical detachment. Or consider the "non-Lockean" elements in the classical liberalism of Locke. His moral vision combines independence with eminently social virtues such as charity and truthfulness. Certainly his political thought is unintelligible apart from the existence of strong associations—churches, scientific fellowships, commercial partnerships and exchanges. Essential elements of liberalism such as toleration, limited government, and the separation of public and private spheres are senseless apart from the assumption of private groups that have powerful holds on their members.

Liberal theorists sometimes represent individuals abstractly, but rarely if ever do they intend such representation to fully describe actual men and women, let alone human nature in general. Their reasons are political. Recall that the notion of self-interest was not devised to deny or devalue altruism or public spirit; it was a political concept, employed against other more destructive and potentially egotistical forces such as religious zealotry or military glory. Self-interest also stood in opposition to deference and paternalism. Similarly the notion of individuals abstracted from social contexts originated in the attempt to counter assumptions about the naturalness and necessity of traditional dependencies or of hierarchical and ascriptive attachments.

In some cases abstract individualism *is* prescriptive; it is a normative concept of the person that values and promotes impersonal relations. Like legal formalism, abstract individualism is part of the discipline of liberal culture. Thinking of oneself and others as if they are simply "persons" bearing rights promotes conduct that supports civil society and constitutional democracy. Liberalism requires people to inhibit the full range and force of their personal judgments and affective ties. In a heterogeneous society cooperation depends on indirectness and impartiality, which in turn requires deliberate indifference to one another of the sort encouraged by market and contractual relations. Abstract individualism is meant to serve a particular kind of sociability. It does not claim that men and women are essentially or only consumers or legal persons. Abstract individualism does not deny eroticism, comradery, ideological affinity, and so on; liberalism asks men and women to ignore all the other things they are in order to treat one another fairly in certain contexts and for certain purposes. This does not mean that men and women are always and in every context strangers, or that if they are strangers, they are aliens.

It is a mistake to represent liberal notions of legal personhood or autonomy as a comprehensive psychology or theory of human nature. The burden is on critics of individualism to show that liberalism requires a particular psychology at all, any more than it does a metaphysics. I have shown how liberalism can accommodate romanticism. The romantic sensibility with its psychology of infinite longing does not conform neatly to autonomy or to calculating utilitarianism—and certainly not to possessive individualism. As Richard Rorty has recently argued, incompatible theories of the self are no more threatening to liberal political thought than incompatible religious beliefs; their existence may even be one more justification for liberalism.[24]

It is hard to believe that contemporary communitarian critics who feel obliged to remind us of our social nature are actually convinced that for liberal theorists "human sociability was a rare feature of human behavior that had to be superimposed by argument on human self-sufficiency."[25] In any case this criticism of abstract individualism is not to the point. For critics want community, not just sociability or interdependence. When community and society are used interchangeably the result is tautology. If "what we are as human beings we are only in a cultural community," then critics who charge that abstract personhood accurately describes men and women prove the existence of cultural communities of alienated souls.[26] This defeats their purpose, which is to show that conventional liberalism and community are incompatible. The importance of pluralist communitarianism is to remind theorists that men and women *are* members, not strangers.

One charge against the excessive abstractness of liberal individualism that cannot be countered so easily appears in feminist writings. Rather than crudely juxtaposing liberal isolation with social interdependence, or liberal egotism with moral connectedness, some feminist theorists focus on the significance of affective connections for the development of adult autonomy. They point out that conventional liberalism simply ignores the essential human interdependence of infancy and childhood. (This relationship is ignored, feminists argue, because the business of caring for dependents in the family has fallen largely to women.) The feminist point is developmental: adult men are able to act and be treated as independent agents, as liberalism prescribes, because of the existence of a sphere of life that its theorists have been reluctant to examine.

By ignoring the family, liberalism misses a chance to demonstrate the affective sources of individualism. And in failing to fully extend its assumptions about equality and justice to the family, liberalism is inconsistent.[27] This is a strong challenge to the adequacy of abstract individualism as applied exclusively to adult males. For communitarians, however, the conventional liberal account of an autonomous self is not just incomplete; it is repulsive.

There are obvious motivations for theorists to use community membership as a way of countering dissatisfaction with liberal accounts of personal existence: giving content to contentless personalities or making thin individualism rich and "thick." These seem like abstractions themselves, though; what is the content of "richness"? Charles Taylor and Michael Sandel accuse liberals of assuming that men and women are disembodied freely choosing agents, and envision instead a community that is constitutive of personality. Yet even these strong advocates of a "socially constituted self" claim only that we are "partly defined by the communities we inhabit."[28] This claim is surprisingly modest, in light of their severe attacks on abstract personhood. To propose that identities are only partly constituted by membership is to allow that not all attributes are intrinsic and inalienable—as they must. Otherwise choice would have no meaning, and characteristically liberal attempts to alter one's status or reform social order would be irrational.[29] Once this is admitted, their picture of an "embedded" and "radically situated" self gives way to the paler image of individuals encumbered to an indeterminate extent by an indeterminate number of social ties.[30] Then ties may appear as creations of individual impulses.

What communitarians do envision as the content of rich and embedded selves is distinctively romantic: spirit, heartfelt attachments, friendship, and love. Like romantic sensibilities communitarians identify conventional liberalism with a kind of philistinism—not bourgeois materialism but impersonality; in community, by contrast, personalities are not cold, empty, or "disempowered," but full of affect and dramatically gripped by commitment.[31] Alongside traditional communitarians whose first concern is social justice are many whose concern is the frustration of romantic longings.

Some critics of conventional liberalism warn that membership in

expressive associations cannot be liberating. For Roberto Unger, pluralist communities are not spontaneous or responsive to personal
needs; they are just one more device for getting individuals to submit
to the demands of a group, one more instrument of domination.[32]
This charge is plausible so long as communitarians do not specify
what kinds of groups provide situatedness and embeddedness. Theorists more sympathetic to liberal pluralism counter with the argument
that associations can enrich abstract persons and warm cold souls,
supplying moral content and self-respect to persons otherwise empty.

John Rawls argues that associations support self-esteem by providing individuals with at least one context in which they do not fail.
Each person needs to belong to some association whose internal life
is adjusted to his or her abilities and wants and sustains a sense of
self-worth. Pluralism increases opportunities to find some group within
which "the activities rational for him are publicly affirmed by others."
Amy Gutmann proposes a "morality of association" that is only possible in a pluralist society. It consists of accepting rules appropriate
to the roles that individuals play in various cooperative associations.[33]
Gutmann sees this "morality of association" as an alternative to pure
autonomy on the one hand and civic education and conditioned virtue
on the other. The problem is that people may learn roles and rules
in associations that are not at all cooperative, and conflicts among
their various roles may produce unbearable tension or fragmentation.
Gutmann portrays groups as scenes of moral development, but their
significance to communitarians has little to do with rules, roles, or
moral education. Groups are vital because they answer longings for
personal plenitude and expression.

Pluralist communitarianism revises standard wisdom about liberalism by demonstrating that community experiences are possible. Within
liberal society there are enclaves for community just as there are for
the family and private worlds of artistic creation and romantic love.
These are imperative for fully realized, expressive selves. However, if
members are not wholly immersed in groups that define them (and
for pluralism to remain liberal, memberships must be partial), then
the puralist revision of liberalism may not have come far enough from
shifting involvements to satisfy longings for immediate, affective attachments. Rawls remarks that liberal citizens "may regard it as simply unthinkable to view themselves apart from certain religious,
philosophical, and moral convictions, or from certain enduring attachments and loyalties. These convictions and attachments are part
of what we may call their 'nonpublic identity.' "[34] For communitar-

ianism of the second type this is no answer to the failings of liberalism, because to think of membership as part of one's "nonpublic identity" is to tolerate fragmentation. In this version of communitarianism, affective attachment and expressivity must be public and expressed in the shared ideals of a political order. Instead of pointing to groups within civil society, they discover community in liberal society as a whole, hidden beneath the surface of pluralism and legal formalism.

Liberalism and Latent Community

In the conventional view the unity of liberal states is political, based on ideological consensus about matters such as privacy, property, limited government, and civil liberties. Liberal consensus lacks appeal for communitarians because principles are not sufficiently affective; they are not lovely or loved. Liberal political thought is an expressively dead ideology of public utility.[35] The second type of communitarianism avoids this impasse by claiming that community does exist, although people are not ordinarily conscious of it. Men and women are bound by more than ideological agreement. Genuine community is "latent" in our deep shared meanings and in our faithfulness to common practices. The task of these communitarians is reclamation.

A growing literature is dedicated to uncovering the expressive impulses and affective ties beneath the liberal "procedural republic." "Few of us have any direct experience of what a country is or of what it means to be a member," Michael Walzer admits, but he insists that a "deeper understanding" of shared social meanings in the United States points to a latent community of complex equality.[36] Roberto Unger discovers latent solidarity in certain legal practices: "the search for this latent and living law—not the law of prescriptive rules or of bureaucratic policies, but the elementary code of human interaction—has been the staple of the lawyer's art wherever this art was practiced with most depth and skill."[37] William Galston arrives at the Aristotelian conclusion that there is a common liberal idea of the good life that its theorists fail to recognize.

Recent efforts to reclaim community from the surface debris of a society of strangers are unusual. In the past critics of liberalism argued that conventional liberal thought is repulsive but correct: liberalism captures the essential nature of autonomy or possessive individualism and mirrors exactly their morally limited and emotionally bankrupt results. Liberalism is perfectly accurate when it portrays men and women relating to one another superficially through law and exchange, associating to receive the protection of the state (and protection from the state in the form of rights), but utterly lacking community, internal cohesion, and a "common project." Typically critics see liberal theory as a powerful self-fulfilling prophecy and civil society as the product of this destructive conceptual apparatus.[38] The traditional communitarian argument is that liberalism must be replaced altogether; there is nothing to be reclaimed.

Theorists of latent community disagree. For them liberalism is not irreparably cold and abstract, but contains hidden assumptions of common values and affective ties. Conventional liberals, intent on constructing a neutral political philosophy, have simply been blind to what is actually (or potentially) best in their own society and tacitly required by their own philosophy. William Galston claims that "a distorted image of liberalism is projected by those of its defenders who have persuaded themselves that liberal theory should not be— and is not—linked to any substantive vision of a worthy human existence." In fact liberalism "contains *within itself* the resources it needs to declare and to defend a conception of the good life that is in no way truncated or contemptible."[39] Theorists of latent community are necessarily sanguine; after all, they must claim more than that common meanings unite every political order not irreparably divided by radically dissimilar cultures; they must claim that liberal democracy is an expressive order, not just an instrumental one.

What these shared meanings are, how widely they are shared, and what degree of conflict is permissible without the loss of latent community remain open questions. Fundamental moral agreement, consensus, and cooperation based on mutual respect are not sufficient for community, but it is not clear what they see in liberalism beyond them.[40] The categories developed by social science to separate communitarian orders from others (size, for example) are ignored. So are the categories social psychologists use to gauge identification with a collectivity. Communitarians rarely specify which aspects of personality are constituted by deep shared meanings or how community penetrates the self. In place of a developed theory of community or detailed empirical studies of exemplary communities communitarians offer illustrations and interpretations.

Some examples of the communitarianism latent within liberalism are drawn from counterculture trends, in which community is said to live on under new guises such as fraternity in participatory workplaces. It is hard to see such pockets of fraternity as anything more than subgroups within civil society. They do not point to tendencies of the whole.[41] Demonstrations of the hidden communitarian character of typical liberal practices are more convincing. Some of the sting can be taken out of legalism and market exchange by showing that even the most impersonal practices rest on underlying community values. Thus the market is said to express the community's distinctive character: "market morality (in, say, its Lockean form) is a celebration of the wanting, making, owning, and exchanging of commodities," and the community expresses itself by setting limits to this celebration—blocking, banning, resenting, or deploring some monetary exchanges.[42]

Legalism is the most grievous aspect of liberalism for theorists of latent community, just as it is for romantic anarchists who follow the law of the heart. Unger argues that "impersonal respect and formal equality edge out communal solidarity."[43] Jerold Auerbach's judgment is even harsher: law begins where community ends. "Litigation expresses a chilling, Hobbesian vision of human nature. It accentuates hostility, not trust. Selfishness supplants generosity. Truth is shaded by dissembling. Once an adversarial framework is in place, it supports competitive aggression to the exclusion of reciprocity and empathy."[44] Not surprisingly, the most common illustrations of latent community are informal norms and alternative ways of resolving disputes. Auerbach looks for "an ideology of communitarian justice" based on reciprocal access and trust among members, and he discovers fraternal conceptions of law.[45] Most appealing of all are instances of "justice without law"—practices like arbitration and mediation. Communitarians see retreat from formalism as a way to soften the hard edges of liberal impersonality. They assume, often without sufficient evidence, that informal justice eliminates the adversary character of proceedings, results in mutually beneficial outcomes, or gives voice to fundamental values.[46] This sort of claim, the result of wishful thinking more than social science, caused Laurence Tribe to caution that "one must be wary of the almost desperate desire to perceive institutions, places, and groups as 'communities' whether or not they can realistically be so described."[47]

Like advocates of civic republicanism, theorists of latent community concentrate on historical revisionism; those who study American law, for instance, search for a countertradition to legal formalism.[48] The use of historical examples reinforces their claim that communitarian criticisms of conventional liberalism are immanent in established practices. It relieves them of the idealist burden of realizing something that does not exist. It defines their work as interpretation of latent community rather than utopian invention. They can claim, as Unger has of critical legal studies, that their vision is "neither just another variant of the mythic, antiliberal republic nor much less some preposterous synthesis of the established democracies with their imaginary opposite." Unger calls his position "superliberalism."[49]

Except for alternatives to legal formalism it is striking how seldom theorists of latent community point to particular practices as defining characteristics of community. By contrast, theorists identified with the political right and the left are clearly committed to specific institutions that further socialist cooperation or participatory democracy, authority or hierarchy or equality. The search for latent community is inspired less by a systematic conception of justice than by a romantic longing for feelings of membership. Affective attachments are more important than political outcomes. In her study of fraternity, for example, Jane Mansbridge concludes that equal power is only a conditional value and that mutual respect and personal growth can be achieved within a community in other ways.[50] For Michael Taylor the importance of the equal distribution of economic benefits is its power to produce identification with the whole: "I never assume nor argue that equality—any sort of equality—is in itself an end or ideal . . . Economic equality is important but only because it is a necessary (though not of course sufficient) condition of community."[51]

Theorists of latent community have good reasons for preferring to aggregate examples rather than to identify specific institutions or practices as characteristics of liberal community. For one thing, they wish to present liberalism as an expressive order rather than an instrumental one, and any focus on particular institutions or principles threatens to bring up immediate political purposes and disagreements about them. For another, amassing a wide array of disparate illustrations both historical and contemporary, strengthens the argument that community is at least conceivable. A particular example may produce a shock of recognition in those who do not ordinarily admit to experiencing community themselves.

The reasons for arguing by example are not all tactical, though. Latent community by its very nature defies detailed description and systematic definition. Community has character, which is latent in an unspecified and unlimited range of practices. Just as individuality cannot be fully encompassed by a list of a person's activities and relations, community cannot be adequately captured by any fixed and determinate set of institutions. Membership cannot be defined by a single practice like political participation, at least not in romantic accounts in which feelings of belonging must be pervasive. The idea is that conduct generally is expressive and reflects shared understanding and affection. Community appeals to romantics by its intimation of wholeness without limitation. As Jacques Barzun describes it, the task of a romanticist is "to reconcile the contraries within him by finding some entity outside himself vast enough to hold all his facts."[52] The idea of latent community exploits this longing.

The Romanticism of Latent Community

Because the existence of an underlying liberal community is not evident in the empirical workings of institutions or in the conscious thoughts and feelings of individuals—orthodox liberals or romantics—theories of latent community rely on interpretation. One recent example is Steven Lukes's approach to studying authority, which he calls "inherently perspectival." In order to identify authority relations one must take into account society's "underlying consensus," which according to Lukes is implicit in, but distinct from, other more easily identifiable official and unofficial perspectives on authority. Lukes does not say how we can know this consensual perspective. He does not contemplate the epistemological difficulties involved in discovering this implicit underlying consensus, but claims it "may be elicited by a sensitive interpretation or reconstruction of a society's beliefs and practices."[53]

Michael Walzer is the ablest proponent of latent community and a model of communitarians' interpretive freedom. In *Spheres of Justice* he argues that a latent community of complex equality exists in the United States. This complex equality is the necessary condition for people to feel that they are members of the community. If there are many autonomous contexts and criteria for distributing goods, comparisons are harder to make, feelings of relative deprivation are minimized, and self-respect is heightened. Thus complex equality "connects the strong and the weak, the lucky and the unlucky, the rich and the poor, creating a union that transcends all differences of interest, drawing its strength from history, culture, religion, language, and so on."

For Walzer community requires a differentiated social structure with plural spheres. It also requires common understanding about the autonomy of spheres, about which goods belong to each sphere, and about criteria—based on deep shared meanings—that govern their distribution. Walzer claims that this common understanding is latent in contemporary practices. At this stage of his argument the strange task of reclaiming community takes over. It is one thing to say that liberal society is structurally pluralistic so that equality is complex. It is quite another to point to a community of complex equality in which shared meanings define what goods belong to which sphere and how they are distributed—much less how shared values should be translated into policy. Walzer finds signs of latent community even in disagreement: "arguments about communal provision are, at the deepest level, interpretations of that union." What might seem like an ordinary pluralist politics of adjustment, or even like a genuine conflict of values, is really "at the deepest level" an interpretation of union.[54]

"Deep" suggests unconscious. Walzer admits that few of us have any direct experience of what it means to be a member. So latent community need not be a felt experience to exist: "if the citizen is a passive figure, there is no political community. The truth, however, is that there is a political community within which many citizens live like aliens."[55] The problem here is not epistemological only—how community is known by us if it is separable from measurable consensus, if alienation is not disproof, and if even disagreement is taken as a manifestation of union. The problem is also how to reconcile latent community with the inestimable value Walzer and others place on feelings of belonging. If community is a "closely held communion of reciprocal expectations," as Unger describes it, how can it be latent?[56] And how can latent community be lovely or loved? Community is more than just consensus; it must be "beautiful to its members." The tension is between metaphors of depth, with their implications of unconsciousness, and analogies between communitarianism and commitment and love, with their implications of immediate personal experience.

The search for latent community brings to mind conservative notions of the "suprarationality" of traditions and establishments, a rationality more elusive but at the same time more real, powerful, and unconsciously attractive than abstract principles or written constitutions. It also evokes earlier definitions of political community in terms of belief systems.[57] Both approaches emphasize bonds that are deep and constitutive but not always expressly acknowledged. However the idea of latent community differs from these conservative and psychological accounts of community. For one thing, contemporary communitarians do not propose a comprehensive system of liberal beliefs or unalterable historic norms and institutions. For another, they are typically unconcerned with the way community buttresses authority or wards off primitive anxiety. The real affinity between conservative theorists and communitarians lies in common opposition to cold, competitive relations and to the conflicts that liberalism tends to generate and even protect.

The whole idea of latent community is elusive. If prevailing practices are taken as expressions of community, they must be scrutinized carefully to determine that they really do express community and not superficial accommodation, apathy, or disagreement (which might by the same logic be "latent too."). Furthermore, if knowledge of latent community depends not on empirical observation but on interpretation of deep levels of shared meaning, what do interpreters "read"? The invocation of literary interpretation and hermeneutics is clear but the choice of "texts" is not. Wittgenstein and ordinary language philosophy come to mind too, as one source for the idea that deep unities of structure and meaning are constitutive of everyday practices. Perhaps a better model for interpretation of hidden meanings, though, is depth psychology, with its distinction between conscious and unconscious thought. Psychoanalytic theory provides a way to think about why some meanings are acknowledged while others are resisted and remain latent. Psychoanalytic theory also illuminates the relation between conscious and unconscious mind and culture, between hegemonic and submerged meanings, which, if accepted, could give interpretations of latent community a radical thrust. This affinity is not remarked on, though, and psychoanalytic concepts play no part in communitarian thought.

Philosophers justify interpretation of latent shared meanings in a number of ways today, most of which are separable from communitarian impulses. For some political philosophers, for example, it is impossible to talk about goods and values without reference to a particular setting and common moral vocabulary. "A language, and the related set of distinctions underlying our experience and interpretation, is something that can only grow in and be sustained by a community. In that sense, what we are as human beings we are only in a cultural community."[58] Taking ordinary discourse and conventions as the starting point for discussing ethics and politics says nothing about whether they are communitarian or speak to affective longings, however; here community is simply synonymous with context. This contextual approach to meaning and value does not reveal the community in which shared meanings operate, its purposes, or its members. In a liberal state the "search for situated subjectivity" is more likely to discover the family or some secondary association as the relevant context rather than the nation as a whole. Among romantic sensibilities it is more likely to be a society of friends or a counter-culture. Or shared meanings can be so general that the relevant community is nothing less than the western European intellectual tradition.[59]

Another account of interpretation assigns it a particular task: discovering within a national political culture inconsistencies of which its members are not ordinarily aware. Walzer performs this work of immanent criticism in *Spheres of Justice* and discovers secondary tendencies in American society, including egalitarian ones. But Walzer is less convincing when he goes on to claim that these disparate ideological strands really make up a whole, and one in which we would all recognize ourselves if only it was made known to us. Walzer's methodology in *Spheres of Justice* suggests romantic motivations. He eschews systematic definition of community because it involves critical self-distancing, and even as a political theorist he wants closeness and identification. His approach is "radically particularist." For him, interpretation from within is the only way to understand community: "if such a society isn't already here—hidden, as it were, in our concepts and categories—we will never know it completely or realize it in fact."[60] Insight is possible only through immersion and genuine affective connection. The method evokes Michael Oakeshott's "pursuit of intimations," which also depends on sympathy for a tradition of behavior that does not fully appear.[61] The very idea of a latent community we may never completely know mirrors romantic impulses in another way; it reflects romantic ambivalence, which arises from desire to belong to a unique expressive order on the one hand and dread of finitude and definition on the other.

Not all contextualists are communitarians, of course; metatheoretical questions about the starting point of philosophical inquiry can take priority over determining whether liberal societies are latently communitarian.[62] But one justification for interpretation is political rather than methodological and relates directly to communitarianism and its romantic roots. Theorists of latent community want more than a liberal society with attributes of community; they want membership to be constitutive of the individual's sense of self. At the same time they reject the hard politics that has always been necessary to produce and maintain community. They suggest that latent community is a force that is expressed in practices and somehow "penetrates" selves to create members. Contemporary romantic communitarians do not look back to Herder and older notions of a unique national character expressing itself unconsciously in literature and other collective cultural creations. Nor do they employ organic metaphors. Their notion of latent community is a way to conceive of community as "constitutive" but not deliberately constituted. It avoids an overtly antiliberal politics.

Community has traditionally been a tutelary ideal, concerned with raising members in the habits of a specific way of life. Rousseau employs the classical myth of a founder and says the just order of *The Social Contract* is conceivable only if the Legislator begins with a generation of children. Even today advocates of civic republicanism argue that participatory democracy requires conscious virtue and its systematic inculcation. By contrast the ethos of latent community is one of spontaneity and soft imperceptible permeation. Deep shared meanings contrast with conditioned virtue; latent community contrasts with education and social control.

Sensitivity about the traditional tutelary nature of community emerges too in the cautious, selective use communitarian theorists make of philosophical authorities such as Aristotle. His writings on character and political community are cited, but without his emphasis on the unity of the virtues, on civic education, or on *patria*.[63] Communitarians also appeal to Hegel, but not to his insistence on teleology, organicism, or the authority of the state. They do not want to go too far in the direction of a theory of political wholeness or approach too closely Hegel's claim that "everything that a man is he owes to the state; only in it can he find his essence."[64]

This sensitivity is consistent with the desire to repair the communitarian failings of liberalism without destroying it. The job is difficult, for one of the chief obstacles has always been the conviction that either community is the imperceptible work of history, language, and culture coming together to produce "collective consciousness" or its creation and preservation require a deliberate system of moral and political education. Both are at odds with liberalism. Heterogeneous liberal societies are not produced by uniform ethnic or cultural forces, but a program of character formation is unpalatable. Civic education and conditioned virtue conflict with liberal antipaternalism and the ethos of independence and choice. Certainly they are unromantic.

The assertion of latent community and deep shared meanings can be seen as an attempt to find a political middle ground between perfect autonomy and conditioned virtue. But it is the wrong middle ground. Conventional liberalism is not indifferent to social attitudes and habits; for example, Mill's recognition that calling a desire or opinion "one's own" is psychologically and sociologically problematic leads him to attend to the institutional framework of political education and the conditions for privatized self-cultivation. Sorting out autonomy and socialization is central to consent theory's interest in the signs of consent that create obligation, the sort of personality capable of consent, and the external conditions of freedom from restraint that make consent meaningful and morally binding. Indeed, it has been said that the essence of liberalism is the balance it strikes between systematic character formation and perfect laissez-faire: "The aim of Liberalism is to assist the individual to discipline himself and achieve his own moral progress; renouncing the two opposite errors of forcing upon him a development for which he is inwardly unprepared, and leaving him alone, depriving him of that aid to progress which a political system, wisely designed and wisely administered, can give."[65] The relevant contrast is not between contentless liberal neutrality and *Bildung,* but between the discipline of liberal citizenship and the notion of latent community, with its implication of a collective unconscious. Theories of latent community, not conventional liberals, are shy about the forces that turn men and women into members and that keep members "faithful" to "shared meanings."

The Philosophy of Expressive Unity

Philosophical efforts to draw unity from diversity are nothing new, but the mix of liberalism and romanticism in recent interpretations of latent community is distinctive. It contrasts sharply with the premier effort to find wholeness in the fragmented, legalistic world of civil society—Hegel's.

In both his theological writings and *The Phenomenology of Mind* Hegel identifies the modern state with the political world of the Roman Empire: cold and formal, dispirited and atomistic. *Philosophy of Right* begins in the same spirit, with Hegel analyzing the limitations of individualism and independence. He criticizes the notion of abstract persons exercising unrestricted independence by bearing rights, making contracts, and indulging in private moralizing. And he criticizes the romantic beautiful soul, who rejects both legalism and the pursuit of pleasure in favor of unbounded self-expression, following the law of the heart into arbitrariness or paralysis.

Yet from this mess of willfulness and fragmentation, of abstract right and romantic anarchism, Hegel draws his philosophical theory of the state. Instead of understanding the modern state as the regulator of external relations among individuals, interests, and spheres, Hegel sees it as the embodiment of an ethical whole of which corporations, the family, market relations, and voluntary associations are all "moments." Because the state is an "expressive unity" of particular and universal, subjectivity and reason, it commands ultimate allegiance from citizens who find their "substantial essence" there.

Hegel moves beyond his initial rejection of legalism as cold instrumentalism. In *Philosophy of Right* he grants the juristic state a new, positive character to carry us beyond pluralism and liberty to genuine wholeness. In a juristic state of rights, he explains, individuals act according to universal norms. They "know and will the universal. They even recognize it as their own; they take it as their end and aim and are active in its pursuit." The individual's "particular satisfaction, activity, and mode of conduct have this substantive and universally valid life as their starting point and their result."[66] As Charles Taylor remarks, by belonging to the state the individual is already "living beyond himself in some larger life."[67]

Hegel rehabilitates legal formalism. It is no longer a falling-off from unity but instead constitutes a distinctive formative culture. It had its own *Sittlichkeit*. Institutions take on "an expressive dimension, as embodying certain conceptions or a certain quality of life."[68] Legalism is a particular discipline that produces an identifiable character in a people. Thus rights and liberty are not purely external, and Hegel's universal class, with its concrete welfare functions and, more important, its own *Bildung,* is the explicit manifestation of this. The universal class knows the discipline of a legalistic culture and demonstrates that universalism signifies unity, no just proceduralism.[69] This is a higher unity, for "as the state comes to its 'truth' as an expression of universal reason in the form of law, it brings the individual with it towards his ultimate vocation."[70]

Hegel promises that legalism produces a unique form of culture and that this common cultural substance can be recognized in what appears to be a world of purely subjective willing. Individuals can escape the arbitrariness of unrestricted independence by understanding their personal connection to actual laws and conventions. Hegel, and T. H. Green and L. T. Hobhouse after him, offer philosophical views of the state that describe an intimacy between personality, practice, and the larger political whole. Their object is to bring this intimacy home to political consciousness. At this point the crucial contrast between Hegel's philosophical account of expressive unity and contemporary theories of latent community becomes clear.

In Idealist thought unity is conceptual. Hegel does not rely on a background of implicit understanding or feelings of belonging to bring unity home to consciousness. The state itself does not provide direct sentimental experiences of community; wholeness and belonging are apprehended through thought. Philosophy is self-sufficient. For Hegel, the *idea* of the state is where the mind finds itself at home.

Contemporary communitarians are attracted to two aspects of Hegel's political thought, his argument that culture constitutes personality and the way his theory of the state avoids simple unity and preserves pluralism and differentiation. They set aside his theory of history and of the hierarchy of forms of thought: "Hegel's answer to the problem of *Sittlichkeit,* the evolution of a society founded on the Idea, is a complete non-starter for us today."[71] Even sympathetic communitarians distance themselves from Hegel because of their continued attachment to elements of both liberalism and romanticism that Hegel rejects. Neither liberal nor romantic sensibilities can acquiesce in Hegel's conclusion that man can find his essence only in the state. Both liberal autonomy and romantic longings for infinitude and self-expression reject the notion of a rational human "essence" and with it the possibility of unconditional obligation.

Most important, contemporary communitarians reject the guiding motivation of Hegel's thought: consolation. For Hegel, individuals identify with the juristic state and pluralistic civil society because philosophy teaches them that they cannot wish it to be otherwise. Hegel's philosophy of history and mind shows that this political culture is a rational necessity. Judith Shklar observes that "freedom of knowledge is not any sort of happiness and Hegel did not claim that it was"; nevertheless it takes him a long way from his initial loathing of atomistic individualism and from the judgment that the modern state is an advanced form of imperial Rome.[72] For Hegel, understanding brings reconciliation. Liberalism and romanticism, however, are activist and expressive; consolation is not their object. For the reconciliation they desire intellectual recognition is insufficient. Community should be lovely to its members, not just understood.

A Community of Direct Relations: Members and Strangers

The notion of latent community leaves a gap between conscious experience and deep shared meanings. This gap is intolerable to those who wish to repair the communitarian failings of liberalism because they want to be gripped by powerful feelings of intimacy and belonging. Followers of the law of the heart seek a perfect lover or friend to arouse emotion, escape banality, and stir them from ennui; communitarians of the third type look for community to excite them in the same way. For them community means friendship, empathy, solidarity, and love. The emphasis is on erotic or emotional ties, on intimacy. Like all political theories inspired by direct personal relations (politics modeled after the family, for example) communitarianism is liable to ignore that personal relations are often occasions for meanness and brutality and that they create tests of loyalty and love that we all inevitably and painfully fail sometimes.

Theorists of direct relations are more adamant about the limitations of conventional liberalism than pluralist communitarians or theorists of latent community. They describe rights and liberties as woefully insufficient: equality "is merely a contingent feature of commensurability and has none of the force that community or fraternity has."[73] Mutual respect lacks spontaneity; it requires self-discipline, not the free flow of feeling. Because we are not called upon to act impartially or respectfully all the time or in every sphere of life, respect for rights cannot be a source of affective bonds. Such residual virtues "permit common ties to wither."[74] Something more active, passionate, and gripping is wanted. As Samuel Beer says, "Freedom and equality can be cold. People may be free and equal—and strangers."

One way communitarians recast the conceptual apparatus of liberalism to get around these limitations is to refer to men and women as members rather than as rights-bearing individuals or moral agents, citizens or possessive individualists. Much of the attraction of being a member derives from its opposite: stranger. The term is evocative; we can immediately sense who is alien. The exclusion of strangers may be what community of direct relations is principally about.

The communitarian concept of membership adds constructively to conventional liberalism by pointing to the discrepancy between formal citizenship and the freedom to enter and exit the various spheres of liberal society. Merely removing legal barriers to political influence cannot produce even "the political equality theoretically required by adversary democracy."[75] In addition to politically estranged citizens there are those separated from the dominant community by poverty and persistent unemployment. If a sense of belonging requires possession of certain material goods associated with community life—if "money buys membership in industrial society"—then poverty can inhibit membership.[76] It can also prevent people from enjoying ideal goods such as respect or recognition as a productive person.

Women may be excluded from full membership by the gender structure of political society. Because their labor in the home is unpaid, economic dependence is "likely to affect power relations within the household, as well as access to leisure, prestige, political office, and so on."[77] If women are forced to lead predominantly domestic lives or to define themselves in terms of private life, they may never participate fully in the array of associations where men learn what John Rawls calls "the content of social ideals given by the various conceptions of a good wife and husband, a good friend and citizen, and so on."[78]

The idea of membership can be used to reinforce liberal notions of equality, mutual respect, and freedom of access to plural spheres. The distinction between members and strangers can be used critically to suggest that everyone is a potential member. Belonging may be inseparable from feeling "at home," but it is not purely subjective and guided by the law of the heart. It has its sources in remediable social arrangements. When affective attraction is at stake, as it is in theories of direct relations, however, membership does not always suggest inclusiveness, much less egalitarianism, and there is real danger of slipping away from liberalism entirely.

The criteria for liberal citizenship are general: place of birth, minimum competence or rationality. Rights at law, universal suffrage, and the principle of toleration are inclusive, but other liberal principles liberate forces of separation and exclusion. The principle of free association, for example, encourages the formation of close and closed groups. It can also generate conflict between a majority community of sentiment and nonconformists—nonmembers who may not belong to an alternative secondary community or who form a community only in the rhetorical sense of a community of oppressed. The term membership reinforces these exclusive tendencies by implying likeness and familiarity, intimacy and trust. These political implications are important: exclusion from membership in self-defined communities has historically been based on religion, sexual preference, race, or some personal characteristic or condition that the community views as alien. There is also a historical connection between communitarianism and militarism.

Liberalism deemphasizes likeness and familiarity as sources of political unity. It is designed to facilitate relations among citizens who may be strangers to one another and profoundly dissimilar; fairness assumes impartiality between friends and strangers. When membership replaces formal citizenship, the consequences of being a stranger can be harsh. The community may treat nonmembers, those who do not seem to belong fully, as strangers in the sense of fearful unfamiliars, moral or psychological aliens.

That is why marginal groups and estranged individuals may reject communitarianism as the goal of reconstructed liberalism. For them heightened community sentiment and direct relations are threatening. Cold impersonal rights and indirect relations are genuine goods: "many of this society's hardest questions take the form of constitutional arguments by marginal groups [the disabled, aliens, and homosexuals, for example] who seek for their members some legal right. The issues raised by such groups cannot be resolved by invoking community sentiment, for these groups challenge too deeply the liberal understanding of *membership*. It is precisely *because* these groups are demanding more than the 'community' or the polity wishes to grant them that these controversies exist in the first place."[79] Alienation may be painful for the excluded, but strangers do not always desire unambivalently to belong. Once a loose consensual society is replaced by affective and constitutive community, membership may require self-distortion. For nonmembers identity may consist of separation; for example, the black man or woman now must choose blackness.[80] It is just this predicament—the possibility of a show of disloyalty— that formal liberal citizenship is designed to avoid.

The obvious advantage of pluralist communitarianism is that multiple associations and flexible entrances and exits allow everyone to be both a member and a stranger, so that no one is everywhere "ignored, patronized, despised, or taken for granted."[81] Walzer pictures each citizen earning self-respect by "reigning in his own company." Pluralism disperses power and limits the capacity of unforgiving communities to injure and inhibit their members, but it is inadequate if what is wanted is direct relations in a community of the whole.

Walzer acknowledges that such a "community of character" preserves its uniqueness by controlling the admission of members and the exclusion of strangers; he is understandably perplexed about the criteria that should govern admission and exclusion from a liberal society, which does not after all put a premium on homogeneity or political agreement. Most theorists are loath to confront this problem directly, even when it seems as if their own ideas would force them to. Jerold Auerbach draws his examples of alternatives to legal formalism from religious communities that excommunicated heretics and from utopian orders that expelled discordant spirits. Auerbach does not propose measures like these, of course, but he does not confront the implications these examples have for his recommendations for "justice without law" either. He is typical in seeing membership as benign, solely in terms of empathy and caring: "as intrusive as the scrutiny seems, and surely was," he observes, "members were reassured of solicitous community concern for their welfare."[82] From the standpoint of pluralism and tolerance it is sobering when Roberto Unger uses tribal relations to illustrate solidarity.[83] It is also sobering to read Walzer's contention that citizens who live as aliens in a political community "are not traitors in the specific sense of that word"— suggesting that they may be traitors in some less specific sense, traitors to some notion of membership and shared public life.[84]

For Walzer it is crucial that the regime appear "lovely" to its members.[85] Perhaps this appearance of loveliness is the test of membership; members are bound not only by common principles but also by tastes and affective attraction. By contrast conventional liberalism requires only self-restraint, not aesthetic delight. The object of our tolerance or respect does not have to appear lovely to us, just unrevolting. Perhaps moral and political principles can be said to be "lovely," but a community of direct relations downplays principles in favor of irrational affections like friendship or love. For Unger the ultimate stakes in politics are always direct passionate dealings among people.[86] Michael Sandel is clear that sheer emotional excitation is a corrective for coldness and impersonality: he wants "embedded" selves to be "gripped" by strong feelings, even "obsessions."[87]

A Community of Direct Relations: Friends and Lovers

Communitarians are still more explicit about wanting to recast society in terms of direct relations when they replace the concept of membership with that of friendship. The desire to transform mutual tolerance and respect into something warmer and closer is unmistakable, as is the fact that rights are pushed into the background. Because friendship implies intimacy, some theorists sympathetic to the charge that liberalism is cold and impersonal worry that friendship is too strong a criterion for community.[88] For others the extravagance of this demand is precisely the point. If impersonal relations are the problem, friendship is the corrective, as are empathy, solidarity, and love.

Michael Sandel suggests that friendship may be crucial for conventional liberal individualism in which the defining characteristic of autonomy is choice. Friendship becomes an important source of self-knowledge: "Where seeking my good is bound up with exploring my identity and interpreting my life history, the knowledge I seek is less transparent to me and less opaque to others. Friendship becomes a way of knowing as well as liking. Uncertain which path to take, I consult a friend who knows me well, and together we deliberate, offering and assessing by turns competing descriptions of the person I am, and of the alternatives I face as they bear on my identity."[89] Liberalism and utilitarianism typically assume a general sort of knowledge of others—knowledge of our mutual self-interestedness, say— but friendship implies intimacy ("a friend is a second self"). Sandel expands the orthodox notion of liberal individualism by showing that even narrow self-interest is enhanced by personal attachments. But there is little here to recommend friendship as the basis for community.

Apart from small intentional communities of friends formed and studied in the 1960s and 1970s, the significance of friendship for transfiguring liberalism is obscure. Most often theorists of direct relations do not derive their ideas from experiments in communal life; they look instead to the philosophical authority on political friendship, Aristotle. Communitarian theorists find support in Aristotle's argument that friendship is a higher virtue than justice. They are also drawn, mistakenly, to the *Politics* as a description of the *polis* as a community without fundamental disagreement, ignoring Aristotle's preoccupation with instability and civil war.[90] Moreover, for Aristotle both citizenship and friendship resting on shared virtue are available only to men of wealth and leisure who enjoy specific physical and psychological capacities for ethical life; the exclusion of women and slaves from both justice and friendship indicates how central election and exclusion are. Communitarians want to move beyond equal rights and mutual respect, and they are not always careful to say whether these will be preserved at all in a community of friends, but they are not prepared to abandon liberal universalism altogether. They at least imply that everyone is a potential friend and that no one is specifically excluded from friendship, as Aristotle (with his belief in a natural hierarchy of superior and inferior types) does not. Thus for Benjamin Barber "a neighbor is a stranger transformed by empathy and shared interests into a friend—an *artificial* friend, however, whose kinship is a contrivance of politics rather than natural or personal and private."[91]

Unger uses the idea of solidarity rather than friendship to move beyond standard rights to a community of direct relations. For him "superliberalism" rests on solidarity, which is "the social face of love."

His ideas diverge from more tempered descriptions of close political bonds. Democratic theorists often speak of the bonds forged by commitment to "common projects," for example, but these are understood to be bonds of mutual purpose, not love. In democratic theory participatory activities may be more important than the relations forged. Solidarity is characterized as a direct unmediated relation, but like democratic fraternity it too is separable from intimacy or love. The crux of solidarity is equality and interdependence in the context of concrete collective action. Because it is a reciprocity that does not calculate benefits and costs, solidarity is often associated with the intensity and comradery of war or the mutual aid and protection of labor movements. Unger's conception of solidarity, by contrast, is removed from the context of shared adversity. He defines it as love. Unger knows that love differs from respect because it attaches to particular objects: "love . . . prizes the loved one's humanity in the unique form of his individual personality."[92] The question is how love can have a "social face," or what it can mean to say that solidarity is love "struggling to move beyond the circle of intimacy."

Unger's elusive notion of "solidarity rights" suggests benefits that go beyond civil liberty and welfare rights, both consistent elements of conventional liberal thought. Only empathy can inspire men and women to provide these benefits for one another. The specific content of solidarity rights is unspecified, though, and does not seem to correspond to available theories of communal rights or ethics of caring. This omission is not surprising; for Unger feelings of solidarity take priority over concrete benefits, and taking care of others is less important than caring for them. In accounts of a community of direct relations, the notions of friendship, solidarity, and love push liberalism beyond the idea that the only thing men and women owe one another is respect for traditional rights and liberties or a minimum concern for one another's welfare—expressed indirectly in public policy. However, the emphasis is more on strong feelings than on obligations. The chief concern is that people experience strong sentiments of attachment. A community of direct passionate relations liberates emotional expressivity; remedying political programs and institutional arrangements is secondary.

From the point of view of liberalism, which values impartiality, the danger of friendship as a criterion for social relations is evident. More interesting is how it poses a threat to romanticism. Today, friendship is intimate; it is a response to purely personal qualities in others that do not necessarily include virtue. After all, it is possible to find someone revolting even though he or she is admittedly good, or lovable though clearly evil. Personal qualities are not like ideology; no one can be persuaded to adhere to them or to be attracted by them. Attraction is mysterious, often spontaneous, and it cannot be explained or generalized. Communitarians look to respirit arid relations, but judging from romanticism, there is no guarantee that intimacy will be edifying or constant. Indeed, affection may not be under our control at all, as romantics of the law of the heart confess.

This ought to discourage those who want friendship to serve community building, but communitarians tend to ignore or deny the pains of private affections and the difficulties that arise when private affections are injected into public life. Oblivious, they want to make public use of the private life of romantic sentiment. They want to bring the impulses and affections that traditional liberalism conceives of as part of private identity into community.

Theorists of direct relations employ a distinctive vocabulary of personal relations even when they do not speak of friendship, solidarity, or love. Consider the phrase "faithfulness to shared meanings," which is used so often by political philosophers today. Meals are shared, but meanings? People can and do mean the same thing. They may have language and intentions in common, as we know from studies of social conventions and body language as well as political discourse. But "shared meaning" suggests something more intimate— meaning the same thing while sitting face to face across a table, where common meaning is deeply affecting and the pleasure comes from the sharing.

Even more striking is the term "faithfulness." It is calculated to bring intimate and erotic relations to mind. The opposite of "faithfulness to shared meanings" is not compromise of principles, as it would be if what were at stake were political values rather than deep meanings; instead the opposite is infidelity, personal betrayal. Unfaithfulness to shared meanings also implies betraying oneself—disobedience to the law of the heart, but its principal thrust is fickleness. There is a moralistic as well as an erotic cast to the language. By implication the charge leveled at those who would leave communities, or dissent from the shared meanings of members, or be content with impersonal relations, is promiscuity. Theorists of direct relations encourage intense spontaneous feeling, but in the context of "embeddedness," not liberation. With this, communitarianism discards not only fundamental elements of liberalism but the lessons of romanticism as well.

The vocabulary of personal and erotic relations and its application to politics is familiar from the 1960s; it is inherited from proponents of counterculture in the United States and from the Freudian language of French radicals. They, not Aristotle, provide the best resources for theories of direct relations. Contemporary communitarians have given this vocabulary a new twist. Originally intimacy was associated with erotic relations and with the comradery of radical dissent. The appeal to personal feelings was associated with liberation and spontaneity and often recalled the law of the heart. It evoked romantic anarchy. Feelings were imperative and dictated attachments but the connections formed were anything but established. Contemporary communitarians defuse the anarchic potential of seeing politics in terms of personal relations. Before, personal politics was ecstatic; now it is domesticated. Communitarians want to combine affect and constancy. They want men and women to be gripped not simply by passion but by passionate commitment.

This impulse to find both expressive personal attachments and stability in community is evident in Walzer's work. Alone among communitarians he asks what becomes of private life if public membership is gripping. He imagines that community and private relations will reinforce one another. Liberal society, Walzer explains, protects private life, especially family life, but in the process imposes an "enormous strain" on these affections since an individual "has no other reference than his relatives in a time of despair."[93] Community relieves the family, and presumably other personal relations as well, of psychic burdens; emotionally intense involvement in community does not compete with private attachments but actually strengthens them. Walzer is surely right that multiplying attachments and affections is desirable. Perhaps susceptibility to betrayal and loss decreases as exclusivity does. In addition the welfare state can mitigate the emotional stress of some economic hardships. However these do not constitute an argument for a community of direct relations, for solidarity, intimacy, friendship, or even deep shared meanings. No political community can alleviate the risks of affection; they are an inseparable part of personal freedom and romantic attachment.

Although community cannot guarantee satisfying affective relations it can intrude on them. A politics of loyalty, empathy, sharing, and eroticism can disrupt and eclipse personal attachments. That is why Humboldt and Constant were reconciled to the impersonal politics of the Rechtsstaat, which offers relief from the emotional demands of both private affections and of public life when it compels shows of feeling. The impersonality of liberal public life can help to insure that private relations remain personal. It is always possible that purely personal relations will be undercommitted, underinstitutionalized, and unsatisfying. Liberalism has traditionally taken a misanthropic view of men and women, recognizing that passions are often egotistical and malevolent. Certainly they appear arbitrary and erratic. Romanticism adds that personal feelings cannot serve communitarianism, for the simple reason that friendship and love, empathy and caring, are not predictable and cannot be willfully sustained. The law of the heart can be erratic and its imperatives exhausting. Arrant emotionalism and enervation are both common experiences. If romantic longings provide motivation for the idea of community of direct relations, romantic sensibilities remind us of its perils.

Romantic Self-Doubt and the Advantages of Liberal Indirection

Ironically, theories of direct relations inspired by romantic longings for emotional expressiveness present a more serious threat to romantic sensibilities than conventional liberalism does. That is because a community of direct relations multiplies possibilities for hypocrisy and inauthenticity. Liberalism requires respect not for men and women personally, but for their rights. It requires that people interact impartially, "as if" they respected one another, and only in certain limited ways and domains. Unger's account of solidarity allows for "maintaining a system of social relations in which men are bound to act, if not compassionately, at least as if they had compassion for each other."[94] However, the two politics of "as if" are not identical: there is a difference between pretending to have feelings of solidarity or to appreciate the community's "loveliness" and abiding by public norms such as impartiality.

Respect for rights is not emotionally coercive. Because it does not force people to esteem others more highly than they deserve or to have any particular emotions toward them, most people can manage respect for rights without feeling enraged and inauthentic. As Judith Shklar observes, "not all of us are even convinced that all men are entitled to a certain minimum of social respect. Only some of us think so. But most of us always act as if we really did believe it, and that is what counts."[95] Men and women can act as if they believe in rights and respect because liberalism does not insist that their attitudes and conduct toward others reflect the character of those they treat with respect, or that acting respectfully mirrors their own true inner selves. Only the extreme romantic sensibility who cannot be reconciled to even the rudiments of liberal discipline would find this behavior hypocritical.[96]

The alternative is a public order in which feelings and intensity of commitment do matter. That means Jacobin fervor, incessant charges of hypocrisy, and a politics of unmasking. It means pretense and ultimately revulsion. Worst of all, it means incessant self-doubt. Adolphe's question to himself—"Am I really in love?"—can take the form of "Do I really feel solidarity?" "Do I really feel that I belong?" The self-inflicted wounds of communitarianism are real. Contemporary communitarians are moved in part by romantic impulses, but they have not learned the lessons of chastened romanticism.

CONCLUSION

Romanticism and the Reconstruction of Liberal Thought

In this book I have confronted formal political concepts and arguments with another constellation of ideas—informal, affective, psychological. This is the methodology behind my picture of "another liberalism." The confrontation must be deliberately staged because typically political theory does not have a place for these romantic concerns. Every political theory has a conceptual apparatus that sets the terms of discussion for its commentators. Liberalism is no exception. Whether theorists investigate the origins of liberal ideas or analyze current usage, they respect and operate within its systematic framework. This means that in conventional formulations of liberalism certain problems remain invisible, or if they do come to light, they appear intractable. One of these is lack of sympathy for the needs of romantic sensibilities.

Romantics reject the terms of political theory; that is what makes their confrontation with liberalism dramatic. They bring personal and aesthetic experience to bear on liberalism. They point up limitations that are imperceptible from within. They express longings that liberalism must acknowledge if it is to become more hospitable to them, if they are to finally make their peace. The romantic perspective also sheds new light on divisions among political theorists and what is at stake in the issues that divide them. But one of the most important things to emerge from this method of confrontation is that romanticism comes to liberalism with resources of its own. These are the materials from which liberalism can be recast.

This romantic perspective has a special importance today. For me and others of my generation the romantic experience of liberalism plays a large part in our judgments of it. This is true even of those of us who are political theorists and are committed to preserving the essential terms of liberalism. In this book I show that reconciliation is possible.

Romanticism's first response to liberalism is antipathy, expressed by militarism and the law of the heart. But romantic sensibilities make their way back to sympathy with liberalism. Reconciliation is born of many things: heroic affirmation and arrant emotionalism have painful failings. They can lead to aloofness and self-absorption. Yet these can be moderated and made compatible with respect for rights and the discipline of legalism. Chastened romanticism can make its peace.

If romanticism can become liberal, it is also possible for liberalism to be romanticized. As liberalism accommodates romantic longings—through heroic individualism, shifting involvements, and communitarianism—it is reformed. I have distilled these principal types of "another liberalism" from a wide range of sources. Still, I cannot claim that my typology is exhaustive; there may be other versions I have missed.

Heroic individualism and communitarianism have real affinities to liberalism. They draw on certain aspects of conventional liberalism such as freedom to form spontaneous associations and inspire revolution. Communitarianism gives priority to feelings of closeness and belonging and to the desire that community appear lovely to its members. Heroic individualism makes self-expression the premier impulse and seeks outlets for the sense of infinite possibility in public and private life. Both extend liberalism by insisting that it is not only dissimilar values that must be accommodated in a tolerant society, but radically dissimilar sensibilities as well. Reconstructing liberalism in a heroic or communitarian vein can have its costs, however. Pushed too far they tend to ignore liberalism's preoccupation with concrete institutions and its sober expectations for daily conduct. Liberal political thought is uniquely attentive to the boundaries, discipline, and constraints that create liberty and cooperation in a pluralistic society. Without these liberalism is nothing.

Shifting involvements is a special case. It is not inclined to excess. It takes up an essential problem of traditional liberal thought—defining the boundaries between separate public and private spheres—and assigns new meaning and value to public and private life. In doing this it speaks to the traditionally intractable problem of how to get individuals to take an interest in both public and private affairs. Self-cultivation and self-expression are its distinctive rationales, and individuality is defined as nothing but the way particular men and women go about exploiting the opportunities liberalism provides. Here longings for plenitude converge with pluralism and liberty.

This type of reconstructed liberalism is appealing because nothing is lost. We do not erase intimacy or repress affect by prescribing impartiality in certain spheres. We do not sacrifice spontaneity by sometimes setting strict legal limits on conduct. We do not lose individuality by insisting that general moral and political demands flow from individualism. Public and private life, personal and impersonal relations, instrumentalism and expressivity require one another.

Besides its positive pictures of plenitude and "beautiful individuality," "another liberalism" can be reactive and self-protective. In fact fearfulness and protection against political abuse have always been more enduring elements of conventional liberalism than hopeful theories of progress. Romantic recastings can be reactive as well. They are not always ecstatic or aesthetically delightful; they have darker sources in fear of paralysis, limitation, and self-hatred. Negative versions of romantic liberalism spring from aversion to being constrained, but they combat excesses of calculation or imagination. Like traditional liberalism, romantic reworkings are chiefly concerned with warding off political usurpations.

Liberalism has historically protected against usurpations and tyranny. Recently, however, theorists have begun to rethink the advantages of beginning with other things to be avoided. In *Ordinary Vices* Judith Shklar describes a "liberalism of fear" in which institutional defenses against cruelty are the only protection from the demeaning effects of fear on individuals.[1] John Dunn offers a version of negative liberalism in "The Future of Liberalism," arguing for prudence in the face of a new wave of utopianism that threatens to make contemporary liberal thought irrelevant.[2] I have tried to capture yet another "negative liberalism": it is designed to avoid cold impersonality on the one hand and the unrestrained eruption of personal, expressive impulses on the other.

"Another liberalism" is not romantic in the dismissive colloquial sense of being unrealistic. Romantic recastings of liberalism may not address immediate political issues or prescribe political action, but they do offer a perspective from which to consider questions such as material distribution. Evaluating the material conditions for free self-expression, for example, is a legitimate project for political theory—and no more or less difficult than evaluating the material bases for democratic equality or mutual respect.

More important than political realism is psychological realism, the reality of longing. If political theory is to effectively justify political life and reconcile men and women to it, then it must address felt needs. Romantic liberalism does. The needs it speaks to are historically contingent and not universal; even where they arise they are not felt by everyone. Nonetheless they exist and exert a powerful hold on men and women in liberal society, and political theory must try to speak to them.

Notes
Index

Notes

1. Romantic Militarism versus Civil Society

1. William Wordsworth, "The Convention of Cintra," in *Political Tracts of Wordsworth, Coleridge, and Shelley,* ed. R. J. White (Cambridge: Cambridge University Press, 1953), p. 192; hereafter citations to this work will appear in parentheses in the text.

2. Romantic militarism must be distinguished, then, from militarism proper, which argues for the social importance of military privileges and virtues. Alfred Vagts, *A History of Militarism* (New York: Meridian Books, 1959).

3. "Cintra" itself is a response to government propaganda justifying the Convention.

4. The phrase "correspondent breeze" is M. H. Abrams's, in his "The Correspondent Breeze: A Romantic Metaphor," in *English Romantic Poets: Modern Essays in Criticism* (Oxford: Oxford University Press, 1975), pp. 37–55.

5. Samuel P. Huntington, *American Politics: The Promise of Disharmony* (Cambridge, Mass.: Harvard University Press, 1981), pp. 39, 12.

6. Wilhelm von Humboldt, *The Sphere and Duties of Government* (London: John Chapman, 1854), pp. 22, 8.

7. Marianne Cowan, ed., *An Anthology of the Writings of Wilhelm von Humboldt: Humanist without Portfolio* (Detroit: Wayne State University Press, 1963), p. 165.

8. Humboldt, *Sphere and Duties,* pp. 41–42, 66, 11, 18, 99.

9. Cowan, *Humanist,* p. 303.

10. G. W. F. Hegel, *Philosophy of Right,* cited in George A. Kelley, *Idealism, Politics, and History* (Cambridge: Cambridge University Press, 1969), p. 347.

11. Humboldt, *Sphere and Duties,* p. 13.

12. Henry Hatfield, *Aesthetic Paganism in German Literature* (Cambridge, Mass.: Harvard University Press, 1964); Humboldt, *Sphere and Duties,* pp. 13, 6, 65.

13. Alfred de Musset, *Confessions of a Child of the Century* (Paris: Mazarin, 1905), p. 10.

14. Benjamin Constant, *L'Esprit de Conquête* (Paris: Grasset, 1918), p. 13, my translation.

15. Albert O. Hirschman, *The Passions and the Interests* (Princeton: Princeton University Press, 1977), pp. 10, 70, 79, 130.

16. Ibid., p. 100. Economic growth made the pursuit of interest a real possibility for increasing numbers of people. Only then did the argument shift from the political effects of commercialism to Adam Smith's argument about the advantages of prosperity per se (p. 40).

17. Even Adam Smith, who recognized the advantages of probity and punctuality, regretted that commerce also results in debilitating luxury and corruption and "universal effeminacy." Hirschman, *Passions and Interests,* p. 106.

18. Musset, *Confessions,* pp. 10–11. On the social setting of the generation of 1830 and the general susceptibility of outcast intellectual youth to these discontents, see Cesar Grana, *Bohemian versus Bourgeois* (New York: Basic Books, 1964), chap. 1.

19. Alfred de Vigny, *Military Servitude and Grandeur* (New York: George Doran, 1919), pp. 243, 118–119.

20. François René Vicomte de Chateaubriand, *The Memoirs of Chateaubriand,* ed. Robert Baldick (New York: Knopf, 1961), p. 290.

21. Ibid., pp. 276, 267, 315.

22. Leo Strauss, *The Political Philosophy of Hobbes* (Chicago: University of Chicago Press, 1936), p. 17.

23. An example of what Durkheim would call *suicide égoiste.*

24. Byron had predicted his death in Greece and anticipated the fame death in a just cause would bring. More important, he thought that his death would constitute a denunciation of the public that had failed to recognize his worth as an artist and a man; the only positive action the world permitted him was death. Harold Nicolson, *Byron: The Last Journey* (London: Constable, 1924), p. 108.

25. Contrast this to the nihilism of Max Stirner, where the point is to live the self out—to assert and squander, exploit and use it up. See *The Ego and His Own* (New York: Libertarian Book Club, 1963).

26. De Vigny, *Military Servitude and Grandeur,* p. 14; hereafter citations to this work will appear in parentheses in the text.

27. For a discussion of later accounts of military brotherhood as an antidote to disaffection see Robert Sayre, *Solitude in Society* (Cambridge, Mass.: Harvard University Press, 1978), chap. 5.

28. Mill, "Coleridge," *The Philosophy of J. S. Mill* (New York: Modern Library, 1961), p. 87.

29. J. S. Mill, "Civilization," in *Dissertations and Discussions* (Boston: William Spencer, 1868), I, 198.

30. Ibid., pp. 192, 205–206. Military organization is another example of how Mill sets his argument in the context of a theory of historical stages.

31. Mill, "Poetry and Its Varieties," in *Dissertations and Discussions,* pp. 97–98.

32. Mill, "The Writings of Alfred de Vigny," in *Dissertations and Discussions,* pp. 332–333.

33. Constant, *L'Esprit de Conquête,* pp. 24–25. It was not until the trench warfare of World War I, however, that military action really lost its association with active aggression. This happened earlier in America, the result of the Civil War. This disillusion is captured in Stephen Crane's *Red Badge of Courage.*

34. Stephen Holmes makes this argument in *Benjamin Constant and the Origins of Modern Liberalism* (New Haven: Yale University Press, 1985).

35. Constant, cited in Guy Dodge, *Benjamin Constant's Philosophy of Liberalism* (Chapel Hill: University of North Carolina Press, 1980), p. 29.

36. Arnold Hauser, *The Social History of Art* (New York: Vintage Press, 1959), III, 182.

37. Gissing, *The Unclassed,* cited by Raymond Williams, *Culture and Society, 1780–1950* (New York: Columbia University Press, 1958), p. 176.

38. William Morris is one example of a romantic sensibility who made this transition to politics, attaching his aesthetic values to the progress of the working class. It has been observed, however, that this ambition required him to set the priority of art aside for revolution.

39. "To submit to politics was an act of resigning to actuality and, as such, an abandonment of romanticism." Judith Shklar, *After Utopia* (Princeton: Princeton University Press, 1957), p. 107.

40. Stendhal, *The Red and the Black* (New York: Signet, 1970), pp. 325, 146, 182, 327.

41. Irving Howe, *Politics and the Novel* (New York: Horizon Press, 1957), p. 34.

42. A detailed national study of the connection between utilitarianism and romantic anomie is Henri Brunschwig, *Enlightenment and Romanticism in Eighteenth Century Prussia* (Chicago: University of Chicago Press, 1974). Another case study in this connection is Robert Wohl, *The Generation of 1914* (Cambridge, Mass.: Harvard University Press, 1979).

43. "Was it all to end in a counting house with a Whig committee dealing out champagne to the rich and margarine to the poor in such convenient proportions as would make all men contented together, though the pleasure of the eyes was gone from the world?" William Morris, cited in Raymond Williams, *Culture and Society,* p. 149.

44. Henry David Thoreau, *Walden* (New York: New American Library, 1960), p. 8.

45. Sheldon Wolin, *Politics and Vision* (Boston: Little, Brown, 1960), p. 324.

46. The classic study of romantic epistemology is M. H. Abrams, *The Mirror and the Lamp* (Oxford: Oxford University Press, 1955).

47. I am following the interpretation of Simone de Beauvoir, *The Second Sex* (New York: Vintage, 1974), pp. 269–285.

2. The Law of the Heart versus Liberal Legalism

1. Judith N. Shklar, *Legalism* (Cambridge, Mass.: Harvard University Press, 1964), p. 21; on degrees of legalism see pp. 59–60.

2. Emile Durkheim associates the first emergence of personalities from "the social mass" with the institution of despotic authority; power becomes autonomous and makes them capable of personal activity. *The Division of Labor in Society* (New York: The Free Press, 1933), p. 195.

3. Duncan Kennedy, "Legal Formality," *Journal of Legal Studies* 11 (June 1973), 351–398.

4. Schiller, *On the Aesthetic Education of Man in a Series of Letters* (New York: Ungar, 1954), p. 41.

5. Max Weber, *Max Weber on Law in Economy and Society* (Cambridge, Mass.: Harvard University Press, 1954), p. 317.

6. Schiller, *Aesthetic Education,* p. 41.

7. John Dunn, "The Concept of 'Trust' in the Politics of John Locke," in *Philosophy in History,* ed. R. Rorty, J. B. Schneewind, and Q. Skinner (Cambridge: Cambridge University Press, 1984), pp. 279–301.

8. Mortimer Kadish and Sanford Kadish, *Discretion to Disobey* (Stanford: Stanford University Press, 1973), p. 145.

9. Jury lawlessness has a political purpose. Juries' actions to acquit, which nullify a law in practice, are the community's way of resisting unjust laws without resort to revolution. Acquittal domesticates and institutionalizes popular protection against the tyranny of officials.

10. Blackstone describes this "fountain of grace" in *Commentaries,* IV, 445–446.

11. Biddle v. Perovich, 274 U.S. 480 (1927).

12. Nahmeh v. U.S., 267 U.S. 122 (1924).

13. Kadish and Kadish, *Discretion to Disobey,* pp. 178, 181.

14. Jerold Auerbach, *Justice Without Law: Resolving Disputes Without Lawyers* (Oxford: Oxford University Press, 1983).

15. A true departure from legalism would be a creative, radical resolution of conflict among individuals proposed by a genius. A similar point has been made about the laws of social science: one source of systematic unpredictability in human affairs is the possibility of radical innovation. See Alasdair MacIntyre, *After Virtue* (Notre Dame, Ind.: University of Notre Dame Press, 1981), p. 89.

16. Auerbach, *Justice Without Law,* p. vii.

17. Alfred de Vigny, *Stello* (Montreal: McGill University Press, 1963), pp. 66–67. On "Kadi-justice" and its relation to the rational administration of justice and to sentiment see Max Weber, "Bureaucracy," in *From Max Weber,* ed. Gerth and Mills (Oxford: Oxford University Press, 1946), p. 221.

18. Edmund Burke, *Reflections on the Revolution in France* (Indianapolis: Library of Liberal Arts, 1955), pp. 87–88.

19. Law is distinguished by the fact that it is guaranteed by coercion. Anarchism dispenses only with this structure of coercion. *Max Weber on Law,* pp. 5, 27.

20. Michael Taylor, *Community, Anarchy, and Liberty* (Cambridge: Cambridge University Press, 1982), p. 91.

21. I will leave aside the special case of judicial review in America,

in which a test of the constitutionality of a statute, the extent of a right, or the validity of a judicial or administrative order requires first that it be breached.

22. Laws that coerce and unjust or oppressive laws are not always thought to be the same, but here the absence of direct consent unites them.

23. See Robert Paul Wolff's argument for unanimous direct democracy, requiring every citizen's consent to every act of government. *In Defense of Anarchism* (New York: Harper and Row, 1970).

24. Friedrich Schiller, *The Robbers* (London: George Bell, 1875), p. xiv.

25. Albert O. Hirschman, *Exit, Voice, and Loyalty* (Cambridge, Mass.: Harvard University Press, 1970).

26. Michael Walzer, *Obligations* (Cambridge, Mass.: Harvard University Press, 1970), pp. 123–126, 131–135, 128, 113, 111.

27. Hannah Arendt, *Crises of the Republic* (New York: Harcourt Brace Jovanovich, 1969), p. 55.

28. Schiller, *Aesthetic Education,* p. 48.

29. De Vigny, *Stello,* p. 19.

30. If only present passions have reality private life will be undercommitted and underinstitutionalized. It is not necessary to explain the eclipse of personal relations by the intrusiveness of a despotic public, as Christopher Lasch does in *The Culture of Narcissism* (New York: Norton, 1979).

31. Cited by M. H. Abrams, *Natural Supernaturalism* (New York: Norton, 1973), pp. 294, 298.

32. The "different voice" Gilligan explores is not supposed to be exclusive to women, but her examples are drawn from interviews with women. Carol Gilligan, *In a Different Voice* (Cambridge, Mass.: Harvard University Press, 1982), p. 38.

33. François René Vicomte de Chateaubriand, *Atala/René* (Berkeley: University of California Press, 1952), p. 96.

34. Benjamin Constant, *Adolphe* (London: Hamish Hamilton, 1948), p. 56.

35. Schiller, *Aesthetic Education,* p. 100.

36. G. W. F. Hegel, *The Phenomenology of Mind* (New York: Harper, 1957), p. 666.

37. Constant, *Adolphe,* p. 35.

38. Stephen Holmes, *Benjamin Constant and the Making of Modern Liberalism* (New Haven: Yale University Press, 1984), pp. 13–14.

39. T. E. Hulme invented the phrase "spilt religion" to capture his distaste for romanticism, in *Speculations: Essays on Humanism and the Philosophy of Art* (New York: Harcourt Brace, 1961).

40. Schiller, *Aesthetic Education,* p. 32.

41. Steven Lukes, *Individualism* (New York: Harper and Row, 1973), pp. 8, 17–18. See also Guido de Ruggiero, *The History of European Liberalism* (Oxford: Oxford University Press, 1927).

42. See John Rawls, *A Theory of Justice* (Cambridge, Mass.: Harvard University Press, 1971). The recent emphasis on impersonality makes this point even

more strongly, as in P. F. Strawson's emphasis on the numerical differences of physical bodies or Thomas Nagel's "personal premise."

43. According to one definition, organization itself is a device to "[allow] mediocrity to transcend its limitations." Sheldon Wolin, *Politics and Vision* (Boston: Little, Brown, 1960), p. 383.

44. Georg Simmel, "Individual and Society in Eighteenth- and Nineteenth-Century Views of Life: An Example of Philosophical Sociology," cited in Lukes, *Individualism*, p. 18.

45. Cited in Lukes, *Individualism*, p. 68.

3. The Penumbra of Privacy

1. The classic distinction between public and private based on force and voluntarism is John Locke, *A Letter on Toleration* (New York: Library of Liberal Arts, 1950).

2. The terms are taken from Albert O. Hirschman, *Exit, Voice, and Loyalty* (Cambridge, Mass.: Harvard University Press, 1970).

3. Wartime is an exception to this, of course.

4. Michael Walzer, *Spheres of Justice* (New York: Basic Books, 1983), p. 205. This conception of citizen as recipient of benefits has two faces: citizen as consumer of services and citizen as patient of the therapeutic state. The political implications are dramatically different; one metaphor emphasizes the dependence of officials on the satisfaction of their "citizen-customers," the other emphasizes the dependence of the "citizen-patients" on the state.

5. Stanley I. Benn, "Privacy, Freedom, and Respect for Persons," in *Nomos XIII: Privacy* (New York: Atherton Press, 1971), p. 22.

6. Locke's state of nature was social, even institutionalized—think of the existence of promises, or money. For a fuller discussion of criticisms of liberalism as a theory of antisocial individualism, see chapter 7.

7. Another element is privacy within government—closed legislative committees allow for debate, decision, learning, and change without publicity.

8. On Alexander Meiklejohn's interpretation see Frederick Schauer, *Free Speech: A Philosophical Inquiry* (Cambridge: Cambridge University Press, 1982), p. 37. On the classification of speech versus action see Thomas I. Emerson, *The System of Freedom of Expression* (New York: Random House, 1970), pp. 80–84, 295-297.

9. Emerson, *Freedom of Expression*, pp. 6–9. From a legal standpoint, this defense of free speech is overinclusive, because self-expression is a rationale for the principle of liberty generally, not speech in particular; on one view all voluntary conduct that manifests inner feelings is self-expressive. See Schauer, *Free Speech*, p. 93.

10. Michael Walzer, *Obligations* (Cambridge, Mass.: Harvard University Press, 1970), p. 221.

11. See for example W. L. Weinstein, "The Private and the Free," in *Nomos XIII: Privacy*, p. 33.

12. W. H. Morris Jones, "In Defense of Apathy," *Political Studies* 2, no. 2 (1954), 25–37.

13. L. T. Hobhouse, *Liberalism* (Oxford: Oxford University Press, 1964), p. 24.

14. Emerson, *Freedom of Expression,* p. 676.

15. Similarly in libel law stringent tests of false and defamatory statements are applied not only when public officials are involved but also in the case of "public figures," on the grounds that "there is a legitimate concern with the performance and qualifications of the president of General Motors, the leader of the Trades Union Council, or the administrator of a major private hospital." Schauer, *Free Speech,* p. 174.

16. Hobhouse's argument for affirmative state action to increase individual liberty in economic life is exemplary: "nominal freedom, that is to say, the absence of legal restraint, might have the effect of impairing real freedom, that is to say, would allow the stronger party to coerce the weaker." *Liberalism,* pp. 75, 86.

17. Some Liberals today argue that the absence of governmental force behind intolerance "is a difference in kind and not a difference in degree," and that individuals ought to be permitted to recover damages against private groups or individuals who interfere with their freedom of speech. Schauer, *Free Speech,* pp. 121, 124.

18. Sheldon Wolin, *Politics and Vision* (Boston: Little, Brown, 1960), pp. 346, 343.

19. Laurence Tribe, *American Constitutional Law* (Mineola, N.Y.: The Foundation Press, 1978), p. 890.

20. Joan Didion sees the family as the cause of the failure of the American center to hold: "At some point between 1945 and 1967 we had somehow neglected to tell these children the rules of the game we happened to be playing . . . Maybe there were just too few people around to do the telling. These were children who grew up cut loose from the web of cousins and great-aunts and family doctors and lifelong neighbors who had traditionally suggested and enforced society's values." *Slouching Towards Bethlehem* (New York: Washington Square Press, 1961), p. 127.

21. For a feminist critique see Frances E. Olsen, "The Family and the Market: A Study of Ideology and Legal Reform," *Harvard Law Review* 96, no. 7 (May 1983), 1499–1578.

22. Walzer, *Spheres of Justice,* p. 239. Christopher Lasch is more vehement: "In our own time, this invasion of private life by the forces of organized domination has become so pervasive that personal life has almost ceased to exist." *The Culture of Narcissism* (New York: Norton, 1979), p. 30.

23. For this and the dangers of an "underinstitutionalized" private life see Peter Berger et al., *The Homeless Mind* (New York: Vintage, 1974), p. 186.

24. Charles Fried, *An Anatomy of Values* (Cambridge, Mass.: Harvard University Press, 1970), p. 142.

25. Ibid., p. 146.

26. Emerson, *Freedom of Expression,* p. 548. Privacy is a product of tort law, which treats the unauthorized exploitative publication of letters and pho-

tographs as a violation of a species of property right, and reputation as a material interest. See Paul A. Freund, "Privacy: One Concept or Many," *Nomos XIII: Privacy*, p. 150.

27. Richard Morgan, *The Law and Politics of Civil Rights and Liberties* (New York: Knopf, 1985), p. 234.

28. Mapp v. Ohio, 367 U.S. 643 (1961), 84.

29. Justice Harlan, in Katz v. U.S., 389 U.S. 347, 351 (1967), raises the question of the constitutionality of government informers in terms of misplaced personal confidences.

30. Griswold v. Connecticut, 381 U.S. 479 (1965).

31. Five of the justices found that fundamental personal liberty protected by the due process clause of the Fourteenth Amendment includes the right of privacy; others discover a basis in the Ninth Amendment protection for nonenumerated rights. See Tribe, *American Constitutional Law*, pp. 893–896.

32. Justice Douglas, in Griswold v. Connecticut.

33. Douglas found a penumbral right of privacy in the First, Third, Fourth, and Fifth Amendments.

34. Ernest Van Den Haag, "On Privacy," *Nomos XIII: Privacy*, p. 150.

35. See Louis D. Brandeis and Samuel D. Warren, "The Right to Privacy," *Harvard Law Review* 4 (1890). Concern to protect individuality informs Brandeis' First Amendment decisions and writings on the tort law of privacy. However, self-development and expressivity have had few repercussions in constitutional law; see Rogers Smith, *Liberalism and American Constitutional Law* (Cambridge, Mass.: Harvard University Press, 1985).

36. "Privacy and Personhood" is the title of Tribe's chapter on the subject in *American Constitutional Law*.

37. Isaiah Berlin, *Four Essays on Liberty* (Oxford: Oxford University Press, 1969), p. 124.

38. Fried, *Anatomy of Values*, p. 141.

39. Benn, "Privacy, Freedom, and Respect for Persons," p. 26.

40. Preoccupation with information marks Thomas Scanlon's essay "A Theory of Free Expression," *Philosophy and Public Affairs* 1 (1972).

41. Schauer, *Free Speech*, p. 176.

42. Tribe, *American Constitutional Law*, p. 966.

43. Carl Friedrich, "Secrecy versus Privacy: The Democratic Dilemma," *Nomos XIII: Privacy*, pp. 115, 116.

44. Emerson, *Freedom of Expression*, p. 549.

45. The phrase is from Berger et al., *The Homeless Mind*, p. 64.

46. Berlin, *Four Essays*, p. xli.

47. "At least in this respect the Kantian state, though a means to something higher than lawful action, is not easily distinguishable from the state based upon utilitarian principles. Both command only externally . . . Neither attempts, or believes it possible, to force people to act from moral laws." Amy Gutmann, *Liberal Equality* (Cambridge: Cambridge University Press, 1982), p. 36.

48. Wilhelm von Humboldt, *The Sphere and Duties of Government* (London: John Chapman, 1854), p. 75.

49. Berlin, *Four Essays*, p. 163.

50. "The exclusive nature of interest rendered it impossible that anyone could really advance the interest of another: impossible not merely because each individual acted primarily from motives of self-interest, but also because an interest existed in the closest possible intimacy to the individual holding it. No outsider, not even one prompted by altruistic motives, could ever know enough to act benevolently." Wolin, *Politics and Vision*, p. 339.

51. Berlin, "Two Concepts of Liberty," in *Four Essays*, pp. 161, 126–129, 171, xlix.

52. Michael A. Weinstein, "The Uses of Privacy in the Good Life," *Nomos XIII: Privacy*, p. 88.

53. Walzer, *Obligations*, p. 179.

54. Harry Clor, *Obscenity and Public Morality* (Chicago: University of Chicago Press, 1969), pp. 187, 200.

55. Harvey C. Mansfield, Jr., *The Spirit of Liberalism* (Cambridge, Mass.: Harvard University Press, 1978), p. viii.

56. Lionel Trilling, "The Fate of Pleasure: Wordsworth to Dostoevsky" in *Romanticism Reconsidered*, ed. Northrop Frye (New York: Columbia University Press, 1963), p. 104.

57. Marxists once focused on the contradictions of capitalist society, but recently they have begun to emphasize how institutions and behavior patterns maintain capitalism. Liberals have taken up the theme of the irony of history, in which a society generates patterns that lead to its own destruction. The focus is on the relation between personal liberty, self-expression, and the destructive impact of expressivism. See Daniel Bell, *The Cultural Contradictions of Capitalism* (New York: Basic Books, 1976); Jon Elster, *Ulysses and the Sirens* (Cambridge: Cambridge University Press, 1979), pp. 33–34.

58. Frye, *Romanticism Reconsidered*, pp. v–vi. Preromantic medieval, renaissance, and Christian humanist poetry divided reality into heaven above, the human and physical orders of nature below, and beneath these the stratum of sin, death, and hell.

59. Frye, "The Drunken Boat," ibid., p. 10. Even antiromantic movements in art have failed to create an alternative to this structure, so poets may be related by imagery although they do not agree "on a single thesis in religions, politics, or the theory of art itself." See pp. 3, 4, 22, 24.

60. M. H. Abrams, "English Romanticism: The Spirit of the Age," ibid., pp. 53–54.

61. Ibid., p. 21.

62. Erich Heller, "The Importance of Nietzsche," in *The Artist's Journey into the Interior*, (New York: Harcourt Brace Jovanovich, 1959), pp. 173–198.

63. Albert Camus, *The Rebel* (New York: Vintage Books, 1956), p. ix.

64. Hannah Arendt, *The Human Condition* (Chicago: University of Chicago Press, 1958), pp. 24, 28.

65. Ibid., p. 38.

66. Burkhardt describes "the different tendencies and manifestations of private life . . . thriving in the fullest vigor and variety." The thirteenth century began to "swarm with individuality; the ban on human personality was dissolved; and a thousand figures meet us each in his own special shape and dress." Cited

in Steven Lukes, *Individualism* (New York: Harper, 1973), p. 24. Like Arendt, Richard Sennett traces privacy to the Romans, in *The Fall of Public Man* (New York: Vintage, 1974), p. 13.

4. Beyond Liberalism and Romanticism

1. Because privatization is a response to powerlessness I call it "antipolitical," though it represents retirement from society as well.

2. The universe may be a rational cosmos governed by thought, penetrable by philosophy, foreseeable by prophecy, but it is still not amenable to human agency or intervention.

3. Marcus Aurelius, *Meditations* (Chicago: Gateway, 1956), p. 18.

4. Tertullian, *The Writings of Quintus Septimus, F. Tertullianus* (Edinburgh: Clark, 1869), I, 53.

5. Ibid., p. 352.

6. The end of persecution and the adoption of Christianity as the official imperial religion did not put an end to Christian antipolitical thought. Beginning with Saint Anthony, the early monk was distinct from the cleric and monasticism was opposed by church authorities as a rejection of the organization of the empire and the solidarity of believers. Its character changed dramatically as monasticism emerged as a social order of rules of which the most important was obedience to one head. See Herbert Workman, *The Evolution of the Monastic Ideal* (London: Epworth Press, 1913), p. 26.

7. Epictetus, *The Discourses of Epictetus* (New York: A.L. Burt, n.d.), p. 17.

8. Marcus Aurelius, *Meditations,* p. 104; Epictetus, *Discourses,* pp. 64–65. Nothing external can really disturb us, only our judgment of it, so that what really troubles us is not the power tyrants have to cut off our heads but our own opinion of the value of our heads. Thus even the slave has it in his power to live free of compulsion; stoicism inverts the political reality of the empire.

9. G. W. F. Hegel, *The Phenomenology of Mind* (New York: Harper, 1967), p. 244.

10. Antipolitical retreat inward is also remote from modern forms of idealism and from the philosophical habits of post-Nietzschean philosophers like Heidegger or Hannah Arendt, for whom philosophy is passionate "life-activity." It is distinct too from contemporary searches for scientific truth, with their activist ethos of intellectual "momentum" and their application of results.

11. Marcus Aurelius, *Meditations,* p. 31.

12. For a full, eclectic 600-year history of the stoics see Ernst Barker, *From Alexander to Constantine* (Oxford: Clarendon Press, 1956). My focus is on the later *stoa.*

13. Seneca, *Morals* (New York: A.L. Burt, n.d.), p. 354; Marcus Aurelius, *Meditations,* p. 13.

14. Epictetus, *Discourses,* p. 32. The *philosophes'* political reading of stoic cosmopolitanism is a later invention. See Peter Gay, *The Enlightenment: The Rise of Modern Paganism* (New York: Norton, 1966), pp. 83, 189.

15. Tertullian, *Writings,* p. 86. The crucial issue in the empire was military

service. "Render unto Caesar" meant that Christians must pay taxes, but they could not serve in the army. They could serve only in the army of God: "you are a foreigner in this world, a citizen of Jerusalem." *Writings*, p. 351. See H. Richard Niebuhr, "Christ Against Culture," in *Christ and Culture* (New York: Harper, 1951), pp. 45–55.

16. Cited in Barker, *Alexander to Constantine*, p. 450. The conflict between membership in two societies did not yet exist for the simple reason that when Tertullian wrote Christianity was not yet a fully institutionalized religion, a competing public. He argued against the idea of the church as episcopate, called laymen priests unto themselves, and elevated faith as an internal disposition over "positive" doctrine, authority, and ritual.

17. Contrast the interpretation of Tertullian by Sheldon Wolin, *Politics and Vision* (Boston: Little, Brown, 1960), chap. 4. Frank Manuel and Fritzie Manuel, in *Utopian Thought in the Western World* (Cambridge, Mass.: Harvard University Press, 1979), provide indirect support for my quietist interpretation. They date utopian thought from the renaissance, but draw connections with Judeo-Christian paradises and Hellenic ideal cities as well. The one period not mentioned in their prehistory of utopia is ancient Rome.

18. The world is the real prison, Tertullian taught: "the world has the greater darkness . . . imposes more grievous fetters . . . contains the larger number of criminals, even the whole race." *Writings*, pp. 2, 3.

19. Hegel is not only the best analyst of this disposition but also its culmination: self-conscious of the severance between mind and world, Hegel's spirit reappropriates the world in thought. See Erich Heller, *The Artist's Journey into the Interior* (New York: Harcourt Brace Jovanovich, 1976), chap. 5.

20. G. W. F. Hegel, *Early Theological Writings*, ed. T. Knox (Chicago: University of Chicago Press, 1948), pp. 43, 157; *Philosophy of History* (New York: Dover, 1956), p. 278.

21. G. W. F. Hegel, *Philosophy of Right* (New York: Oxford University Press, 1952), p. 9.

22. Hegel, *Early Theological Writings*, pp. 156, 164; *Phenomenology of Mind*, p. 503.

23. Hegel, *Early Theological Writings*, pp. 43, 157.

24. The description is in Heller, *Artist's Journey*, p. 103.

25. Hegel, *Philosophy of History*, p. 312; *Phenomenology of Mind*, p. 502; *Early Theological Writings*, p. 162. Hannah Arendt writes in the same vein: "The experiences of inner freedom are derivative in that they always presuppose a retreat from the world, where freedom was denied." "What is Freedom?," in *Between Past and Future* (New York: Penguin, 1977), p. 146. Isaiah Berlin links stoicism and detachment to political powerlessness in *Four Essays on Liberty* (New York: Oxford University Press, 1969), p. 140n.

26. Hegel, *Philosophy of Right*, p. 92.

27. Hegel, *Philosophy of History*, p. 279. Guido de Ruggiero calls stoicism "liberal" because of this connection between property rights and political order, referring to "the corrosive liberalism of an Epictetus or a Marcus Aurelius." *The History of European Liberalism* (Oxford: Oxford University Press, 1927), p. 26.

28. Judith Shklar discusses this dual history in *Freedom and Independence* (Cambridge: Cambridge University Press, 1976), pp. 108–109.

29. Hegel, *Philosophy of History,* p. 279.

30. For Hegel, Kantian morality is already a journey inward since it opposes the individual conscience to the demands of utility and external authority.

31. Hegel, *Philosophy of Right,* p. 255; Friedrich Schleiermacher, *On Religion* (New York: Harper and Row, 1958), pp. 36–37, 599. On the difference between romanticism and pietism and other forms of inner light, see Paul Tillich, *A History of Christian Thought* (New York: Harper and Row, 1968).

32. Hegel, *Philosophy of Right,* p. 5.

33. M. H. Abrams, "English Romanticism: The Spirit of the Age," in *Romanticism Reconsidered,* ed. Northrop Frye (New York: Columbia University Press, 1963), p. 58.

34. Hegel, *Phenomenology of Mind,* p. 391.

35. Henri Brunschwig develops this thesis with reference to the rise of romanticism in Prussia in *Enlightenment and Romanticism in Eighteenth Century Prussia* (Chicago: University of Chicago Press, 1974) pp. 98, 151, 224–225.

36. Alfred de Musset, *Confessions of a Child of the Century* (Paris: Mazarin, 1905); François René Vicomte de Chateaubriand, *Atala/René* (Berkeley: University of California Press, 1952), p. 100.

37. The epithet "philistine" is also wielded against individuals who represent these classes; Lenin uses it to attack the "renegade Bernstein" in *State and Revolution* (Moscow: Progress Publishers, 1972), p. 50.

38. Originally the term "philistine" was applied to townspeople by German university students to indicate their parochialism and hostility to ideas. For a history of the term see Estelle Morgan, "Bourgeois and Philistine," *Modern Language Review* 57 (January 1962), 69–72.

39. Matthew Arnold, *Culture and Anarchy* (London: Cambridge University Press, 1969), pp. 59, 102.

40. The definition of taste is from T. S. Eliot, *The Use of Poetry and the Use of Criticism* (Cambridge, Mass.: Harvard University Press, 1933), p. 27.

41. This argument is made by Hannah Arendt in "The Crisis of Culture," in *Between Past and Future,* p. 211. In the same vein, the middle class has been accused of using art as an intoxicant, a way of dissolving the care of the world. See Hilton Kramer, "High Art and Social Chaos," *The New York Times,* December 28, 1969.

42. Henry David Thoreau, *Walden and Civil Disobedience* (New York: New American Library, 1960), p. 10.

43. For instance, literature is "not only a trade, but is carried on by the maxims usually adopted by other trades which live by the number, rather than by the quality of their consumers." Alexis de Tocqueville, cited in J. S. Mill, "De Tocqueville on Democracy in America," in *Essays on Politics and Culture* (New York: Doubleday, 1962), II, 262.

44. Arendt, "The Crisis of Culture," p. 200.

45. "O nameless Multitude! You are the born enemy of names!" Alfred de Vigny, *Stello* (Montreal: McGill University Press, 1963), p. 165.

46. Heinrich Heine, *The Romantic School* (New York: Henry Holt and Co., 1982), p. 250.

47. J. S. Mill, *On Liberty* (New York: Norton, 1975), p. 62; "Civilization," in *Essays on Politics and Culture*, p. 60.

48. Ralph Waldo Emerson, "Aristocracy," in *The American Transcendentalists*, ed. Perry Miller (New York: Anchor, 1957), pp. 289–290.

49. J. S. Mill, "Civilization," p. 60.

50. In this century the romantic perception of monolithic philistinism does not distinguish liberal governments from totalitarian states. See, for example, Henry Read, *Politics of the Unpolitical* (London: Routledge, 1943), pp. 6, 13.

51. De Vigny, *Stello*, pp. 6, 165. Artists in every age have protested patronage arrangements, academies, and audiences, regretting the absence or corruption of good taste—so much so that the artist's situation has been described as "one long story of persecution and flight from authority." Jacques Barzun, *Classic, Romantic, and Modern* (Chicago: University of Chicago Press, 1961), pp. 42–43.

52. Jean Jacques Rousseau, *The First and Second Discourses* (New York: St. Martin's, 1964), p. 50.

53. J. S. Mill, "The Writings of Alfred de Vigny," in *Dissertations and Discussions* (Boston: William Spencer, 1868), p. 349.

54. De Vigny, *Stello*, pp. 175, 179, xxi, 182.

55. "I never wrote one single line of poetry with the least shadow of public thought," Keats affirmed. Cited in M. H. Abrams, *The Mirror and the Lamp: Romantic Theory and the Critical Tradition* (Oxford: Oxford University Press, 1953), p. 26. The characteristics marking art since the nineteenth century that have been described as compensation for estrangement include esotericism, the growth of studio art to a size and quality that makes it "homeless," music that can be played by virtuoso performers only, and so on.

56. Percy Bysshe Shelley, *A Defense of Poetry* (New York: Library of Liberal Arts, 1965), p. 80.

57. Cited in Arnold Hauser, *The Social History of Art* (New York: Vintage, 1959), IV, 80.

58. Frieda Fromm-Reichmann considers loneliness the prerequisite for the conception of "nearly all works of creative originality." Cited in Michael A. Weinstein, "The Uses of Privacy in the Good Life," *Nomos XIII, Privacy* (New York: Atherton Press, 1971) p. 100.

59. Arendt, *Between Past and Future*, p. 217.

60. Annie Dillard observes that "when the arts abandon the world as their subject matter, people abandon the arts . . . the arts are free to pursue whatever theories led them to abandon the world in the first place. They are as free as wandering albatrosses or stamp collectors or technical rock climbers; no one is looking." *Living by Fiction* (New York: Harper and Row, 1982), pp. 78–79.

61. On the complex history of "art for art's sake" and its historical center in the second half of the nineteenth century, see Raymond Williams, *Culture and Society: 1780–1950*, (New York: Columbia University Press, 1958), pp. 166–167.

62. Abrams, *The Mirror and the Lamp,* pp. 272, 278. Modern critical methods work on texts from any century or culture: "In the contemporary modernist view, the work of art . . . is a self-lighted opacity, not a window and not a mirror. It is a painted sphere, not a crystal ball." Dillard, *Living by Fiction,* pp. 47–48. This position resonates with contemporary assertions about the provisional and relative nature of scientific hypotheses. If from a relativist point of view art is no more the creation of context than everything else, how false or trivial can it be? "It has always been possible for artists of every kind to sniff at science and claim for art special, transcendent, and priestly powers. Now it is possible for artists to have and eat that particular cake by adding that, after all, science is in one (rather attenuated) sense 'mere' art; art is all there is." Dillard, p. 61.

63. Cited in Raymond Williams, *Culture and Society,* p. 136.

64. Flaubert, cited in Abrams, *The Mirror and the Lamp,* p. 328. The religious analogy of martyrdom to art was common. Chateaubriand called "art for art's sake" "the pageant of the bleeding heart." Cited in Cesar Grana, *Bohemian Versus Bourgeois* (New York: Basic Books, 1964), p. 78.

65. The phrases are Annie Dillard's, describing contemporary fine writing. *Living by Fiction,* p. 115.

66. Cited in Heller, *Artist's Journey,* p. 105.

67. For the view that role-playing in general is a way of achieving ironic distance from the deadly routine of daily life, see Christopher Lasch, *The Culture of Narcissism* (New York: Norton, 1978), p. 94.

5. Heroic Individualism and the Spectacle of Diversity

1. For a consideration of interpretations of Thoreau as a transcendentalist and for specific comparisons between this reading and others see Nancy L. Rosenblum, "Thoreau's Militant Conscience," *Political Theory* 9: 1 (February 1981), pp. 81–110.

2. Leon Edel, "The Mystery of Walden Pond," in *Stuff of Sleep and Dreams* (New York: Avon, 1982), p. 48.

3. Henry David Thoreau, "Civil Disobedience," in *Walden and Civil Disobedience* (New York: New American Library, 1960), p. 233.

4. "There will never be a really free and enlightened State, until the State comes to recognize the individual as a higher and independent power, from which all its own power and authority are derived, and treats him accordingly." "Civil Disobedience," p. 240.

5. Samuel Huntington, *American Politics: The Promise of Disharmony* (Cambridge, Mass.: Harvard University Press, 1981), pp. 3–4.

6. Thoreau, "Civil Disobedience," p. 222.

7. "Paradise (To Be) Regained," in *Antislavery and Reform Papers* (Montreal: Harvest House, 1963), p. 90; "Life Without Principle," ibid., p. 139. The only activist he lauded was John Brown; for a discussion of Thoreau's identifi-

cation with Brown's "killing of slavery" see Rosenblum, "Thoreau's Militant Conscience."

8. Cited in Leo Stoller, *After Walden* (Stanford, Calif.: Stanford University Press, 1967), p. 17.

9. "Civil Disobedience," p. 226.

10. Ibid., p. 239.

11. *Walden*, p. 147.

12. Acting in his continuing capacity as citizen, the civil disobedient distinguishes his purpose from revolution or subversion by inviting punishment and making his conduct both public and nonviolent. The facts argue against Thoreau as civil disobedient: he stopped paying the poll tax before the Fugitive Slave Law was enacted and did nothing to encourage his arrest or stay in the Concord jail. He considered his night there an injury and an injustice and hoped that the spread of disobedience would be fatal to the courts.

13. "Civil Disobedience," pp. 14, 226. Leon Edel, following James Russell Lowell, shows the self-deceptive quality of Thoreau's claims for independence: "Thoreau, then, lived one kind of life and fancied he lived another; his fancy may have ruled him so completely that he believed he was really a solitary." "The Mystery of Walden Pond," p. 52. The essay is a study of the psychopathology that generated Thoreau's personal myth. I am not concerned with the psychologically compensatory functions of Thoreau's writings, but with their import for political theory. What is important is not the facts of Thoreau's self-sufficiency but his consideration of what conditions are necessary for consent or detachment.

14. "A Plea for Captain John Brown," in *Antislavery and Reform Papers*, pp. 60–61.

15. "The Last Days of John Brown," in *Antislavery and Reform Papers*, p. 72.

16. "Last Days of John Brown," p. 62. This running down makes the whole debate over capital punishments "a needless ado."

17. "Civil Disobedience," p. 224.

18. "Plea for Captain John Brown," p. 58.

19. Ibid., p. 61.

20. "Civil Disobedience," p. 238.

21. Wendell Phillips "does himself an injustice when he reminds us of the American [Antislavery] Society which he represents; really he stands alone. "Wendell Phillips before the Concord Lyceum," in *Antislavery and Reform Papers*, p. 101.

22. *Walden*, p. 10.

23. "Plea for Captain John Brown," p. 50.

24. Stanley Cavell, *The Senses of Walden* (New York: Viking, 1972), p. 88.

25. Thoreau did not think of slavery as an institution that takes a variety of historical forms; he had no use for prevailing social theories that interpreted American politics in terms of the organized interests of producing and nonproducing classes, or in terms of labor or aristocratic and democratic factions.

26. "Life Without Principle," p. 154.

27. Henry Miller, *Life without Principle* (Stanford, Calif.: Stanford Uni-

versity Press, 1946) and Stanley Hyman, "Henry Thoreau in Our Time," in *Walden,* ed. Owen Thomas (New York: Norton, 1966), p. 316.

28. "Civil Disobedience," p. 238.

29. Ibid., p. 232.

30. Ibid., p. 229.

31. *Walden,* p. 3.

32. Ibid., p. 10.

33. "Plea for Captain John Brown," p. 51.

34. *Walden,* p. 95.

35. Joseph Moldenhauer, "Paradox in Walden," in *Twentieth Century Interpretations of Walden* (Englewood Cliffs, N.J.: Prentice-Hall, 1968), p. 78; Cavell, *The Senses of Walden,* pp. 14, 33.

36. "Paradise (To Be) Regained," p. 90.

37. "Civil Disobedience," p. 234.

38. Cited in James Russell Lowell, "Thoreau," in *The Shock of Recognition,* ed. Edmund Wilson (New York: Farrar, Straus, and Cudahy, 1943), pp. 235–236. "Let us love by refusing not accepting one another," Thoreau wrote. *Early Essays* (Princeton: Princeton University Press, 1975), pp. 275–276. His poem "Friendship" begins: "Let such pure hate still underprop/Our love, that we may be/Each other's conscience/And have our sympathy/Mainly from thence." Cited in *The American Transcendentalists,* ed. Perry Miller (New York: Anchor, 1957), p. 233.

39. *Walden,* pp. 15, 104.

40. Ibid., p. 156.

41. "I love to see that Nature is so rife with life that myriads can be afforded to be sacrificed and suffered to prey on one another; that tender organizations can be so serenely squashed out of existence like pulp—tadpoles which herons gobble up, and tortoises and toads run over in the road; and that sometimes it has rained flesh and blood." *Walden,* p. 211. There is the echo of Max Stirner here, for whom life is not the occasion to realize one's true self but to live oneself out—to assert and squander ourselves. *The Ego and His Own* (New York: Libertarian Book Club, 1963).

42. Edel, "The Mystery of Walden Pond," p. 63.

43. "Civil Disobedience," p. 240.

44. Ibid., p. 226.

45. The classic statement is Friedrich Schiller, *The Beautiful and the Sublime.* See also M. H. Abrams, *Natural Supernaturalism* (New York: Norton, 1971).

46. Abrams, *Natural Supernaturalism,* p. 377.

47. Walt Whitman, "Preface to *Leaves of Grass,*" in *The Portable Walt Whitman* (New York: Penguin, 1945), p. 5.

48. G. W. F. Hegel, *The Philosophy of History* (New York: Dover, 1956), p. 72.

49. Edmund Burke, *Reflections on the Revolution in France* (Indianapolis: Bobbs-Merrill, 1955), p. 87.

50. Whitman, *Democratic Vistas,* in *The Portable Walt Whitman,* p. 323.

51. Ibid., pp. 332, 337. D. H. Lawrence read in Whitman only the erotic longing for fusion and identity, and nothing of the cult of personality: "Oh Walter, Walter, what have you done with it? What have you done with yourself? With your own individual self? For it sounds as if it had all leaked out of you, leaked into the universe." Cited in Wilson, *Shock of Recognition,* p. 1064. McWilliams argues that "Whitman's American nationalism has no specifically American content. It was merely a part of his cosmic unity, a democratic pantheism." Wilson Carey McWilliams, *The Idea of Fraternity* (Berkeley: University of California Press, 1973), p. 417.

52. Whitman, *Democratic Vistas,* pp. 348, 324.

53. For a discussion of liberal cosmopolitan nationalism, see Friedrich Meinecke, *Cosmopolitanism and the National State* (Princeton: Princeton University Press, 1970). I leave aside romantic versions of nationalism incompatible with liberalism, such as "blood and soil" nationalism, as well as those that attribute romantic individuality only to the group.

54. George Kateb, "Democratic Individuality and the Claims of Politics," *Political Theory* 12: 3 (August 1984), p. 344.

55. Samuel H. Beer, citing Emile Durkheim, "Liberty and Union," *Political Theory* 12: 3 (August 1984), p. 366.

56. Of course self-completion is only one possible view of friendship; likeness rather than difference could be at its heart, or kindliness, or the friend could be seen in metaphysical terms as an "other me" that unites one person to all of humanity and to nature, as in transcendentalism. McWilliams, *The Idea of Fraternity,* p. 285.

57. Herbert Read, *Education Through Art* (New York: Pantheon, 1956), p. 4.

58. Samuel Beer, "Liberty and Union," *The New Republic,* January 23, 1984, pp. 26–30; and "Liberty and Union," *Political Theory* 12:3 (August 1984).

59. Emile Durkheim, *The Division of Labor in Society* (New York: The Free Press, 1964), p. 400. "The human person . . . is considered as sacred, in what one might call the ritual sense of the word . . . It is conceived as being invested with that mysterious property which creates an empty space around holy objects . . . Such a morality is therefore not simply a hygienic discipline or a wise principle of economy. It is a religion." Cited in Steven Lukes, *Emile Durkheim: His Life and Works* (New York: Harper and Row, 1972), pp. 340–341.

60. Durkheim, *Division of Labor,* p. 80.

61. Durkheim, *Division of Labor,* pp. 361, 37. Compare L. T. Hobhouse: "The common good . . . is founded on personality, and postulates free scope for the development of personality in each member of the community." *Liberalism* (Oxford: Oxford University Press, 1964), p. 70. So long as differentiated activities are distributed spontaneously on the basis of natural talents, individuals are prevented from being degraded to cogs in a machine.

62. Beer, "Liberty and Union," *Political Theory,* p. 375.

63. John Rawls, *A Theory of Justice* (Cambridge, Mass.: Harvard University Press, 1976), p. 565.

64. Beer, "Liberty and Union," *Political Theory,* p. 367.

65. To the extent that diverse conditions add to the sublimity of democratic liberalism, even the monstrous, the impoverished, and the cruel may be aesthetically justifiable. For Whitman the dark side of aesthetic spectacle is cities "crowded with petty grotesques, malformations, phantoms, playing meaningless antics." Cited in Robert Penn Warren, *Democracy and Poetry* (Cambridge, Mass.: Harvard University Press, 1975), p. 8.

6. The New Face of Pluralism

1. I take the name from the title of Albert O. Hirschman's book, *Shifting Involvements: Private Interest and Public Action* (Princeton: Princeton University Press, 1982).

2. William Kornhauser, *The Politics of Mass Society* (Glencoe, Ill.: Free Press, 1959), p. 136.

3. J. S. Mill, *Considerations on Representative Government* (Indianapolis: Bobbs-Merrill, 1958), p. 55.

4. Mill is an excellent guide to the intricate relation between democracy and the authority of expertise. He does not say that individuals always know their own interests best or how to advance them, only that excluded groups are not likely to have their interest protected. See Richard Friedman, "An Introduction to Mill's Theory of Authority," in *Mill: A Collection of Critical Essays,* ed. J. B. Schneewind (Notre Dame, Ind.: University of Notre Dame Press, 1969), pp. 379–425; Nancy L. Rosenblum, "Studying Authority: Keeping Pluralism in Mind," *Nomos: Authority Revisited* (New York, 1987).

5. Mill, *Representative Government,* pp. 38, 51; *On Liberty* (New York: Norton, 1975), p. 66. Even religion is selfish; the desire for personal salvation "identifies the votary as little in feeling with the rest of his kind as sensuality itself." *Representative Government,* p. 39.

6. Mill, *Representative Government,* p. 53.

7. See *Representative Government,* pp. 205, 208; and Dennis Thompson, *John Stuart Mill and Representative Government* (Princeton: Princeton University Press, 1976), pp. 104–105.

8. The difference, of course, is that Madison's statesmanship is largely a matter of neutralizing conflicting classes or factions, while Mill's altruism is the application of the principle of utility to the nation in general. It is the difference between political balancing and a feeling of identification with the general good that makes public action a labor of love.

9. Mill, "M. de Tocqueville on Democracy in America," *The Philosophy of J. S. Mill* (New York: Modern Library, 1961), p. 141.

10. Mill, "Tocqueville," p. 139. He discusses the consequences of the institution of marriage for men and women in *The Subjection of Women* (Cambridge, Mass.: MIT Press, 1970), p. 80. Mill was concerned about cultivating other feelings as well. As well as a policy of government forbearance from interference with others, tolerance is a personal quality, an inner disposition. It is a combination of feeling and imaginative identification with others. This mutual

identification also creates nationality, the minimum condition for permanent political cohesion; but beyond this minimum of empathic feeling liberal democracy also requires altruism. "Coleridge," in *The Philosophy of J. S. Mill*, pp. 78–79.

11. Mill, *Representative Government*, pp. 25, 28.

12. J. S. Mill, *Autobiography* (Indianapolis: Bobbs-Merrill, 1957), p. 90. For a fuller discussion of the laws of the association of ideas—chronological, instrumental, and affective—see "Thoughts on Poetry and its Varieties," in *Autobiography and Literary Essays*, ed. J. Robson and J. Stillinger (Toronto: University of Toronto Press, 1981), pp. 348–349.

13. Mill, *Representative Government*, p. 38.

14. Mill, "Periodical Literature: *Edinburgh Review*," in *Autobiography and Literary Essays*, p. 322; *On Liberty*, p. 15.

15. Wilhelm von Humboldt, *The Sphere and Duties of Government* (London: John Chapman, 1854), pp. 53, 114, 116–117, 188.

16. Hirschman, *Shifting Involvements*.

17. Marianne Cowan, ed., *An Anthology of the Writings of Wilhelm von Humboldt: Humanist without Portfolio* (Detroit: Wayne State University Press, 1963), pp. 144–145; Humboldt, *Sphere and Duties*, pp. 107, 36. Humboldt looks on limited government as a stage in the "natural sequence of revolutions of human energy."

18. Friedrich Meinecke, *Cosmopolitanism and the National State* (Princeton: Princeton University Press, 1970), pp. 36–38.

19. Cited in Mill, *On Liberty*, p. 2.

20. Mill did not oppose altruism to self-interest; he respected legitimate concern for one's material welfare and thought breach of assignable obligations to support and educate one's own should be punishable.

21. Mill, *On Liberty*, p. 57.

22. Ibid., p. 58.

23. Ibid., p. 58.

24. Mill, *Autobiography*, pp. 86, 92–93. To say as Jean Elshtain does that "Mill's is the philosophy of the external man" is simply wrong; see Jean B. Elshtain, *Public Man, Private Woman* (Princeton: Princeton University Press, 1981), p. 136.

25. Mill, "What is Poetry?" in *Essays on Literature and Society*, ed. J. B. Schneewind (New York: Collier, 1965), pp. 104, 105–106, 119; "Thoughts on Poetry and Its Varieties," pp. 348–349.

26. For more on types of sensibility and the distinctiveness of artists see Mill, "Thoughts on Poetry and Its Varieties," pp. 345–346, 355–357. His friend John Roebuck was a "lover of poetry" but failed to realize the value of poetry for the cultivation of feelings. *Autobiography*, p. 98; "Coleridge," p. 85.

27. Mill, *Autobiography*, p. 96.

28. Mill, "Inaugural Address," in *Essays on Literature and Society*, pp. 409–410.

29. Mill, "Thoughts on Poetry and Its Varieties," p. 348.

30. Mill "contributes to the emergence in England of the history of ideas

as an intellectual discipline which satisfies the criterion of interestingness that is different from that of philosophy." Eldon Eisenach, "An Illiberal Defense of Mill's Liberalism," unpublished paper delivered to the North American Society for Social Philosophy, 1985, p. 5.

31. Compare Robert Penn Warren: the poem is a model of the organized self; it brings freshness and immediacy of experience that returns us to ourselves. Poetry serves democracy because it reaffirms the worth of individuals; it is an antidote to passivity because it demands participation. *Democracy and Poetry* (Cambridge, Mass.: Harvard University Press, 1975), pp. 69, 72, 89.

32. Mill, *Autobiography,* pp. 94, 91.

33. Friedrich Schiller, *On the Aesthetic Education of Man in a Series of Letters* (New York: Ungar, 1954), pp. 87, 101, 91.

34. Mill, "Inaugural Address," p. 371.

35. See Gertrude Himmelfarb, who accuses Mill of not seeing how liberty would lead men to "explore the depths of depravity." *On Liberty and Liberalism* (New York: Knopf, 1974), p. 321. Mill distinguished strong feelings from the wild and intemperate in *On Liberty,* p. 65. See too his attack on sentimentalism in "Edinburgh Review," pp. 312, 322–325.

36. Mill, *Autobiography,* p. 89; "Two Kinds of Poetry," in *Essays on Literature and Society,* p. 120.

37. "Ordinary education and the ordinary course of life are constantly at work counteracting this quality of mind and substituting habits more suitable to their own ends . . . when will education consist, not in repressing any mental faculty or power . . . but in training up to its proper strength the corrective and antagonistic power?" "Two Kinds of Poetry," p. 126.

38. Lionel Trilling, "On the Teaching of Modern Literature" and "The Two Environments: Reflections on the Study of English," in *Beyond Culture* (New York: Viking, 1955).

39. For a discussion of Constant, the use of classical forms by revolutionaries to arouse sentiments of obedience, and the liberating thrust of romantic styles in art, see Susan Tennenbaum, "The Coppet Circle: Literary Criticism as Political Discourse," *History of Political Thought* 1:3 (1980), 453–473.

40. Cited in Guy Dodge, *Benjamin Constant's Philosophy of Liberalism* (Chapel Hill: University of North Carolina Press, 1980), p. 29.

41. See William Kornhauser for a contemporary account of the difference between liberal pluralism and "naked" society. *The Politics of Mass Society,* pp. 23, 41, 77.

42. Cited in Dodge, *Constant's Philosophy,* p. 35.

43. "For twenty years you have commended to these men sobriety, attachment to their families, assiduousness in their work; but it is necessary to invade the World! They are arrested, they are carried away, they are stirred to contempt for the virtues inculcated in them for so long. They are dizzied by intemperance, they are roused to debauchery: that is what is called reviving public spirit." Benjamin Constant, *L'Esprit de Conquête* (Paris: Grasset, 1918), p. 33, my translation.

44. This is the central argument in Stephen Holmes, *Benjamin Constant*

and the Making of Modern Liberalism (New Haven: Yale University Press, 1984).

45. Cited ibid., p. 19.

46. Cited in Holmes, *Benjamin Constant,* p. 45.

47. For a contemporary expression of this theme see Richard Sennett, *The Fall of Public Man* (New York: Vintage, 1978).

48. Hirschman, *Shifting Involvements,* pp. 10, 21, 134.

49. Carol Gilligan, *In a Different Voice* (Cambridge, Mass.: Harvard University Press, 1982), p. 159.

50. Judith N. Shklar, *Ordinary Vices* (Cambridge, Mass.: Harvard University Press, 1984), p. 101.

51. Ibid., p. 136.

52. Daniel Levinson et al., *Seasons of a Man's Life* (New York: Ballantine, 1978), pp. 41, 323n.

53. Levinson et al. refer to developmental periods in literary terms as acts of a play or major divisions of a novel. *Seasons,* p. 19. For a discussion of the unity of a human life and narrative unity see Alasdair MacIntyre, *After Virtue* (Notre Dame, Ind.: University of Notre Dame Press, 1981), chap. 15.

54. There is the possibility of being "stuck," of course. Indeed individuality is clearest from the point of view of pathology, in the infinite and unpredictable ways individuals can deviate from the course of development toward wholeness. Levinson et al., *Seasons,* pp. 139–140.

55. "Life planning" focuses on developing identity, not just discrete purposes like career planning or family planning. See Peter Berger et al., *The Homeless Mind* (New York: Vintage, 1974), pp. 72–76.

56. Erikson's report to the White House Conference on Childhood and Youth is one example: "The sense of autonomy which arises . . . is fostered by a handling of the small individual which expresses a sense of rightful dignity and lawful independence on the part of the parents and which gives him the confident expectation that the kind of autonomy fostered in childhood will not be frustrated later. This, in turn, necessitates a relationship of parent to parent, of parent to employer, and of parent to government which reaffirms the parent's essential dignity within the hierarchy of social positions." Erik Erikson, *Identity and the Life Cycle* (New York: Norton, 1980), p. 76.

57. Levinson et al., *Seasons,* p. 200.

58. David Norton, *Personal Destinies: A Philosophy of Ethical Individualism* (Princeton: Princeton University Press, 1976), p. 21.

59. Wholeness connotes an assembly of diversified parts "that enter into fruitful association and organization." Erik Erikson, *Insight and Responsibility* (New York: Norton, 1964), p. 92.

60. Erikson, *Identity,* p. 125.

61. Levinson et al., *Seasons,* p. 47. With this comes a new critical perspective on liberalism: the conventional liberal view might oppose bureaucratization because it inhibits democratic control or teaches obedience rather than independence; for the romantic, bureaucratization reduces the degree to which spheres are differentiated and impedes personal construction of "life structures."

62. Erikson, *Insight and Responsibility,* p. 125.

63. Erikson, *Identity,* p. 104.

7. Repairing the Communitarian Failings of Liberal Thought

1. Wilhelm von Humboldt, *The Spheres and Duties of Government* (London: John Chapman, 1854), p. 8.

2. Charles Taylor, *Hegel and Modern Society* (Cambridge: Cambridge University Press, 1979), p. 140; Roberto Unger, "The Critical Legal Studies Movement," *Harvard Law Review* 96:3, p. 587.

3. Alasdair MacIntyre, *After Virtue* (Notre Dame, Ind.: University of Notre Dame Press, 1981), pp. 238, 147.

4. See Michael Walzer, *Spheres of Justice* (New York: Basic Books, 1983) and Roberto Unger, *Law and Modern Society* (New York: Free Press, 1976).

5. Samuel H. Beer, "Liberty and Union," *The New Republic,* January 23, 1984, p. 26.

6. George C. Lodge, *The American Disease* (New York: Knopf, 1984).

7. The public household "has always existed to meet common needs, to provide goods and services which individuals cannot purchase for themselves." Daniel Bell, *The Cultural Contradictions of Capitalism* (New York: Basic Books, 1976), pp. 224, 176, 194, 226–227.

8. Samuel H. Beer, "Liberty and Union," *Political Theory* 12:3 (1984), p. 362.

9. MacIntyre, *After Virtue,* p. 234.

10. Unger, *Law and Modern Society,* p. 144.

11. MacIntyre, *After Virtue,* pp. 234, 233.

12. Walzer, *Spheres of Justice,* p. 279.

13. Charles Taylor, *Hegel and Modern Society,* pp. 115, 121. The decline of pluralism is explained variously: through slow erosion, the assault of uniform public policy, or the destructive atomizing power of the concept of autonomy. Taylor treats destruction and neutralization as identical.

14. Michael Sandel, "Morality and the Liberal Ideal," *The New Republic,* May 7, 1984, p. 17.

15. Laurence Tribe, *American Constitutional Law* (Mineola, N.Y.: Foundation Press, 1978), p. 979.

16. Ibid., p. 988.

17. R. M. MacIver, *The Modern State* (Oxford: Oxford University Press, 1926), p. 474. "The community is the matrix of all its inclusive and exclusive forms. It is not an organization but the source of organization" (p. 482).

18. George Sabine, *A History of Political Theory* (New York: Holt, Rinehart and Winston, 1937), p. 750.

19. One notable exception is heads of families; the assumption that the typical individual is a male head of family plays a significant and often unacknowledged part in liberal thought.

20. Unger, *Law and Modern Society,* p. 202.

21. Charles Taylor, *Hegel and Modern Society,* p. 129.

22. Benjamin Barber, *Strong Democracy* (Berkeley: University of California Press, 1984), p. 68. Bruce Ackerman's phrase for this is "asocial monads"; see *Social Justice and the Liberal State* (New Haven: Yale University Press, 1980), p. 100.

23. George Sabine, referring to T. H. Green. *History of Political Theory*, p. 737.

24. Richard Rorty, "The Priority of Democracy to Philosophy," unpublished paper delivered at Harvard University, November 1985.

25. Sabine, *History of Political Theory*, pp. 749–750.

26. Charles Taylor, *Hegel and Modern Society*, p. 87. Theorists sometimes conflate society and community for political purposes of their own, as Barber does in support of "strong democracy": "If we accept the postulate that humans are social by nature, then we cannot tend to regard citizenship as merely one among many artificial social roles that can be grafted onto man's natural solitariness. It is rather the only legitimate form that man's natural dependency can take." Barber, *Strong Democracy*, p. 217.

27. Susan Okin, "Justice and Gender," *Philosophy and Public Affairs* 16:1 (Winter 1987), p. 44.

28. Sandel, "Morality and the Liberal Ideal," p. 17. Charles Taylor writes, "Our experience is what it is, shaped in part by the way we interpret it; and this has a lot to do with the terms which are available to us in our culture." *Hegel and Modern Society*, p. 87. Peter Berger and Thomas Luckmann are just as unspecific: "Every individual is born into community and owes its life to community . . . community is always there." *The Social Construction of Reality* (New York: Doubleday, 1966), p. 183.

29. Amy Gutmann makes this point in "Communitarian Critics of Liberalism," *Philosophy and Public Affairs* 14:3.

30. By pointing in an unsystematic way to membership as a partial source of personal identity, communitarians evade the political questions at the heart of liberalism. It is disturbing but not surprising that communitarians are vague when it comes to addressing questions of political conflict and civil liberty; after all, connectedness, not liberty, is their chief concern.

31. Michael Sandel, *Liberalism and the Limits of Justice* (Cambridge: Cambridge University Press, 1982), p. 62.

32. Unger, *Law and Modern Society*, p. 146.

33. John Rawls, *A Theory of Justice* (Cambridge, Mass.: Harvard University Press, 1971), p. 441. Amy Gutmann, "Should Public Schools Teach Virtue?" *Report from the Center for Philosophy and Public Affairs* 5:3 (Summer 1985), pp. 12–13. We can question whether there is a direct course from "winning the battle against amoralism and egoism" to political independence, or from piety, love, and patriotism to critical thinking about politics, as she suggests.

34. John Rawls, "The Independence of Moral Theory," *Proceedings and Addresses of the American Philosophical Association* 48 (1975), pp. 5–22, 231, 241. See also Charles Larmore, "Review of Liberalism and the Limits of Justice," *Journal of Philosophy* 81:6 (June 1984).

35. Charles Taylor, *Hegel and Modern Society*, p. 132.

36. Walzer, *Spheres of Justice*, p. 35.

37. Unger, *Law and Modern Society*, p. 242.
38. See Charles Taylor, *Hegel and Modern Society*, p. 129. Michael Taylor writes: "The second argument against the liberal justification of the state . . . is that the state tends to undermine the conditions which make the alternative to it workable, and in this way makes itself more desirable. It does this by weakening or destroying *community*." *Community, Anarchy, and Liberty* (Cambridge: Cambridge University Press, 1982), p. 57.
39. William Galston, "Defending Liberalism," *American Political Science Review* 76 (1982), p. 629. "We have seen that Rawls' theory of justice requires for its coherence a conception of community in the constitutive sense, which requires in turn a notion of agency in the cognitive sense, and we have found that Rawls' theory of the good can allow for neither." Sandel, *Liberalism*, p. 161; see also p. 49.
40. For an extended account of the difficulty with "latent community" see Nancy L. Rosenblum, "Moral Membership in a Postliberal State," *World Politics* (August 1983), pp. 581–596.
41. See, for example, Jane Mansbridge, *Beyond Adversary Democracy* (Chicago: University of Chicago Press, 1980).
42. Walzer, *Spheres of Justice*, pp. 104–105, 97. Another account that reinterprets possessive individualism as having developed its "own forms of *Sittlichkeit*" is Charles Taylor, *Hegel and Modern Society*, p. 133.
43. Unger, *Law and Modern Society*, p. 144.
44. Jerold Auerbach, *Justice Without Law* (Oxford: Oxford University Press, 1983), p. vii.
45. Ibid., p. 4.
46. Auerbach's enthusiasm is not diminished by the fact that contemporary examples of mediation and arbitration are justified by efficiency and applied to a "marginal" clientele of disadvantaged groups—the poor, criminals, and so on—who cannot afford counsel and full litigation of their rights; or by the fact that the arbitration of consumer grievances is an alternative to class-action lawsuits, undercutting their power. An alternative paradigm is that negotiation is a manipulative technique for getting what you want in a hostile world. See David Luban, "Bargaining and Compromise: Recent Work on Negotiation and Informal Justice," *Philosophy and Public Affairs* 14:4 (1985), pp. 397–416.
47. Tribe, *American Constitutional Law*, p. 980.
48. For example, Laurence Tribe's history of the "gradual evolution of shared values." "Structural Due Process," *Harvard Civil Rights–Civil Liberties Law Review* 10 (1975), p. 269.
49. Unger, "The Critical Legal Studies Movement," p. 602.
50. Mansbridge, *Beyond Adversary Democracy*, p. ix. She is sceptical about communitarian practices, pointing out that rules of unanimity can be employed to protect individual interests rather than to express a strongly held consensus; see pp. 260–261.
51. Michael Taylor, *Community, Anarchy, Liberty*, p. 96.
52. This is consistent with a view of the state as the embodiment of wholeness, but not, Jacques Barzun argues, with political authoritarianism. *Classic,*

Romantic, and Modern (Chicago: University of Chicago Press, 1961), p. 56.

53. Steven Lukes, "Perspectives on Authority," *Nomos;* see Nancy L. Rosenblum, "Studying Authority: Keeping Pluralism in Mind," *Nomos* (1987).

54. Walzer, *Spheres of Justice,* pp. 82–83.

55. Ibid., p. 35; Michael Walzer, *Obligations: Essays on Disobedience, War, and Citizenship* (Cambridge, Mass.: Harvard University Press, 1970), p. 210.

56. Unger, *Law and Modern Society,* p. 61.

57. For example, Sebastian De Grazia, *The Political Community: A Study of Anomie* (Chicago: University of Chicago Press, 1948).

58. Charles Taylor, *Hegel and Modern Society,* p. 87.

59. If we take nuclear, ecological, or economic conditions into account, interdependence and associated feelings of connectedness are truly global.

60. Walzer, *Spheres of Justice,* p. xiv. Unger proposes a similar approach when he refers to "counterprinciples." "The Critical Legal Studies Movement," pp. 569, 619, 620, 625.

61. Michael Oakeshott, "Political Education," in *Philosophy, Politics, and Society,* ed. Peter Laslett (Oxford: Basil Blackwell, 1975), pp. 12–13.

62. We can understand why "metatheoretical" questions about the foundations of political philosophy arise in the context of criticisms of liberalism. They are inseparable from the attack moral philosophers level against liberalism's alleged moral neutrality.

63. An exception is a declared antiliberal like Alasdair MacIntyre. "This notion of the political community as a common project is alien to the modern liberal individualist world. This is how we sometimes at least think of modern hospitals or philanthropic organizations: but we have no conception of such a form of community concerned, as Aristotle says the polis is concerned, with the whole of life." *After Virtue,* p. 146.

64. Charles Taylor, *Hegel and Modern Society,* p. 86.

65. R. G. Collingwood, "Introduction," in Guido de Ruggiero, *History of European Liberalism* (Boston: Beacon Press, 1959), p. viii.

66. Hegel, *Philosophy of Right* (Oxford: Oxford University Press, 1952), pp. 160, 156.

67. Charles Taylor, *Hegel and Modern Society,* p. 51.

68. Ibid., p. 126.

69. Hegel, *Philosophy of Right,* p. 189.

70. Charles Taylor, *Hegel and Modern Society,* p. 51.

71. Ibid., p. 129.

72. Judith Shklar, *Freedom and Independence: A Study of Hegel's Phenomenology of Mind* (Cambridge: Cambridge University Press, 1976), p. 208.

73. Barber, *Strong Democracy,* p. 78.

74. Ibid., p. 223.

75. Mansbridge, *Beyond Adversary Democracy,* p. 125.

76. Lee Rainwater, cited in Walzer, *Spheres of Justice,* p. 105.

77. Susan M. Okin, "Justice and Gender," *Philosophy and Public Affairs* 16:1 (Winter 1987), p. 50.

78. Rawls, *Theory of Justice*, p. 468; cited in Okin, "Justice and Gender," p. 51.

79. H. N. Hirsch, "The Threnody of Liberalism: Constitutional Liberty and the Renewal of Community," *Political Theory* 14:3 (August 1986), p. 424.

80. Walzer, *Spheres of Justice*, p. 52.

81. Isaiah Berlin, "Two Concepts of Liberty," in *Four Essays on Liberty* (Oxford: Oxford University Press, 1969), p. 155.

82. Auerbach, *Justice Without Law*, p. 52.

83. Unger, *Law and Modern Society*, pp. 143–144.

84. Walzer, *Obligations*, p. 210.

85. Walzer, *Spheres of Justice*, p. 64.

86. Unger, "The Critical Legal Studies Movement," p. 586.

87. Sandel seems to call for this. *Liberalism and the Limits of Justice*, p. 62.

88. Michael Taylor, *Community, Anarchy, Liberty*, p. 31.

89. Sandel, *Liberalism and the Limits of Justice*, p. 181.

90. MacIntyre, *After Virtue*, p. 146. Bernie Yack has argued that these are misreadings of Aristotle, who understands political community as a scene of conflict, not unity. Yack also argues that Aristotle's friendship is a source of accusation and recrimination, of distrust as well as connection. "Community and Conflict in Aristotle's Political Philosophy," *Review of Politics* 47:1 (January 1985), pp. 92–112.

91. Barber, *Strong Democracy*, p. 189.

92. Unger, *Law and Modern Society*, pp. 206–207.

93. Walzer, *Obligations*, p. 188.

94. Unger, *Law and Modern Society*, p. 209.

95. Judith Shklar, *Ordinary Vices* (Cambridge, Mass.: Harvard University Press, 1984), p. 77.

96. Ibid., p. 50.

Conclusion

1. Judith Shklar, *Ordinary Vices* (Cambridge, Mass.: Harvard University Press, 1984); she explains the reasoning behind beginning with "what is to be avoided" on p. 5.

2. John Dunn, "The Future of Liberalism," in *Rethinking Modern Political Theory* (Cambridge: Cambridge University Press, 1985), pp. 154–170.

Index